How to Program Your IBM PC BASIC for Beginners

Carl Shipman

Publishers: Bill & Helen Fisher
Executive Editor: Rick Bailey
Editorial Director: Theodore DiSante
Art Director: Don Burton
Book Design: Leslie Sinclair

Published by HPBooks, P.O. Box 5367, Tucson, AZ 85703   602/888-2150
ISBN: 0-89586-263-8   Library of Congress Catalog No. 83-85907
©1983 Fisher Publishing, Inc.   Printed in USA

About This Book

This book is for beginners. No programming knowledge is necessary because this book starts at the *beginning* and tells you what you need to know about programming in a simple and interesting way.

You should have access to an IBM Personal Computer (PC). The computer must have one or two disk drives installed. Any type of display is OK if it displays 80-character lines. The IBM Personal Computer Display is fine, as is any color display intended to work with a computer. Image quality on a home TV screen will probably not be satisfactory with 80-character lines. A printer is not necessary, but can be used if you have one. Shown below are the IBM display, system unit with two disk drives, and keyboard.

The programming language used in this book is called *BASIC*. It is the most popular programming language for personal computers and is the language you should start with.

With this book you learn from simple programming examples that you type and then run on your computer. Your understanding is reinforced by doing. For best results, place this book beside your computer while typing the examples. It's designed to be used that way.

By the end of the book, you will know a lot about computers and programming. You'll be able to write programs that will help you enjoy and benefit from your computer.

WHAT DOES *BASIC* MEAN?

BASIC is an acronym, formed from the initials of its full name, *Beginner's All-Purpose Symbolic Instruction Code.* This is why BASIC is written in capital letters.

The BASIC programming language was developed at Dartmouth College in the 1960s by John G. Kemeny and Thomas E. Kurtz. Its original purpose was to teach the ideas of programming by using a programming language that was simple and easy to understand.

It proved to be so useful that it was adopted by computer makers and gradually became a practical programming language rather than just a teaching method. Today, BASIC has matured and become one of several standard programming languages. It is the standard language for personal computers.

Computers and programmers use BASIC more than any other language.

1 Getting Started

You should have access to an IBM Personal Computer with one or more *disk drives*. The disk drive reads computer programs and data that you store on 5-1/4-inch diskettes. Diskettes store information magnetically, like an audio tape cassette. If you don't have diskettes for your computer, get some. They're sold in boxes of ten, which isn't too many to start with.

There are two different types of diskettes, depending on the disk drive you have. One uses only one side of the diskette. The other uses both sides. If you don't know the correct type of diskette, ask your local computer-equipment dealer.

You should also have the instruction books that come with the computer. They're discussed later in this chapter.

THINKING BASIC

Although there are only about 300 words in the BASIC programming language, it's very powerful when used well. With BASIC, you can program virtually anything your mind can conceive.

The fun and accomplishment of programming is to have an idea, express it logically and precisely in a program, and then polish and improve it until the program does *exactly* what you intend.

The main purpose of this book is to help you have useful programming ideas and make them work. Learning the BASIC programming language as used with the IBM Personal Computer is the best way.

People who study the human mind have an interesting theory: We cannot have a thought or an idea that we don't have words to express. This implies that the power of your mind is limited by your vocabulary— *not the opposite*. I think that is basically true, and you may agree. Certainly language is the means by which we *extract* thoughts from our minds.

When you "have an idea," you probably have it in fully formed words in your mind. Whatever you are thinking, right now, you are thinking in words. If you didn't know those words, you probably couldn't express that idea. More important, you probably would never have had the idea in the first place. That's why learning the BASIC words and their practical meanings will put programming ideas into your mind.

Some people try to learn the theories and grand strategies of programming and then "look up" the BASIC words to express them. That's doing it backward. Until you know the words really well, and what they do, you can't understand the theories. And no grand strategies will occur to you.

The way to learn BASIC is through experience—specifically, through your fingers. You *must* type a BASIC program, run it on your computer and see what it does.

GETTING READY

If your computer is new, your dealer should have shown you how to connect the cables, turn it on and make a backup copy of the Disk Operating System (DOS) diskette.

With your computer you received an IBM Personal Computer book entitled *Guide to Operations*. If you haven't done so already, read through this book. Most of it is easy to understand and immediately useful. There will probably be some things you don't understand. If so, don't worry about them. The things you may not understand aren't important right now. Later, you *will* understand them.

If you need help in connecting the cables and checking out your computer, refer to Sections 2, 4 and 5 of *Guide to Operations*. It's easy to do when you know how.

The Disk Operating System—With the disk drive unit in your computer, you received an IBM Personal Computer publication entitled *Disk Operating System*. In the back of this book is an IBM Personal Computer diskette labeled *DOS*. Stored on this diskette is a program called *Disk Operating System* (DOS). It's a special computer program for operating disk drives and assisting you in using the computer.

It's not necessary to read the *Disk Operating System* book now. You can look through it, if you wish, and locate the DOS diskette. After you've read this book, you will be better able to understand important parts of the *Disk Operating System* book.

To operate the computer with one or more disk drives, it's necessary to use the program stored on the DOS diskette. For protection against accidental loss or damage to the original copy, make one or more duplicates. These are called *backup* copies.

Back Up the DOS Diskette—If you have not yet made a backup copy of the DOS diskette, do it now. When you've made one or more backup copies of the original DOS diskette, put the original back in the *DOS* book and never use it again—except to make more backups if you need them. If you make two copies of the DOS diskette—as I do—store one and use the other with your computer.

In the IBM Personal Computer *Guide to Operations* book, the backup instructions are in Section 3, under the heading *An Important Exercise: Backing Up Your DOS Diskette*. There is one set of instructions for a computer with a single disk drive and another set for use with two disk drives. Follow the instructions exactly, and it will be easy. Be sure to type the commands exactly as you see them in the IBM book.

This is how the disk should be inserted into the disk drive. The notch on the left side, near the label, is the *write-protect notch*. To prevent recording data on a diskette, and thus protect data that is already there, cover this notch with a piece of tape. Write-protect tape is supplied with diskettes. This diskette is not write-protected.

To prevent accidental erasure, store all diskettes a foot or more away from electrical devices such as computers, audio equipment, television sets and telephones. Keep them in the paper envelopes they're packaged in. Store them in boxes or containers that keep out airborne dirt particles, in a place that doesn't get wet or hot.

To run the programming examples in this book, I will ask you to put a backup copy of the DOS diskette into disk drive A of the computer.

THE IBM PERSONAL COMPUTER REFERENCE BOOK ON BASIC

You should also have received an IBM Personal Computer book entitled *BASIC.* It's written by Microsoft, the company that wrote the version of BASIC used in the IBM Personal Computer. This is an excellent reference book about the BASIC programming language. It is thorough and comprehensive, but it may be difficult for beginners to understand.

It's organized to make it easy to look up information about a specific BASIC programming word or procedure—similar to a dictionary or encyclopedia. You don't need to read the IBM *BASIC* book now. You can look through it, if you wish.

This book and the IBM *BASIC* book both discuss programming, but this book is organized differently. It helps you learn, step by step, starting with the fundamentals. This book is not a complete discussion of programming. It tells you only what a beginner needs to know and understand.

Use this book to learn programming at the beginner's level. Use the IBM Personal Computer *BASIC* book as a *reference* when you want more details or information about specific topics.

THE KEYBOARD

You communicate with your computer by typing on the keyboard. The IBM Personal Computer has an astonishing range of capabilities, all of which you can command from the keyboard. This makes the keyboard seem complicated because it must do a lot of different things.

This discussion will give you a general introduction to the keyboard and ask you to use some of the keys so you can see how they work. To do that, you must turn on the computer and do some preliminary operations.

IF YOU HAVE A PRINTER

If a printer is connected to the computer, it should be turned on when the computer is turned on. Otherwise, it is possible to lose data. This may happen if the computer sends data to the printer with the printer turned off. The demonstration programs in this book do not send data to the printer, except in the chapter that discusses using the printer.

But good habits are better than bad habits. If you *never* turn on the computer without first turning on the printer, you will *never* make a mistake and lose some data.

Form the habit of first turning on the printer, then turning on the computer. When you are through using the equipment, turn off the computer and then turn off the printer.

Using the ENTER Key—When you type letters, numbers or punctuation symbols at the keyboard, the computer displays what you typed so you can see it. It does not accept or use the typed information until you press the ENTER key. This allows you to make changes, if you wish, before pressing ENTER.

This key is engraved with a special arrow symbol as shown in the accompanying illustration. I'll call it the *ENTER* key, even though it's not engraved with the word *ENTER*.

TURNING THE COMPUTER ON

If you have a printer connected to your computer, turn it on first. Then put a backup DOS diskette in drive A and turn the computer on. You should hear the fan motor start running. The computer takes a short time to do an automatic internal check and then beeps if it doesn't find anything wrong. Then you will hear clicking and buzzing sounds that mean the disk drive is operating.

Loading the Disk Operating System—DOS is loaded automatically if the DOS diskette is in drive A when you turn on the computer. When the disk drive stops running, DOS has been loaded. It has been read from the disk in drive A and fed into the computer so it can be used.

DOS Versions—There is more than one version of the Disk Operating System. Each is identified by a number, such as 1.00 or 1.10. If you don't know which you have, the version number is shown on the DOS diskette. It is also shown by the computer. You'll see that soon.

This book can be used with any version of DOS. Version 1.00 is used with single-sided diskettes. Version 1.10 is used with double-sided diskettes. There are a few differences in the way they operate.

You'll notice only one difference while using this book. Version 1.10 asks you to enter date and time as soon as DOS is loaded. Version 1.00 doesn't, but you can enter it if you wish. Your instruction book will tell you how. For the examples used in this book, it is not necessary to enter date and time.

The following discussion of date and time applies to DOS Version 1.10. If you have the earlier version of DOS, skip the date and time entry procedures.

Entering Date and Time—When the Disk Operating System has been loaded into the computer, the display for DOS Version 1.10 shows something like this:

```
Current date is Tue 1-01-1980
Enter new date:
```

Notice that the number zero has a diagonal slash through it when displayed on the screen. This is to help you distinguish it from the capital letter O. The IBM Personal Computer Printer prints the number zero without the diagonal slash. In addition, the number zero is shaped differently from the letter O. You should have no trouble distinguishing them.

The short blinking line after the word *date* on the second line is called the *cursor*. It shows where the next letter or number will appear on the screen when you type something on the keyboard.

You are being asked to enter the correct date. Then, if you use the computer to put information on a diskette, the information will be labeled with that date. This is often useful.

The current date shown on the first line doesn't mean anything. It serves as a dummy to show you the correct form.

For the year, you can use four-digit numbers from 1980 to 2099. If the year is 1980 to 1999, you can type only the last two numbers.

Using the number keys along the top of the keyboard, type numbers for month, day and year, separated by dashes as shown on the display. If you prefer, you can use the slash symbol (/) instead of a dash. Do not use any spaces—follow the format exactly. Do not type the day of the week—the computer will reject it and ask you to type the date again.

The BACKSPACE Key is in the top row of the keyboard, marked by a left-pointing arrow. The ENTER key is just below it, marked by a "down-and-then-left" arrow. These are international keyboard symbols.

Check the date to be sure you typed it correctly. If not, use the *backspace* key to move the cursor to the left until the incorrect numbers disappear. Then type them correctly.

The backspace key is engraved with an arrow pointing to the left, as shown in the accompanying illustration. Even if you typed the date correctly, use the backspace key for practice. Remove part of the date and retype it.

When the date is correct, press the ENTER key. As an example, I have entered 2-22-1983. If you leave the computer turned on, the date will automatically advance at midnight.

Entering the date causes the computer to display a request to enter the time of day. The screen looks like this:

```
Current date is Tue 1-01-1980
Enter new date:   2-22-1983
Current time is   0:0:13.07
Enter new time:
```

The current time shown on the screen is a dummy to illustrate the format: hours:minutes:seconds.hundredths of seconds.

Hours are based on a 24-hour clock. One AM is 1:00, one PM is 13:00 and midnight is 00:00. The computer has a built-in clock. Once set, it will run as long as the computer is turned on. You can display time and date on the screen, print them on a printer and use them in programs, if you wish. It isn't necessary to enter seconds and hundredths of seconds unless you need to keep time that accurately. Just enter hours and minutes, then press ENTER.

If you are not going to put information on a diskette, or use time and date in a program or display, you may wish to skip these two steps. If so, just press ENTER twice, without typing anything. The computer will use the displayed date and time *even though* they are wrong.

When you've completed the date and time exercise, the screen display is as follows. I entered 10:15:00.00 as the time.

```
Current date is Tue 1-01-1980
Enter new date:   2-22-1983
Current time is   0:0:13.07
Enter new time:   10:15:00.00
```

DOS Is Ready—When DOS has been loaded and you've responded to the date and time routine, if asked to, you then see a message that includes the version number.

```
The IBM Personal Computer DOS
Version 1.10 (C) Copyright IBM Corp 1981, 1982
A>_
```

The first line of the new message on the screen tells you that DOS has been loaded. The second line shows the version number, such as 1.00 or 1.10. When the DOS program is changed and improved, it is given a new version number. Larger numbers are given to later versions.

The bottom line is called a *prompt* symbol. Here's what you see:

```
A>_
```

This is the prompt for DOS, which is different from other prompts. Learn to identify the prompt displayed because it helps you know what is happening and indicates the computer's status. When you see this prompt, you know that DOS is loaded and ready to do something.

There are a lot of useful things you can do when you see the DOS prompt, but the computer is not yet ready to accept BASIC or run programs written in BASIC. Because I want you to see how the keyboard operates when you program in BASIC, we won't do anything with DOS.

Loading BASIC—To use BASIC, you must load a second program that is on the DOS diskette. This prepares the computer for that language. Even though this program enables the computer to use BASIC, it's not written in BASIC. It and the DOS program are written in *machine language,* also called *assembly language* or *assembler language.*

The cursor after the DOS prompt symbol shows where the next character will appear on the screen. Type the word

```
BASIC
```

and press the ENTER key. You can type upper or lower case, or even a combination such as *BaSic.* The computer will recognize the command as long as you spell it correctly.

The disk drive runs again, and the display at the top of the screen shows something like:

```
The IBM Personal Computer Basic
Version D1.10 Copyright IBM Corp. 1981, 1982
40959 Bytes free

Ok
_
```

The first line tells you that BASIC has been loaded, so you can use it. The second line shows the version. The letter will be C, D, or A. I'll explain these later. The number, such as 1.00 or 1.10, is the version number of BASIC.

The third line shows how much computer memory is available for use by a BASIC program. Computer memory is expressed in units called *K.* In general use, that letter stands for 1000 units. When used to specify computer memory, however, K represents 1024 units known as *bytes.* There's a technical reason why 1K equals 1024.

The amount of memory shown on the third line is the amount that is installed in the computer, such as 64K, *minus* the amount of memory used to store DOS and BASIC.

The prompt for BASIC is the word *Ok.* When you see Ok, the computer is ready to use the BASIC programming language. Now's the time to see how the keyboard works when you are using BASIC.

There are 10 special-function keys, labeled F1 through F10, along the left side of the keyboard. They can be programmed to type words or short phrases automatically.

GETTING ACQUAINTED WITH THE KEYBOARD

There's a lot to know about the keyboard. This discussion will get you started.

Function Keys — At the left are 10 keys labeled *F1* through *F10*. You use them to type standard BASIC expressions with one keystroke rather than several.

Ten different expressions are produced by pressing the function keys, as shown along the bottom of the screen. For example, if you press key F1, the word *LIST* is displayed on the screen. Try it. Then press ENTER, and the prompt for BASIC returns to the screen.

The word *LIST* commands the computer to display the program in memory by printing it on the screen — if the program is *written* in BASIC. You have loaded two programs so far — DOS and BASIC — but neither is *written* in BASIC, so neither will be listed by this command. That's why when you pressed ENTER, the screen listed nothing.

Press F2. This commands the computer to RUN the loaded program, if it's written in BASIC.

It ran nothing because there isn't a BASIC program loaded. Then it displayed the BASIC prompt symbol again, to tell you that it's ready for your next command.

The keyboard's typewriter keys are arranged the same as on a standard typewriter.

Typewriter Keys—In the center of the keyboard is a group of keys that are lighter in color than the others. These are similar to the keys on a standard typewriter and are used in a similar way. Type

```
hello
```

and then press ENTER. The computer prints an error message saying *Syntax error* and displays the prompt again.

```
hello
Syntax error
Ok
_
```

The *error message* tells you that the word *hello* has no meaning in the BASIC programming language. In the rest of this chapter, most things I will ask you to type and enter will produce error messages. Please ignore them. This is a keyboard lesson, not a programming lesson.

The better typist you are, the easier it will be to write programs. As you will see, the programmer's greatest problem can be typographical errors.

Look at the light-colored keys and familiarize yourself with the symbols and locations of the keys. You'll see a few that are not on an ordinary typewriter keyboard.

HOW TO TURN THE COMPUTER OFF

To use this book, you should have the computer turned on. This way you can type and enter the programming examples to see what they do. You know how to turn it on—*printer first, then computer*—if you have a printer.

Of course, you won't turn the computer on and type all of the examples in this book without ever turning the computer off. You can go partway through the book and turn the computer off. When you are ready to resume, turn it back on again.

Before turning off a computer, there is one important thing to consider. If you have a program *of any kind* in the computer memory, it will disappear from memory if you simply turn off the computer. The main computer memory stops working when the power goes off, and *everything* in it disappears.

That's why computers use disk drives. If you have a program in computer memory that you don't want to lose when the power goes off, you can send it from memory to the disk drive and copy it onto the disk in the drive. This is called *saving* the program.

Programs on disks are permanent until you erase them. You can run the disk drive and send any program on the disk into computer memory. This *does not remove the program from the disk*. It's like playing music that's on an audio tape cassette.

If you are running the computer and using a program that you brought into memory from a disk, there is no need to save the program back to disk when you want to turn the computer off. The program is still there. DOS and BASIC are examples. Any program that you brought into the computer *from a disk* remains on the disk.

On the other hand, if you entered a new program from the keyboard, it is in computer memory but not yet on the disk. Before you turn off the computer, you should save that program—unless you don't want to keep it.

While reading this book, you can turn off the computer any time you want to. Before you   , think about what is in memory. If you want to keep it, and it is not already on the disk, save it to disk before you turn off the computer. When you need to know how to save programs to disk, this book will tell you how.

After you have saved the program in memory, if you decide to save it, then you can turn off the computer. Turn off computer first, then printer.

Typematic Feature—Most of the keys will repeat if held down longer than a half second. These include the keys that print a character on the screen. Try it with letter and number keys. Then press ENTER.

SHIFT keys are marked with arrows that point up. The Caps Lock key serves a special purpose, not the same as standard typewriters.

Caps Lock—The key labeled *Caps Lock* affects *only* the alphabet keys. Press it once to turn it on, press it again to turn it off. At one setting, all of the letters type as capitals. At the other setting, all of the letters are lower-case.

Try using it a few times to see how it works. Try it both on and off while typing letters. Then press ENTER.

If you're accustomed to using a typewriter, you will notice that this key is like a shift lock, except that it affects letters only.

In programs, all of the letters in BASIC words are upper case. With the IBM Personal Computer, you can type them either way, and the computer will automatically convert lower-case letters to upper case when it stores the program in memory—even though you see lower case on the screen.

Old-time programmers are accustomed to seeing capital letters on the screen. That's what the Caps Lock key is for—to make the screen show capital letters when you program, even though it doesn't matter to the computer.

Now try using the Caps Lock key while typing numbers. You will see that it has no effect. Either way, pressing number keys produces numbers.

Shift Keys—Shifting is done by holding down either of the shift keys at the lower left and lower right of the keyboard. They're identified with an arrow that points up.

Among the typewriter keys, all that are not letters are engraved with two symbols—one above the other. If a shift key is *not* pressed, these keys produce the lower of the two symbols. If shifted, the upper symbol is produced.

Try using a shift key with the number keys along the top of the keyboard. Then press ENTER.

When you are typing letters, holding down a shift key will temporarily reverse the setting of the Caps Lock key. If the Caps Lock is set to produce capital letters, holding down the shift key will cause the letters to appear in lower case. If the Caps Lock key is set to produce lower case, the shift key causes upper-case letters to appear on the screen. Try it. Then press ENTER.

If you are accustomed to a standard typewriter keyboard, it will take a while to learn to use this keyboard. It's designed for programmers. When programming, you can set the Caps Lock key to produce capital letters, which is standard for all words in BASIC. It works *just as well* if you type BASIC words in lower case even though it doesn't "look right" on the screen.

Either way, you must use one of the shift keys to select the "shifted" or upper-case symbols on the other keys—such as # instead of the number 3.

The shift keys are used mainly with the light-colored typewriter keys and the light-colored keys at the far right—called the *keypad*. There is no way to lock a shift key—it operates only when you hold it down.

These numbered keys are called the *keypad*. They have two purposes, controlled by the Num Lock key. At one setting, they are used to type numbers. At the other setting, the keys marked with arrows move the cursor in the display.

Keypad—Most of these keys have two functions, controlled by the Num Lock key just above. The Num Lock reverses its effect each time you press it.

To see the main function of the keypad, it will help to have a clear screen. Here is one way to do that. Press ENTER to be sure that everything you've typed has been accepted by the computer—possibly with an error message—and the BASIC prompt symbol is visible. Then type

CLS

in either upper or lower case. Press ENTER. CLS is the BASIC word that *CLears the Screen*. The screen is cleared and the cursor moved to *home,* the upper left corner of the screen.

Now you need to find out which way the Num Lock key is set. To do that, press the keypad key marked *2.* If it prints a 2 on the screen, the Num Lock key is set wrong for this demonstration. If so, press and release it.

At this setting, the lower symbols on the keypad indicate what the keys do. Notice that there are four arrow symbols—up, down, left and right. Place the middle finger of your right hand on the key marked *5.* Use your index finger to press the left arrow, your ring finger to press the right arrow. Move your middle finger up or down to press the other two arrows.

Press the arrows to see what they do. This is called *cursor control.* It has several purposes. One is to establish where a character will print on the screen. Move the cursor somewhere and then type a letter. Notice that the cursor-control keys will repeat if held down.

Move the cursor anywhere near the center of the screen. Press the key labeled *Home.* Notice that the screen is not cleared but the cursor goes home to the upper-left corner of the screen.

The other function of the keypad is to enter numbers conveniently. Some office calculators have a similar keypad. To see this, press the Num Lock key. Now, numbers and the decimal point will be produced by these keys. Type some numbers and then press ENTER.

Using the Keypad as a Calculator—When you see the BASIC prompt symbol, you can use the keypad as a calculator. First type the word *PRINT.* Notice that there are + and − keys just to the right of the keypad. Clear the screen as you did earlier. If you get an error message, do it again.

When you see the BASIC prompt symbol, type

```
PRINT 2 + 3
```

and press the ENTER key. The display will show

```
PRINT 2 + 3
 5
Ok
_
```

In BASIC, these key symbols are used for mathematics:

+   Add
−   Subtract
*   Multiply
/   Divide

    You can print * with either upper-case 8 in the row of numbers at the top of the keyboard or with the *PrtSc* key just to the left of the keypad. For now, I suggest using upper-case 8.

    If a printer is not connected to the computer or is connected but turned off, and you press the PrtSc key with a shift key down, the computer will lock up and be unresponsive for about a minute, but no harm is done. I'll discuss that later. I want you to know about it now so you won't be alarmed if it happens.

    Try using the keypad to do arithmetic for a while. If you have never used a computer before, this is a milestone. You've found a way to do something useful with it. You can use it instead of a $12 pocket calculator!

The key with left and right arrows is the tab key. Unless specially programmed, it tabs only to the right, similar to the tab key on a typewriter. Esc, Ctrl and Alt keys have special purposes.

Tab Key—Among the darker keys to the left of the keyboard is one with a left and right arrow. This is the tab key. In ordinary use, it tabs only to the right.

    Type a row of characters on the screen. Then move the cursor down to the beginning of the following line. Operate the tab key and notice how many spaces it moves the cursor.

Control Key—This key is labeled *Ctrl*. You use it in combination with other keys to produce special functions. Hold it down, then press another key, then release both keys.

For example, hold the control key down while pressing the letter G. I'll write this combination of keys as *Ctrl-G.* It makes the beeper beep. That's how computer programmers call for the butler.

Try holding down the control key while pressing the key marked *Home* on the keypad. This is another way to clear the screen and send the cursor home. You now know two ways to clear the screen when it is cluttered.

Alt Key—This key provides another way to write BASIC words with a single keystroke. Hold it down while pressing one of the letter keys on the keyboard. Try Alt-R, for example. You will get *RUN,* a BASIC word. Try as many keys as you wish. Notice that the beginning letter of the BASIC word is the same as the letter that you pressed. If there is no word, the letter prints.

PRACTICE HELPS

There is more to know about the keyboard, but you've just had a good start. It takes two kinds of skills to program a computer: knowledge of programming, and finger skills to type correctly. Getting your fingers to do what your mind says is often the most frustrating part.

I suggest that you spend a few minutes reviewing the keyboard discussion in this chapter and training your fingers to find the keys. A little practice will pay off.

USING THE ALT KEY

Alt-(letter)	BASIC Word
Alt-A	AUTO
Alt-B	BSAVE
Alt-C	COLOR
Alt-D	DELETE
Alt-E	ELSE
Alt-F	FOR
Alt-G	GOTO
Alt-H	HEX$
Alt-I	INPUT
Alt-K	KEY
Alt-L	LOCATE
Alt-M	MOTOR
Alt-N	NEXT
Alt-O	OPEN
Alt-P	PRINT
Alt-R	RUN
Alt-S	SCREEN
Alt-T	THEN
Alt-U	USING
Alt-V	VAL
Alt-W	WIDTH
Alt-X	XOR

2 How To Write A Simple Program

This chapter begins with some general information about the computer and then helps you write some simple programs. After that, there's some more general information about programming.

From now on, I will use the word *disk* instead of *diskette*. At one time, 8-inch disks were called *disks* and 5-1/4-inch disks were called *diskettes*. The distinction has become blurred by common usage.

THE SYSTEM DISK

The DOS disk is often called a *system disk* because one of the programs stored on it is the Disk Operating System for the computer. The operating system is a program that operates disk drives, keeps track of where information is placed on a disk, and does a lot of other "housekeeping" chores that you wouldn't want to be bothered with.

Why Use a Disk?—Disks are used to store permanent records of computer programs and data. Unless you erase them, programs stored on a disk remain there and can be transferred, or *loaded,* into the computer. When you "play" a disk in a disk drive—send a program or data into the computer—the disk is not erased. The program or data remain on the disk, unaltered by having the program or data read.

For a program to operate, it must be loaded into the computer. You can change the program while it's in the computer. You can then send the revised version out of the computer and store it on the disk, either replacing the original program or as a different version of the original. Data used with computer programs, such as a list of names and addresses, can also be sent out of the computer and stored on a disk.

COMPUTER MEMORY

Programs and data loaded from a disk go into a part of the computer called *memory.* The computer memory that stores these programs is called *Random Access Memory* (RAM). You can put information into this memory, change it as you wish and get it back out again whenever you want.

Random access memory is not permanent. If you turn off the computer, or if there is a power failure, whatever is stored in RAM vanishes. We use disks to store programs and data because they can't be stored permanently in RAM.

Another type of memory is called *Read Only Memory* (ROM). Information is put into this memory when the computer is manufactured. The information is permanently stored. The computer can read and use what is on ROM, but cannot change it. Neither turning off the computer, nor a power failure will erase information in ROM.

Because information in ROM cannot be changed, this memory is not suitable for most programs or for information that you may wish to change at some future time. The IBM Personal Computer has both ROM and RAM.

LEVELS OF CAPABILITY

When the DOS system has been loaded and the DOS prompt is in view, the computer can display a directory of programs and data files on disk, transfer programs from disk into computer memory, transfer programs and data from one disk to another, and similar functions.

As mentioned, it can run programs written in machine language—also called *assembly* language or *assembler* language. You can write a program in that language, but it is difficult and takes a lot of time. Most assembly-language words are not familiar to us—examples are XLAT, RCL and SBB.

Low-Level Language—Assembly language is considered a low-level language. This means that although it's not easy for people to understand, it is easy for the computer. The computer operates most efficiently when running an assembly-language program.

High-Level Languages—To make it easier for people to write programs, high-level languages have been developed. Some of them are Fortran, Pascal and BASIC. Many words in these languages are ordinary English words and are easy for people to understand. Here are some examples from BASIC: PRINT, RUN, STOP.

Writing programs in a high-level language is easier for you, but they take a little longer to run on the computer.

With the IBM Personal Computer, you have a choice of three types of BASIC.

CASSETTE BASIC

If you do not put a system disk in drive A before turning on the computer, or if the computer doesn't have a disk drive at all, the computer will operate with Cassette BASIC. The version number displayed on the screen will begin with the letter *C,* signifying Cassette.

ROM permanently stores Cassette BASIC. It is always there and available, without loading it. Other programs are loaded into RAM.

With this type of BASIC, you can plug an audio cassette tape machine into a connector on the back of the System Unit. You use audio tape cassettes to store programs and data and send this information back and forth to the computer memory. This method is slower and less convenient than using disks, but satisfactory for some applications. Using cassettes is not discussed in this book.

DISK BASIC

Disk BASIC is an *addition* to Cassette BASIC. It has additional features that allow the computer to use disks and other added features. The added part is stored on the DOS system disk and must be loaded into computer RAM memory before you can use it. When the DOS prompt is displayed, you load disk BASIC by typing the word BASIC and pressing ENTER, something you've already done.

When Disk BASIC is loaded, the version number displayed on the screen begins with the letter *D.*

When the computer uses Disk BASIC, it uses the BASIC stored in ROM and that stored in RAM. Programs that are written in Cassette BASIC will operate with Disk BASIC loaded into the computer. However, programs written in Disk BASIC may not operate correctly if only Cassette BASIC is used. This is called *upward compatibility.*

All programs in this book use Disk BASIC.

ADVANCED BASIC

This is another addition to Cassette BASIC. It does everything that Disk BASIC does plus more, such as providing advanced graphics on the screen.

When Advanced BASIC is loaded, the version number displayed on the screen begins with the letter *A.*

Programs written in Cassette BASIC or Disk BASIC will run correctly when Advanced BASIC is loaded, but programs written in Advanced BASIC may not operate with one of the other versions.

Advanced BASIC is not used in this book.

COMMAND OR STATEMENT

Most BASIC words are either a *command* or a *statement.* There is a small difference in meaning.

Usually, a command tells the computer to do something that relates to operations, such as loading a program.

Usually, a statement tells the computer how to execute the program. A statement is a single BASIC word or a group of BASIC words that together provide an instruction to the computer— similar to a sentence in the English language.

The distinction between commands and statements is not important. Some BASIC words are both commands and statements.

LOADING DISK BASIC

If your computer is not turned on, with BASIC loaded, please do it. As a reminder, here's how: With the computer turned off, place a backup DOS diskette in drive A. If a printer is connected, turn it on. Then turn the computer on. When you see the DOS prompt symbol, the disk operating system has been loaded into RAM. Type the word *BASIC,* in either upper or lower case, and press ENTER. This loads Disk BASIC into memory.

This procedure is sometimes called "Bringing up BASIC." When you see the BASIC prompt symbol, the computer is ready.

BOOTING A PROGRAM

An expression often used to mean loading a program is *booting the program.* This is derived from the old expression, "He lifted himself up by his bootstraps." The word *bootstrap* has been shortened to *boot* and its meaning expanded to include loading nearly anything.

In the early days, when a computer was turned on, it just sat there because it didn't have enough "intelligence" to do anything. Programmers entered short "bootstrap" programs that enabled it to accept and execute longer programs.

The bootstrap routine for the IBM Personal Computer is part of ROM. When you turn the computer on, the bootstrap routine is the first thing that happens. It happens automatically.

THE BASIC INTERPRETER

When you load BASIC, what is actually loaded into memory is a program called a *BASIC interpreter.* It translates or interprets BASIC words, which people can understand, into machine language that the computer can understand and execute.

THE COMMAND MODE

When you see the BASIC prompt symbol, *Ok,* the computer is in the *command mode.* You can type commands in the BASIC language and the computer will execute them *immediately,* as soon as you press the ENTER key. The command mode is also referred to as the *immediate* mode, the *direct* mode and occasionally the *calculator* mode.

Pressing the ENTER key tells the interpreter that you have finished typing a command or statement that can be executed. This is called *entering* the command or statement into the computer.

Pressing the ENTER key also returns the cursor to the left side of the screen and moves it down one line. Then the BASIC prompt symbol is displayed again to show that the computer is ready for another command. When you are asked to type a command or statement, type it and then press the ENTER key.

PRINT

If you see the BASIC prompt symbol on the screen, your computer is in the command mode. Please type and enter this statement:

```
PRINT "HELLO"
```

The simplest way to display capital letters, so your statement looks like my statement, is to use the Caps Lock key. If you make a mistake in typing, use the backspace key to correct it.

PRINT is a statement that tells the computer to display something on the screen. The word *HELLO* is what you have told the computer to print.

Pressing ENTER tells the interpreter to execute the statement you've just typed.

If you do it right, HELLO appears at two places on the screen. You see the *statement* that you typed. Under it, on the next line, you see the *result* of that statement after execution by the computer—the HELLO displayed on the screen. Below that is the BASIC prompt again.

From now on, when I ask you to enter something, I actually mean *type and enter.*

SYNTAX ERRORS

BASIC is absolutely unforgiving of errors in spelling, punctuation and sometimes even the spacing between words. If you type something incorrectly and the BASIC interpreter recognizes that you've made a mistake, it will display the words *Syntax error.* Here's an example. Type and enter

```
PRANT "HELLO"
```

The computer says that you made a *Syntax error* because you typed PRANT instead of PRINT. When I ask you to type something, it will be shown exactly as it should be typed, including spaces and punctuation. If you see capital letters, please type capital letters.

Don't add anything or delete anything unless you want to see what happens. Quotation marks have special significance in BASIC. If you see them in a line that I ask you to type, please type them. If not, don't!

Not all keystrokes result in a display on the screen. For example, ENTER causes the computer to accept and execute the statement, and it causes the cursor to move down on the screen. But it doesn't cause a character or symbol to appear on the screen.

NUMERIC OR LITERAL EXPRESSIONS

When you type characters on the keyboard, they can be treated in either of two ways by the computer—*numeric* or *literal.* Numeric means that the computer will handle them as numbers and do arithmetic with them if requested. A literal expression is not operated on arithmetically or changed in any way. When you enter a literal expression, it always remains exactly as you entered it.

The symbols ''HELLO'' are a literal expression. It's a greeting, not a mathematical symbol or expression. One way to identify a literal expression is to type it inside quotation marks, as you just did when you typed ''HELLO''.

Notice that the computer did not print the quotation marks when it executed the statement. The computer recognized the quotation marks as a signal that the characters typed inside the marks were a literal expression. When asked to print it, it did so—exactly as you typed it, but without the quotation marks.

If you do not put an expression inside quotation marks, the computer treats the expression as a numeric—which means *number.* Here are a couple of examples. Enter

```
PRINT 7
```

The computer considers 7 a number because it is not in quotation marks. It prints the number, as instructed. Now enter

```
PRINT "X"
```

The computer treats X as a *literal expression* because it is in quotation marks. All it does is print it because that's all you've asked it to do.

EVALUATING AN EXPRESSION

If you give the computer some unfinished arithmetic to do, it will immediately finish the job. Please clear the screen by typing Ctrl-Home and then enter

`PRINT 2 + 2`

The statement *PRINT 2 + 2* is treated as a request to do arithmetic because there are no quotation marks. The computer complies by doing the indicated arithmetic first and then printing the answer.

The characters *2 + 2* form an *arithmetic expression*.

Determining the value of an arithmetic expression is called *evaluating the expression*. If you tell a computer to do something with an arithmetic expression, such as PRINT, it will evaluate it first and then print the result.

Literal expressions in quotation marks are not evaluated or changed in any way. Demonstrate this by entering

`PRINT "2 + 2"`

The quotation marks tell the computer to treat this *literally,* so it prints just what you told it to and does not evaluate the expression.

TWO WAYS TO MAKE A COMPUTER DO SOMETHING USEFUL

You can type in statements, one at a time, and the computer will *execute each one immediately* in the command mode. That's what you've done so far.

Or, you can type a series of statements and *store them in the computer's memory,* to be executed later. A series of statements is called a *program.*

When you run the program, the computer accepts the statements just as though you had typed each one separately on the keyboard. The program simply replaces your fingers. When you have it right, a program doesn't make any more typographical errors. You can run a program as many times as you want, without having to type it each time.

When you type statements and store them in memory to run later, you are *programming the computer.* It will not execute the commands as you type them. It merely stores them in its memory for execution later.

When you run the program, it takes charge of the computer. You can watch the program run or you can take a nap. When the program has finished running, the computer returns to the BASIC command mode and displays the BASIC prompt symbol again.

DOING IT MY WAY

Often, I will explain a statement and then ask you to enter it and observe the result. Or, I will ask you to enter it and then I will explain what happened.

If you see something that puzzles you, please do it my way and then read the following paragraphs to find the explanation. I will always tell you what is going on, but I may not do it when you expect me to.

LINE NUMBERS

To write a program, you must tell the computer the order of what you intend to do. It's easy. Just type a number at the beginning of each statement line. This *line number* tells the computer that you are writing a program. The computer will automatically store the statement and its line number in memory, to run later. When you run the program, the statements will be executed in sequence, one line at a time.

It's conventional to start with line 10 and use every tenth number after that. For example, the second line will be 20, the third is 30 and so on. This allows you to go back and insert other lines later, to improve a program or correct a mistake. For example, if you type a line numbered 15, the computer automatically places it in correct sequence in your program—between lines 10 and 20.

Program lines look like this:

```
10 PRINT "2 + 2"
```

Don't bother to type this line. Notice that it's practically the same as the statement you entered earlier from the command mode—except that it has a line number at the beginning. When you entered it without a line number, it was executed immediately. If you enter it with a line number, it will be stored in memory as line 10 of a program. It will not be executed until later, when you run that program.

WHAT IS A LINE?

There's a difference between a line on the screen and a line in a program. The screen normally displays lines that are 80 characters long, including spaces and punctuation marks. If you type more characters than that, the screen performs a *wrap-around*. When one screen line is full, it automatically drops down and starts filling the next screen line.

Type a long line of anything and watch the wrap-around happen.

LENGTH OF ONE PROGRAM LINE

Program lines begin with a line number and include everything you type until the keystroke ENTER. The maximum number of keystrokes that can be stored as a program line is 255, counting the line number and the ENTER keystroke.

If you enter more than 255 keystrokes, everything you type will appear on the screen. But only the first 255 keystrokes will be stored as that program line! The remaining characters will be cut off. The process is called *truncation.*

Nothing obvious happens when you enter a program line that is truncated due to excessive length. However, when you try to run the program, it will not run correctly.

PHYSICAL LINES AND LOGICAL LINES

A program line may occupy more than one screen line. The two kinds of lines are called *physical lines* and *logical lines.* A physical line is one line on the screen. A logical line is one complete program line, no matter how many physical lines are required to display it.

MULTIPLE STATEMENTS ON A LINE

BASIC allows more than one statement in a program line. Each statement must end with a colon, except the last statement in the line, which ends with the keystroke ENTER. Pressing the ENTER key does not print anything visible on the screen.

This is a program line 50 with three statements. Don't bother to type it.

```
50 PRINT 3: PRINT 9: PRINT 27
```

When this line is executed, the numbers 3, 9 and 27 will appear on the screen.

HOW TO CHANGE A PROGRAM LINE

If you notice an error while typing a program line, or any time before you press the ENTER key, change it by backspacing past the error. Then retype it correctly.

If you have entered the line and then want to change it for any reason, start over. Type a completely new line, including the same line number. When you press ENTER, the new line *replaces* the previous line with that number.

Changing program lines is called *editing*. There are other ways to do it, and they're discussed in Chapter 5. For now, use one of the two methods just described.

CLEAR THE SCREEN

The first rule of programming is to clear the screen early in the program—before the program causes anything to be displayed. This removes the "garbage" from whatever was happening earlier. Then, the display will relate only to the program that's running. It looks professional and neat.

In the command mode, the simplest way to clear the screen is to use Ctrl-Home, as you've been doing. However, Ctrl-Home is not a BASIC word, so you can't use it in a program.

The BASIC word to clear the screen is *CLS*. You can use it in the command mode or type it on a program line.

DON'T USE LETTERS INSTEAD OF NUMBERS

If you are accustomed to using a typewriter, you may have the habit of using a lower-case letter l instead of the number one. Don't do that on a computer. It interprets the letter l as a letter, even though you intend it to be the number one.

You may habitually use the upper-case letter O for the number zero. Don't do that either. It will make the computer run your programs incorrectly. When you want the number zero, use the number key at the top of the keyboard or the zero key on the keypad.

A THREE-LINE PROGRAM

Here's a short program for you to enter. This program uses words from the BASIC programming language, meaning that it's written in BASIC. The first line begins with the number 10. Because the lines begin with numbers, the computer knows that you are writing a program. Each line ends with an ENTER keystroke, telling the computer to accept that line and store it in memory.

Use Ctrl-Home to clear the screen before starting to enter this program. If you make a mistake, fix it. Type in

```
10 CLS
20 PRINT "HELLO"
30 END
```

The END statement at line 30 tells the computer, "That's all." With an IBM Personal Computer, an END statement is optional, except in special cases. If you don't use it, the computer will stop running the program automatically when it executes the last program line. The program is now in the computer's random access memory (RAM), waiting for you to use it.

RUNNING A PROGRAM

To run this program, type and enter

```
RUN
```

When you enter RUN, the computer will run any BASIC program that's in RAM. If there is no program, the computer will display only the BASIC prompt symbol again.

IMPROVING THE DISPLAY

The program runs and displays the word *HELLO*. However, the prompt symbol appears on the following line because the computer returns to the command mode when the program finishes running.

Sometimes, the prompt symbol makes the display difficult to interpret. In this case, the display seems to say *HELLO Ok*.

The screen always looks neater and more professional if the prompt is moved downward on the screen, so it doesn't appear to be part of the display created by the program. Do this by adding a line to the existing program. Enter

```
25 PRINT: PRINT: PRINT
```

Notice that one program line contains three statements, separated by colons. It will produce three blank lines because it says to print nothing three times. Because you typed 25 at the beginning, this line will be placed automatically between lines 20 and 30, which is where you want it. Run the program again by entering

```
RUN
```

Notice the improvement in the display.

LIST

When writing a program, you'll often want to see what you wrote. Enter

```
LIST
```

and the computer will display the program, starting at the beginning. You should now be looking at the four-line program you just wrote. Enter

```
RUN
```

and it will run again.

Listing with Function Key F1 — A shortcut method of listing a program is to press the function key F1 at the left side of the keyboard. The display at the bottom of the screen shows what each function key will type.

Press F1 and notice that the word *LIST* is displayed. To actually list the program, you must then press ENTER. The F1 key won't do that for you. Try it and see.

LISTING PART OF A PROGRAM

When a long program is being listed, it will first fill the screen with lines. Then the low-numbered lines will move off the top while higher-numbered lines become visible at the bottom. This is called *scrolling*. It's very difficult to read a program while it is scrolling. If anybody is watching, I sometimes pretend I can do it.

There are several ways to prevent scrolling. One is to tell the computer the line numbers you want to see. Enter

```
LIST 10
```

Line 10 is displayed. Now enter

```
LIST 10-25
```

You see three lines. Now enter

```
LIST 10-100
```

The computer lists as much as it could—all four lines.

To list from a specified line number to the end of the program, you don't have to type the last line number. Just type the starting line number followed by a hyphen. Enter

```
LIST 20-
```

The computer starts at line 20 and goes to the end, wherever it is.

To list from the beginning to a specified line number, type a dash followed by the ending line number. Enter

```
LIST -20
```

The computer starts with the first line of the program and lists all lines through 20.

SUMMARY OF LIST COMMANDS
(The # symbol represents a line number.)

LIST	Lists the entire program. The display may scroll.
LIST #	Lists only the specified line number.
LIST #-#	Lists all lines from the first specified line number to the second specified line number.
LIST -#	Lists all lines from the beginning of the program to the specified line number.
LIST #-	Lists all lines from the specified line number to the end of the program.

SPACING DOWN FROM THE TOP

When a program prints a short message on the screen, it usually looks better and is easier to read if the message is not at the very top. Insert another program line that moves the message down on the screen. Enter

```
15 PRINT: PRINT: PRINT: PRINT
RUN
```

Notice the improvement. Now list the program.

In most programs, many of the lines are not essential to make the program run. This program prints the same result without lines 15 and 25, but those lines serve to make the display look better.

Some program lines simply make the program easy for a person to run. Some make the display easier to read. Some are used to tell the keyboard operator about a typing error and then provide an opportunity to correct the mistake. These features make programs *user-friendly* and are always worth the time and effort it takes to put them in.

Please look at this little program one more time. Be sure you understand each line.

```
10 CLS
15 PRINT: PRINT: PRINT: PRINT
20 PRINT "HELLO"
25 PRINT: PRINT: PRINT
30 END
```

USING FUNCTION KEY F2 TO RUN A PROGRAM

So far, you've typed the word *RUN* and pressed the ENTER key to make a program run.

A faster way is to press the F2 key. Notice in the function-key display at the bottom of the screen that key F2 prints the word RUN followed by a small arrow symbol. The arrow means that the ENTER keystroke is also provided by the F2 key. One keystroke does the whole job.

The program you typed is still in memory. Run it again by pressing F2. Just for practice, list it and RUN it a few times using function keys F1 and F2.

TO DELETE A PROGRAM LINE

One way to delete an entire program line is to type the line number and then press the ENTER key. This enters a line with nothing on it, replacing the previous line with that number. The BASIC interpreter recognizes that the line is "empty," so it deletes it entirely from memory.

This won't change the following line numbers. If you have lines 10, 20, 30, 40, and you delete line 30, then you have lines 10, 20, 40.

Later, you can enter line number 30 again, if you wish, with a new statement.

HOW TO STOP READING THIS BOOK

While working your way through this book, you enter short programs and run them to see what happens. Some of the programs are used several times, at different places. If you turn off the computer, these programs will disappear from memory.

If you have a program in memory and want to stop reading this book, you should save the program on a disk. Then, when you resume reading, you can load the program from the disk back into memory and resume where you left off.

To do this, you should have a backup DOS disk in Drive A. The write-protect notch on the disk should not be covered with tape. This means it is not write-protected and the computer can put the program on that disk.

To copy the program from computer memory onto the disk, enter

```
SAVE "PROGRAM"
```

When you do that, the word *PROGRAM* is the name under which the program is stored on the disk. It is just a temporary name that is easy to remember. The quotation marks are part of the statement. When you enter the statement, the red light on Drive A will glow and you will hear the disk drive operating. When it stops, you can turn off the computer. You can leave the backup system disk in the disk drive if you wish. Put a book mark in this book so you will know where to resume, or record the page number.

When you want to resume, turn on the printer, the computer, and load BASIC in the usual way. Then enter

```
LOAD "PROGRAM"
```

Drive A will operate again. When it stops, the program you saved will be back in computer memory. To be sure, list it. Run it to double-check.

This is just a way to save a program temporarily, using the word *PROGRAM* as a temporary name. Whatever you are working on, save it as PROGRAM. When you want to resume working on it, load it as PROGRAM.

To save a program permanently, use a permanent name for the program, such as DIARY. That way the word *PROGRAM* is always available to use as a temporary name.

NEW

The command NEW erases or *clears* everything in memory. If you are writing a program and make a bad start, sometimes it's simpler just to clear the memory and begin aNEW. If you've been running the program that does nothing but print HELLO, and are completely bored with it, enter

```
NEW
```

The computer memory should be empty. To see if it is, enter

```
LIST
```

or press F1. All you get is the prompt symbol. This means that nothing exists to list. The NEW command cleared out everything in RAM.

When you start to write a program, enter NEW to be sure that nothing is in memory. Otherwise, if lines are there from an old program, they may intermingle with the new program and cause big problems.

Suppose a program in memory has lines 10, 15 and 20. You decide to type a new program and do it without using NEW to clear memory. Your new program has lines 10, 20 and 30.

New line 10 will replace old line 10. New line 20 will replace old line 20. Nothing deletes or replaces old line 15, so it is still in memory. When you run your new program, it will include old line 15. It will execute like this:

```
10 new program line
15 OLD PROGRAM LINE
20 new program line
30 new program line
```

The new program probably won't run correctly. Always clear memory before writing a new program.

NOW YOU WRITE ONE

For practice, write a program that prints the letters A, B and C on lines 4, 5 and 6 of the screen, counting from the top.

When you have it working, insert additional program lines so the letters print on screen lines 4, 6 and 8 instead.

My programs that do this are at the end of this chapter, page 45.

DELETE

Use the DELETE command to delete one or more program lines. DELETE, followed by a line number, removes that line. For example, if a program has a line 170, the command

```
DELETE 170
```

will remove it.

DELETE followed by line number-line number deletes that range of lines. For example, if a program has lines from 10 to 500,

```
DELETE 100-200
```

deletes all lines from 100 to 200, *including lines 100 and 200.*

To delete an entire program, you must type the beginning line number and the ending line number as part of the DELETE command. You must use the actual line numbers in the program.

You can find both numbers by listing the program. For example, if a program has lines from 10 to 2200,

```
DELETE 10-2200
```

deletes the entire program.

You can use the DELETE command to delete all program lines from the beginning, up to and including a specified line number. For example,

```
DELETE -500
```

deletes all lines through 500.

You *cannot* use the DELETE command to delete from a specified line number to an indefinite ending line number. This means that the command

```
DELETE 100-
```

will not work. You will get an error message saying *Illegal function call,* but the program will not be affected.

In all of these DELETE command formats, any line number that you specify must actually exist in the program. If it doesn't, an error message results and the program will not be changed.

SUMMARY OF DELETE COMMANDS
(The # symbol represents a line number.)

DELETE #	Deletes the specified line.
DELETE #-#	Deletes from the first specified line number to the second specified line number, inclusive.
DELETE -#	Deletes from the beginning of the program to the specified line number.

PRACTICE DELETING

Here's a program you can use to practice deleting. Enter

```
NEW
5 CLS: PRINT: PRINT: PRINT
10 PRINT 10
20 PRINT 20
30 PRINT 30
100 PRINT 100
200 PRINT 200
300 PRINT 300
500 PRINT: PRINT: PRINT
```

Press F2 to make the program run and see that it works. Notice that the numbers printed are the same as the line numbers that cause them to be printed.

Now DELETE a single line, using the DELETE command, by entering

```
DELETE 100
```

List it to check the deletion. Run it to check the result. Now, DELETE a group of lines by entering

```
DELETE 30-200
```

List the program to see the result. Lines 30 and 200 are gone. If there had been any lines between 30 and 200, they would also be gone. Remaining are lines 5, 10, 20, 300 and 500.

Try to delete the entire program by entering

```
DELETE 5-
```

As mentioned, the computer considers the command illegal and displays an error message. Deleting program lines is serious business. If you remove something that you didn't intend to, it can be very difficult to reconstruct. This is why the computer requires you to tell it exactly where to stop deleting lines.

Type and enter

```
DELETE -10
```

List it and then run it. It looks better when you clear the screen early in the program, doesn't it?

THE SPACE AFTER THE LINE NUMBER

Program lines are displayed on the screen as you type them. If you don't enter a space after the line number, there will be no space on the screen as you are typing the line. But, the line as saved in memory will have a space added automatically. Try this by clearing the screen and entering

```
NEW
10 CLS
20PRINT "X"
```

List it. Notice that there is now a space in line 20, between the line number and PRINT.

SPACES BETWEEN WORDS IN STATEMENTS

Some versions of BASIC allow you to omit spaces between words. If you do omit the spaces, and you later read the program to see why it doesn't work, there will be problems. You end up TRYINGTOREADSTATEMENTSTHATLOOKLIKETHIS.

It used to be fashionable to omit spaces in program lines because shorter lines require less memory to store. In those days, computer memories were small and expensive. Today, computer memories are larger and relatively cheap.

Remember: The BASIC used by the IBM Personal Computer requires spaces between BASIC words.

END

Your IBM Personal Computer does not require an END statement in a simple program. However, some programs do require an END statement to work properly, as you will see a bit later.

GOTO

Sometimes, you need to skip some lines in a program, jumping either forward or backward. The statement GOTO 100 causes the computer to go immediately to line 100, execute it and then continue with the lines following 100.

We type GOTO as one word, rather than as two, so the expression stands out as a BASIC statement. The statement causes an *unconditional* jump. The computer has no choice—when it arrives at a GOTO statement, it must jump to the specified line.

If line 50 is GOTO 100, the program will skip all of the lines between 50 and 100.

Please clear the screen and then enter this program.

```
NEW
10 CLS: PRINT: PRINT: PRINT
20 PRINT "Howdy,"
30 GOTO ******
40 PRINT "Pardner."
50 PRINT "Youall."
60 PRINT: PRINT: PRINT
```

When I became interested in computers, I learned some things about programming by spending a lot of late-night hours reading books and entering demonstration programs. For me, demonstration programs are often boring because they are trivial, useless except to demonstrate something, irrelevant to what interests me, and too long. Although I may not be doing much better, at least my demonstration programs are short.

It may relieve your boredom if you will imagine, with me, that this little program does the talking for a lonely cowboy, camped by a trail somewhere. This is a greeting from the cowboy to a party approaching his camp. Don't run it yet.

In case you're not familiar with the subtleties of cowboy grammar, a single individual is addressed as *Pardner* and a group of people is addressed as *Youall*. The essence of this exciting program is to arrange it so the cowboy gives the correct greeting.

Notice that the greetings are literal expressions, inside quotation marks. The computer will store and recall them exactly as typed.

Both upper- and lower-case letters are used in these literal expressions. This is to remind you that you can type a literal expression any way you wish. It may also demonstrate that your fingers don't do that very well. I made incorrect settings of the Caps Lock and shift keys just now while trying to type those upper- and lower-case letters.

Please list the program and check your typing. Obviously, line 30 isn't finished yet. When writing a long program, you may know that you want a GOTO statement at some line, but you don't know yet what line to go to. When this happens to me, I usually put a string of asterisks with the GOTO statement because they're easy to see when I come back to complete that program line.

Now, finish line 30. Imagine that several people are approaching on the dusty trail, so enter

```
30 GOTO 50
```

List it again and be sure line 30 is typed correctly. Now let's follow the program flow:

Line 10   Clears the screen and prints three blank lines.
Line 20   Prints *Howdy,*
Line 30   Provides an *unconditional* jump to line 50.
Line 40   IS NOT EXECUTED BECAUSE THE PROGRAM JUMPS OVER IT.
Line 50   Prints *Youall.* and demonstrates correct cowboy grammar.
Line 60   Prints three blank lines so the prompt will be moved down a bit.

Run it by pressing F2. It should give you a great feeling of accomplishment. With the GOTO statement, you can jump *forward or backward* in a program. Right now you probably can't think of many reasons to do that. But when you write real programs you will. There are other types of jumps, described later.

Keep this program in memory or on disk because we will use it again.

INTERRUPTING PROGRAM EXECUTION

Computers have procedures to stop program execution while a program is running. When done from the keyboard, this is called *breaking*.

Do it from the keyboard by pressing and holding down the Ctrl key while pressing the Scroll Lock/Break key at the upper-right corner of the keyboard. This keystroke combination is written *Ctrl-Break*.

When you stop execution this way, the computer displays a special symbol to indicate that it stopped because of Ctrl-Break rather than a program malfunction or some other reason.

The special symbol is an upside-down *v*, called a *caret*, followed by the letter *C*. On the next line of the screen, the line number of *the last line executed* is shown by a message such as *Break in 1600*. Then the computer returns to the command mode and waits for you to tell it what to do next. It looks like this:

```
^C
Break in 1600
Ok
_
```

STOP

You can also stop program execution by a line *in the program*. The command is STOP. This command tells the computer to stop and then display the number of the last line that was executed. It then returns to the command mode. I'll demonstrate this soon.

CONT

This makes the program continue. After stopping program execution, either from the keyboard by Ctrl-Break or in a program line using the STOP command, you can do something in the command mode, get something to drink or answer the phone. When you're ready for the program to start running again, enter

```
CONT
```

Program execution will resume just as though it had never been interrupted, *unless you changed the program while it was stopped*.

It's a great temptation to stop a program that seems to be running wrong, change a line or two and start it up again. The computer won't cooperate. It will display the words *Can't continue* on the screen. You have to start again at the beginning using the RUN command.

FORMING A LOOP

In my opinion, the greatest advantage of a computer is its ability to do a simple task repeatedly without making any mistakes or becoming bored. You can tell it to count to a million three times and it will do it contentedly.

Repeated operations are done in a program formation called a *loop*. There are several good kinds and one bad kind. First, I will show you the bad kind. It's called an *endless loop*.

Suppose line 50 of a program says GOTO 10. When the program first begins to run, it starts at line 10 and executes one line at a time until it reaches line 50. At line 50, it is sent back to line 10 to do it all over again. Each time it reaches line 50, it jumps back to line 10 again. It will do this continuously until you stop it somehow. The *loop* from 50 back to 10, to 50 again and so on is *endless,* hence the name.

When a program is in an endless loop, you can stop it by pressing Ctrl-Break to interrupt execution. Then you can list the program, fix the problem and run it again to see if you corrected it.

THE SOCIABLE COWBOY

If the cowboy program is still in memory, list it. If you put it on disk, bring it back and then list it.

When you last ran the program, it executed the last line, line 60, and stopped because it ran out of program lines to execute.

Let's prepare the cowboy to greet the next party that comes down the trail by putting in a jump back to line 20 so he can say "Howdy" again.

When adding or inserting a line in a program, don't type NEW because you certainly don't want to erase the existing program in memory. Enter

```
70 GOTO 20
```

List it and check to be sure line 70 is correct. Now run the program.

The program is in an endless loop. You are looking at the evil ailment called *scrolling.* When you can't stand it any longer, interrupt the program by pressing Ctrl-Break. Press it repeatedly if necessary. Execution will stop at some line number, depending on when you pressed Ctrl-Break. The screen will show the line number at which execution stopped.

Notice that the Scroll Lock/Break key also stopped the scrolling. This is a coincidence. The key has *Scroll Lock* engraved on the top surface and *Break* engraved on the front surface. It can serve two functions. In BASIC Versions 1.00 and 1.10, the Scroll Lock function has not been provided. The Break function operates when you also press Ctrl. If a program is in an endless loop, stopping the program by Ctrl-Break also stops the scrolling—but it was pressing Break that did it.

Just for fun, start the program again by entering

```
CONT
```

Then stop it again by Ctrl-Break. Do it a few times. When you have it stopped, try pressing function key F5. Add that key to your repertoire. Pressing it does the same as entering the CONT command.

Stop it and list the program again. Do you see that it loops from 70 back to 20 and stays in that loop forever?

A Quick Fix—Line 35 isn't being used in this program. Let's put a STOP there to prevent the program from looping endlessly. Enter

```
35 STOP
```

Run it again. The program has an endless loop. I did that on purpose so you'll know how it feels to be in big trouble. You are really messing up this program!

Stop execution using Ctrl-Break. Then list the program and figure out why the STOP statement at line 35 didn't stop execution. Start at line 10 and see where the program "goes" at each step.

You're right. The program jumps from line 30 to line 50 every time it goes through the loop, so it never "sees" the STOP statement at line 35.

Complicated programs sometimes have many jumps of various kinds. A common problem is jumping over a necessary statement or group of statements, making the program not work. If this happens, you have to follow the program flow step by step until you find the trouble.

Delete lines 35 and 70 by typing the line numbers and then pressing ENTER. As you know, entering a line with nothing on it deletes that line number, but list it to be sure. Keep the program in memory for when we need it again.

RESETTING THE COMPUTER

Sometimes, due to a mistake in a program or a quirk in its execution, the computer leaves the program, goes off into never-never land and won't come back. The entire keyboard is dead and the computer is completely unresponsive to commands. In computer jargon, this is called a *lockup* or a *hangup*.

One way to regain control of the computer is to turn off the power and start over. The penalty is that you *lose everything* in RAM. The computer memory used for programs that you write or load is temporary—when the power goes off, RAM forgets everything. By saving programs to disk, you can protect against such disasters.

Another way to start the computer again has the same penalty. You do it by pressing three keys—Ctrl, Alt and Del—at the same time. Don't try it because we still need the program in memory. This is called a *reset*. The result is the same as if you had turned the computer off and back on again, but resetting is a little faster.

ASSIGNMENT STATEMENTS

When you do arithmetic in a program, you deal with quantities called *variables*. You give each one a name or label, so the computer can keep track of it. This is *assigning variable names*.

Early versions of BASIC used a LET statement to do this. For example, LET X = 2 assigns the *name* X to the *quantity* 2. Some people prefer to say that it assigns the value 2 to the name X, which means the same thing.

As a result of this assignment, the computer stores the number 2 in memory and remembers that its name is X. When you ask the computer to retrieve X, it will go to the place where it stored the number 2 and then deliver it.

If you assign a different value to the variable name X, such as the number 3, the new value will replace the old value in memory. When you ask for X, you get the number 3.

The BASIC you are using does not require the word LET at the beginning of an assignment. But it's OK if you use it anyway. Try it by entering

```
LET X = 2
PRINT X
```

Notice that this is done in the Command mode. It does not affect the program stored in memory. The BASIC prompt symbol appears on the screen between the two lines you typed. Then the number 2 is displayed and the prompt symbol shows again.

Test again without LET.

```
X = 3
PRINT X
```

The computer changes the value of X because you told it to. It prints the number 3. It does not require LET in assignment statements.

INTERACTIVE PROGRAMMING

The advantage of a BASIC interpreter is that you can quickly see what a program does and change it as needed. Then you can run it again and fix it again if necessary.

You can interrupt a running program to make changes or try statements from the command mode.

The computer responds immediately. You say, "Let's try this." The computer says, "OK. Here's the result. Now what?" This type of *interactive* programming is a great aid to learning.

Not all BASIC programming is done this way. Instead of a BASIC interpreter, computers can use a BASIC *compiler*. After the program is written in BASIC, the programmer uses the compiler to translate each program line into machine language without running the program.

With a compiler, you write a program, then compile it as a separate step, then run the compiled version. If the program needs fixing, you can't change the compiled version directly. You must change the original program in BASIC, compile it again, then run it again.

Compiled BASIC programs will run faster, but they are not as easy to write because you can't do it interactively. Some people write and test a program using an interpreter and then compile it after the *bugs,* or mistakes, are out.

USING THE COMMAND MODE WHILE PROGRAMMING

The command mode uses the same interpreter that is used to run programs. BASIC statements will have the same result in either mode. When you are writing a program and you want to check a statement to see exactly what it does, stop programming and try it in the command mode. That's what you just did to see if your computer requires the word *LET.*

YOU CAN'T HARM A COMPUTER FROM THE KEYBOARD

When your computer is new and you still remember how much you paid for it, it's natural to be afraid of breaking it and concerned about the possibility of a big repair bill.

The worst thing you can do to the computer from the keyboard is something unusual that locks it up so it does not respond to commands. You already know what to do. Just reset it. You haven't harmed the computer at all.

Even though you can't harm *the computer* from the keyboard, you can lose programs by forgetting to save them on disk before turning off the computer, or alter programs by deleting something that should not have been deleted.

If you damage a program, the repair cost is not measured in dollars—it's measured in time. Usually the only repairperson who can fix it again is you. When the light in my window is on long after midnight, that's usually what I'm doing.

NEVER USE A NUMBER TO BEGIN A STATEMENT

Suppose you want to assign the value 62 to the variable name X. If you enter

```
62 = X
```

in the command mode, the computer thinks you just wrote line 62 of a program. The line doesn't make sense because it says $= X$. If you have a program in memory, it gets line number 62—which can cause big trouble. Later, when you run the program it will stop and display *Syntax error in 62.*

If you are writing line 120 of a program, and you enter

```
120 62 = X
```

the computer thinks you never give up. It stores $= X$ as line 12062 of the program. The space between 120 and 62 is irrelevant.

Either of these assignment statements would work fine if written

```
X = 62
```

The variable name is always first. Variable names *must begin with a letter.* If you try to begin one with a number, that number gets mixed up with the line number and you get the feeling of being in big trouble again.

Write this on the wall above your computer: *Never use a number to begin a statement.*

VARIABLE NAMES

I once wrote a program to calculate the future retirement income for employees of a small company. The formula was provided by the personnel department. It involved the number of years of service, age at retirement, average earnings during the last five years and some other factors.

The program itself wasn't difficult, but I got tangled up in variable names and finally started over again.

I needed to identify a lot of different years. I assigned the variable name YB to year of birth, YS to the year when employment started, YR to the year of scheduled retirement. Employees needed 15 years of service at retirement, so I assigned YS to years of service.

When the program wouldn't give correct answers, I finally saw that I had used the variable name YS for two different things.

Variable names are important and should be assigned carefully and thoughtfully. It's best to have a plan at the beginning and to write the assigned variable names on a piece of paper beside your computer as you assign them. You may think that you will remember them, but you won't.

The best variable names are *mnemonic* (pronounced *nee-mon-ic*), meaning that they explain themselves to your mind.

Some computers limit variable names to two characters, which makes life simple unless you use YS twice. The IBM Personal Computer allows up to 40 characters per name! Long variable names can be more self-explanatory but are tedious to type.

Nevertheless, it's best to use a name that is long enough to be useful and not confusing after a few months, when you return to the program to change or fix it.

Illegal Names — Words that are BASIC commands or have some special meaning to the computer can't be used as variable names. These are called *reserved words.* Examples are LOAD, RUN, STOP. A complete list of reserved words is in Section 3, *GENERAL INFO,* of the IBM book entitled *BASIC.*

If the computer finds an illegal variable name while a program is running, it will stop and display *Syntax Error* along with the line number containing the mistake. This helps you find it.

Embedded Reserved Words — A reserved word can be used in a variable name if it is part of a longer word. For example, you can't use NEW or END, but you can use NEWS or SEND.

RULES FOR VARIABLE NAMES

LENGTH	Up to 40 characters. You can type longer names, but characters past 40 will be ignored and truncated in the listed program.
FIRST CHARACTER	The first character must be a letter. You can use A1, but not 1A.
SPACES	No spaces. If spaces are used, the computer displays *Syntax error* when the program runs.

IF-THEN-ELSE

Most programs have *decision points*. The program checks or tests something at that point and makes a decision depending on the result of the test.

A very powerful programming technique uses the words *IF-THEN-ELSE.* The third part, *ELSE,* is optional, so I'll start with the first two.

The idea is this: IF it is raining, THEN stay indoors.

How an IF-THEN Statement Works—The IF part states a condition that will either be met or not be met. That is, it will be true or false. If the condition is met, the program then does whatever is specified by the THEN part of the statement.

If the condition is not met, the program does not execute the THEN part of the IF-THEN statement. Instead, it jumps *to the next numbered program line.*

This is a very important fact: When an IF condition is not met in an IF-THEN statement, the program leaves that line *immediately* and goes to the next program line.

When the IF condition is met, the program moves to the next statement, whether it is on the same line or a following line.

Here's a simple example. Please enter it in the command mode, without line numbers.

```
X = 2
IF X = 2 THEN PRINT "YES"
```

The computer displays YES because the condition is met. The computer ''knows'' that $X = 2$ because you made that assignment. Now try this:

```
IF X = 3 THEN PRINT "YES"
```

The computer does not print YES because the condition is not met. In a program, it would jump to the next numbered line.

How an IF-THEN-ELSE Statement Works—This has three parts. The IF portion states the condition to be met or not met. The THEN part says what to do if the condition is met. The ELSE part says what to do if it is not met.

Remember that you set X equal to 2. Try these statements:

```
IF X = 2 THEN PRINT "YES" ELSE PRINT "NO"
IF X = 3 THEN PRINT "YES" ELSE PRINT "NO"
```

In the first statement, the condition is met. The THEN part executes. In the second statement, the condition is not met. The ELSE part executes.

You can use IF-THEN or IF-THEN-ELSE statements in a program to make *conditional* jumps to specified program lines. If the condition is met, the program jumps. If not, it proceeds to the next statement.

One form is like this. Don't type it.

```
50 IF A = 20 THEN GOTO 100
60
```

This will send the program to line 100 if the condition is met. If the condition is not met, line 60 will be executed—whatever it is. Notice that the word *LINE* is not needed to identify a line number.

This statement can be shortened. All of the following statements will have the same result:

```
IF A = 20 THEN GOTO 100
IF A = 20 GOTO 100
IF A = 20 THEN 100
```

Another form is

```
50 IF A = 20 THEN GOTO 100 ELSE GOTO 300
60
```

In this form, the program *must jump* somewhere at line 50. If the condition is met, it goes to line 100. If the condition is not met, it jumps to line 300. This means that the program cannot proceed directly from line 50 to line 60. However, the program can execute line 60 by jumping to it from somewhere else.

BACK IN THE SADDLE

Let's rejoin the sociable cowboy and put a decision point in the program. Let's agree that only one or two people can be greeted. To allow more than two requires some BASIC that I haven't discussed yet. Please list the program in memory and change it to look like this:

```
10 CLS: PRINT: PRINT: PRINT
20 PRINT "Howdy,"
30 NP = 2
35 IF NP = 2 THEN GOTO 50
40 PRINT "Pardner."
50 PRINT "Youall."
60 PRINT: PRINT: PRINT
```

List it and check to be sure it is typed correctly. Here's how the program should work: In line 20, the cowboy begins his cheerful greeting. In line 30, NP means *Number in Party.* The program assigns NP = 2, which means two people. Later, I'll show you a better way to do the same thing.

In line 35, the program tests the value of NP to see which greeting is appropriate. If the party has two people, the program jumps to line 50, and the cowboy finishes his greeting with good grammar by saying "Youall."

If the condition at line 35 were not met, line 40 would automatically execute the greeting for a single person. But, to make that happen, you would have to change the assignment statement in line 30. Run the program to double-check my explanation.

Keep Testing—In my experience, it's a good idea to test portions of programs as you write them, rather than write the whole program and then try to find the bugs. When testing, try all possible values of variables, especially extreme values—the *limits*.

You've seen that the program works when NP = 2. Let's test it when NP = 1. Retype line 30 so it reads

```
30 NP = 1
```

Run it. The cowboy gives both greetings! List the program to see the problem. The IF-THEN statement at line 35 does not execute because NP = 1. Line 40 is executed, followed immediately by line 50—which is the normal flow of the program as it is now written.

When the cowboy gives either of his greetings, the program should end right there. If line 50 executes, he says "Youall," and the program proceeds to the end. If line 40 executes, he says "Pardner," but the program then proceeds to line 50. This doesn't make sense because the program should end after line 40 executes. Here's one way to do that. Enter

```
45 END
```

Run it. The program almost works. Now, the cowboy seems to say "Howdy, Pardner. Ok"

The reason is that line 60 never executes to move the prompt symbol down on the screen. This will fix it:

```
45 PRINT: PRINT: PRINT: END
```

Try changing line 30 back and forth between NP = 1 and NP = 2. Notice that the program works correctly either way. Leave NP set to 1 when you've finished.

Another Way—There's usually more than one way to solve a programming problem. Typically, you do it one way and then eventually see a better solution. For example, list the program again and I will show you a better way.

Notice that what should happen after line 40 is already happening at line 60—three PRINT statements and the program end.

Instead of writing a new line 45 to do that, the program could jump from line 40 to line 60 using a GOTO statement. Here's how:

```
40 PRINT "Pardner.": GOTO 60
```

Retype line 40 to read that way. Then delete line 45. Run it to be sure it works as planned.

List it again and check the program flow from line 35. If NP = 2, the program jumps to line 50, then 60 and ends. If NP = 1, the program moves from line 35 to line 40, then jumps to line 60 and ends. Line 60 ends the program no matter which path is followed.

USING MULTIPLE STATEMENTS ON THE SAME LINE

As you know, you can put more than one statement on the same line. You just did it. To use multiple statements, you must put a colon at the end of each statement except the last one. Each statement will be executed completely, and then the next statement on the line will be executed.

In the old days, programmers used multiple statements to make the program compact, so it took less room in memory. There are some good reasons to use multiple statements, but today that isn't one.

You should use multiple statements on the same line only when there's a logical connection between the statements and when the program will be easier to understand that way. Line 40 is a good example.

REM

When you are writing a program, everything about it is clear in your mind, and you think you will never forget the clever things you did. But you will.

REM means *REMark*. You put remarks in your program to explain your cleverness. This helps another person read and understand your program. It also helps you later, when you want to change something.

Remarks can be on individual lines, all alone, but usually they are put on a line that also has a statement. Separate a statement from a following remark by putting a colon between them. The remark explains that statement or section of the program.

Remarks are not executed. When the computer sees REM, it stops executing *that line* and proceeds to the next line.

If you put a statement on a line, followed by a remark, followed by another statement, the computer will never execute the second statement. Therefore, *always* put remarks at the very end of a line.

If the cowboy program is not already on the screen, list it. Add this remark to clarify the program:

```
30 NP = 1: REM NP is Number in Party
```

What this remark does is explain the variable NP. When writing remarks, don't bother to state what the line does if it is obvious. In this case, it is obvious that NP is being given a value, but it is not obvious that NP is the Number of People to be greeted.

An overenthusiastic remarker might add a remark to line 35, saying "Jump to line 50 if NP = 2." That doesn't add anything that isn't already obvious.

Beginners use too many remarks, or too few, and usually explain the wrong things. Old-timers do the same.

Apostrophe—You can use an apostrophe instead of REM. Consider putting a remark on a line by itself to give your program a name. Enter

```
5 ' COWBOY'S DECISION
```

and it will look pretty fancy. List it. Run it to be sure line 5 doesn't execute or cause a problem.

In addition to a title, you should use remarks at the beginning of the program to indicate what it does, any special things that a user or another programmer should know, and perhaps your name as author.

IDENTIFYING THE OPERAND

Statements and commands in BASIC have two parts: the *operator* and the *operand.* The operator states what operation is to be done, such as SAVE. The operand supplies the rest of the information needed by the computer, such as "COWBOY."

The *operator* "operates" on the *operand.* In the command, SAVE "COWBOY", the operator is *SAVE* and the operand is *COWBOY.*

When the computer sees a statement, it identifies the operator and the operand and then executes the statement. Usually, there is no doubt about the operator. Sometimes, you may be uncertain about the operand, unless you know the rules. This discussion will use the operator PRINT to illustrate some rules about operands.

What Type of Operand is It?—The first question about an operand is this: Is it a numeric or a literal string? The word *numeric* means a number or something representing a number. The term *literal string* means something that is not treated numerically. The computer will handle a literal string exactly as typed and will not do arithmetic with it.

The term *literal string* means a series of characters that are treated literally. The series is called a *string* because the characters are like beads on a string—they are connected and handled as a unit. The term *literal string* is usually shortened to *string.*

So far, you have seen only one way to identify an operand as a literal string. That is to type the string in a program line and put it in quotation marks, such as "Howdy".

If you don't do that, the computer treats the operand as a numeric. Please type and enter these examples:

```
PRINT "Hello"
```

The operand is identified as a string because it is typed inside quotation marks. The computer prints the string, just as you typed it. Try this

```
PRINT 2
```

The operand is clearly identified as a numeric, so the computer prints it as a number.

```
PRINT 2 + 2
```

The operand is a numeric *expression,* with some unfinished arithmetic to be done. The computer first *evaluates* the expression—which means that it does the indicated arithmetic. Then it prints the result.

Stating the Operand Directly—In all of the examples just entered, the operand is stated *directly*. It is typed as part of the statement. The computer doesn't have to look somewhere else to find the operand because it is already there, right behind the operator.

Stating the Operand Indirectly—An operand can be stated *indirectly* by giving it a name and then using the name instead of typing the operand itself. Giving an operand a name is done by an *assignment statement*. For example, enter

```
X = 2
```

When the computer executes the assignment statement, it stores the number 2 in memory, under the name *X*. If another statement uses X as the operand, the computer goes to memory, gets the *value of X* and uses the *value of X* as the operand instead of the symbol *X*. Enter

```
PRINT X
```

and the computer prints the value of X. Now enter

```
PRINT X + 2
```

The computer has no difficulty doing that. It looks up the value of X, evaluates the numeric expression, then prints the result.

If you use a name without first assigning it a value, the computer assumes that the value is zero and proceeds accordingly. Enter

```
PRINT Y
```

The computer prints zero because no value has yet been assigned to Y.

Variable Names—As used here, X and Y are called *variable* names because their values can change. A program can cause X to be 2 for a while and then change it to 33. The program will always use the most recent value given to a variable name.

Kinds of Variable Names—When a variable name is used instead of typing the operand directly in the statement, the computer must go to memory and find the value of that name. To do that, the computer must know if the variable name represents a numeric or a string variable. That's because the computer files numbers by one method and literal strings by another.

The variable names X and Y are treated as numerics, as you have seen. With a special symbol added to the end of the variable name, they can be identified as string variables rather than numeric variables. The special symbol is a dollar sign, $, which we read as the word *string*. For example, the variable name X$ is pronounced *X string*.

Now, you can make two kinds of assignment statements. You can assign a *number* to a numeric variable name or you can assign a *string* to a string variable name. Try it both ways. Enter

```
X = 3
PRINT X
```

The numeric variable name, *X,* receives the value *3*. In the statement using X as the operand, the value of X is printed. Now enter

```
X$ = "Hello"
PRINT X$
```

The string variable, X$, receives the string "Hello" as the result of the assignment statement. In the statement using X$ as the operand, the string "Hello" is printed.

Type Declaration—The string symbol, $, is called a *type-declaration* symbol. It identifies the variable as literal. There are other type-declaration symbols, discussed later.

Things to Remember—Operands can be stated directly by typing them on the program line, or indirectly by using a variable name.

When operands are stated directly, strings are typed inside quotation marks. If quotation marks are used, the operand is literal. PRINT 3 asks the computer to print the number 3. PRINT ''Hello'' asks the computer to print the string *Hello*.

When stated indirectly, using a variable name, the name of a string must have the type-declaration symbol, $. If that symbol is not used, the variable name is a numeric. PRINT X asks the computer to print the number represented by X. PRINT X$ asks the computer to print the string represented by X$.

String assignment statements must use $ as part of the variable name and quotation marks enclosing the string on the right-hand side of the equation. Numeric assignment statements do not use $ or quotation marks. X$ = ''Hello'' assigns the string ''Hello'' to the string variable name X$. X = 3 assigns the number 3 to the numeric variable name X.

Implied Operators and Operands—Sometimes, the operator or operand is implied in a statement, rather than actually being there. For example, PRINT: PRINT: PRINT will print three blank lines. The operators are PRINT statements. The operands are implied.

HOW TO GET INPUT FROM THE KEYBOARD

The existing cowboy program is impractical because it requires you to change line 30 to change the program flow. Rewriting a program line to change the value of a variable is not practical. In the real world, things like that are done by the person at the keyboard—without changing a program line.

The form of the statement is

```
INPUT X
```

It does several things. INPUT prepares the computer to receive a typed message from the keyboard. It will stop the program and wait until something is typed, displaying a question mark as a prompt.

Because X is a variable name, whatever is typed will be assigned to that name. In this form, the statement requires the program user to type in a number because X is a numeric variable. You can use any other numeric variable, such as NP, if you wish.

Because the program user is expected to type a number, the program must provide an instruction on the screen that will cause him to respond appropriately. Enter these lines:

```
12 PRINT "Are 1 or 2 people approaching? Type 1 or 2."
14 PRINT "Then press ENTER key."
16 INPUT NP: REM NP is Number in Party
18 PRINT: PRINT: PRINT
```

Then delete line 30 because the program doesn't need it any more. The value of NP is determined by a keyboard input at line 16. List the program. It should look like this:

```
5 ' COWBOY'S DECISION
10 CLS: PRINT: PRINT: PRINT
12 PRINT "Are 1 or 2 people approaching? Type 1 or 2."
14 PRINT "Then press ENTER key."
16 INPUT NP: REM NP is Number in Party
18 PRINT: PRINT: PRINT
20 PRINT "Howdy,"
```

(Program continued on next page.)

```
35 IF NP = 2 THEN GOTO 50
40 PRINT "Pardner.": GOTO 60
50 PRINT "Youall."
60 PRINT: PRINT: PRINT
```

Run it twice. Enter 1 the first time and 2 the second time. Even though the program is trivial, it accomplishes what I want to show.

Unless the programmer is highly skilled and experienced, most programs go through several improvements after they're first written. A program is changed and improved until satisfactory—just like this program was developed.

But this program doesn't protect against user error. Do that with techniques called *error trapping,* discussed later. Look again at line 35 and you will see that entering 2 produces one result and entering *any number* other than 2 produces the other result. If the user entered 3 or 50, the program path would be the same as if the number 1 had been entered.

HOW TO TRACE PROGRAM FLOW

When a program has decision points and jumps, as this one does, it's sometimes useful to know which lines are executing. This helps in troubleshooting.

There are two BASIC commands for this purpose. TRON means *trace on.* It prints line numbers on the screen as they're executed, along with the results of running the program. Line numbers are in square brackets like this: [50]. Once on, TRON remains on until turned off.

TROFF means *trace off.* It disables TRON. Both commands can be entered either from the command mode or as program lines. In the command mode, TRON is entered by pressing function key F7. TROFF is F8.

Press F7 to enable TRON. Press F2 to run the program. Enter the number 1 from the keyboard.

Refer to the current program listing starting on page 39 and look at the screen display. Line numbers 5 and 10 were printed on the screen by TRON when they executed, but a statement on line 10 cleared the screen, so those two numbers disappeared.

From there, the program flow is shown on the screen: lines 12, 14, 16, 18, 20, 35, 40, 60. Look at the program listing to review what happened when those lines executed.

Now press F2 to run the program again. Enter the number 2 from the keyboard. This time, the executed lines were 5, 10, 12, 14, 16, 18, 20, 35, 50, 60. The program followed a different path. Check the program listing to review what happened when these lines executed.

Do this as many times as you wish. It's important that you understand how this little program works. When you've finished, press F8 for TROFF. Run it again and you will see that the line numbers no longer print.

HOW TO SAVE A PROGRAM

Earlier in this chapter, you saw a simple procedure to save and load a demonstration program named PROGRAM. This discussion gives you more information about saving programs.

Right now, you have a program in memory. You can run it as many times as you can tolerate. If there is a power interruption, or if you turn off the computer, the program will disappear from memory. It will be lost unless you have it on disk. I assume that you are still using a backup copy of the DOS system disk in drive A with the write-protect notch on the disk uncovered.

Before you can save a program, you must give the program a name, called a *filename,* so you know what to ask for when you want to load it back into the computer.

The filename is not part of the program. It does not *have to* appear anywhere in the program, but I usually show the filename as a remark at the beginning of the program anyway.

When I'm ready to put a program on disk, I look at the beginning of the program to be sure I know its correct filename. This way, I don't file it one time as EXCELLENT and then file it the next time as SUPERB.

A filename is a group of eight or fewer characters. They can be letters or numbers, in any order. Examples: INCOME83 or 83TAXES. Spaces are allowed, and some punctuation marks and special symbols are OK, too. For a list of allowable punctuation marks and special symbols, see the filename discussion in the IBM *DOS* book, Section 3, under the heading *DOS Command Parameters*.

Sometimes I write a program in two or more different ways to see which works best. I use numbers as part of the filename to designate different versions, such as EXPENS1, EXPENS2 and so forth. I also include a remark early in each program to say how one is different from another.

Use a name that gives a clue as to what the program does. For the program you now have in memory, you could use CWBYDCSN, meaning *Cowboy's Decision*. Instead, let's use COWBOY for the filename and add it to line 10 as a remark. Change line 10 to read

```
10 CLS: PRINT: PRINT: PRINT: REM filename "COWBOY"
```

If you want to see it in print, add your name as author. Notice the quotation marks around COWBOY. Remember, when saving and loading files, the opening quotation marks are necessary, the closing set optional. Type and enter

```
SAVE "COWBOY
```

It doesn't matter whether you use upper or lower case to type the filename. The filename will end up with upper case letters no matter how you do it.

Disk drive A should run. You'll hear it hum and see a red light. When it stops, the BASIC prompt appears and the save operation is done. The computer merely assigned the name in the SAVE statement to the program in memory. It *did not* read the name in the remark at line 10.

Now you can turn off the computer if you wish. The program should be safely stored on the disk in drive A.

Once a program is saved, you don't need to save it again *unless you change it* while it is in computer memory. If you change the program, you must save it again. Otherwise, the next time you load it from disk, you will get the earlier version.

HOW TO GET IT BACK AGAIN

You already know how to do this. With the computer operating, BASIC loaded and the BASIC prompt displayed on the screen, type and enter

```
LOAD "COWBOY
```

Quotation marks at the end of the filename are optional. Loading a program from disk clears the computer memory as a first step, so it's not necessary to enter NEW before loading. Drive A should run briefly and a prompt symbol should appear on the screen. Then list it or run it to be sure you got it back again.

USING FUNCTION KEYS TO SAVE, LOAD, LIST AND RUN PROGRAMS

By now, your fingers should be automatically using the F1 key to list a program from memory and the F2 key to run it. It's time to add F3 and F4 to your repertoire.

As you can see in the display at the bottom of the screen, pressing F4 automatically types *SAVE"*. It provides the first set of quotation marks for the following filename, which is the only one necessary when saving a program. All you have to do is type the filename, in either upper or lower case, and press ENTER.

The F3 key automatically types *LOAD"*. It also provides the necessary quotation marks. All you have to is type the filename, in either upper or lower case, and press ENTER.

Spend a few minutes practicing with function keys F1 through F4. Use the COWBOY program.

HOW TO LOAD AND RUN A PROGRAM WITH ONE COMMAND

If you want to run a program, and it is not already in memory, two steps are required: loading it and running it. You can do these in sequence by using the LOAD and RUN commands or by using function keys F3 and F2.

An easier way is to use the RUN command with the filename. If the filename is not already in memory, the computer will look for it on Drive A. If it finds the filename on the disk, the computer will automatically load it into memory and then run it.

To try this, first clear memory by entering NEW. Then enter

```
RUN "COWBOY
```

You should hear the disk drive operate and then see the results of running the program.

You can't use function key F2 this way because it automatically types RUN followed by ENTER. This will run the program in memory, but it doesn't allow you to type a filename between RUN and ENTER to be called from the disk.

SAVE OFTEN

If there's a power interruption while you are writing a program, the program will disappear from memory. Power failures are unpredictable. The best way to protect against losing a lot of whatever you have in memory is to keep most of it saved on disk.

Usually, you will write a program in short segments, each of which does a specific thing. Form the habit of saving the program each time a segment is completed, using the same filename each time.

As the program grows longer in memory, it also grows longer on the disk. If you lose some of it due to a power interruption, it will be just the segment you were working on. Usually, you can easily reconstruct that part because it's fresh in your mind.

When you save a program, it is copied to the disk but also remains in RAM. You don't have to load it again to continue working on it.

CHECKING THE DIRECTORY

When the computer is first turned on, the Operating System automatically reads the list of files on the disk in drive A and puts this information in memory. This is called the *directory.* If you add new files, the directory is automatically updated to include new filenames.

You can see the list of files on the disk in drive A both when the Disk Operating System is loaded and also when BASIC is loaded.

If BASIC is loaded, use the BASIC command

```
FILES
```

Type it and press ENTER. You'll see all the files on that disk, including COWBOY. Look around until you find it. What you see is the file specification (filespec) of that program: COWBOY .BAS

The first part, COWBOY in this example, is the filename. The second part, .BAS, is the *filename extension.* The extension either identifies the programming language the file uses or provides some other special information about it. The extension can use up to three characters and must be separated from the filename by a period.

On the screen, there are spaces between COWBOY and .BAS, but they don't mean anything. They merely make a neat display. When you type a filespec, don't put spaces between the filename and the period.

The extension .BAS means that the program is written in BASIC. When you save a program written in BASIC, the computer supplies the extension automatically, so you don't have to type it. You saved COWBOY, but the directory entry becomes COWBOY .BAS automatically.

When you are using BASIC to load a program with the extension .BAS, you don't have to type the extension.

To See the Directory for Drive B—If you have two disk drives, there will be times when you want to see what is on the disk in drive B. The command is

```
FILES "B:*.*"
```

Both sets of quotation marks are necessary.

USING DRIVE B

To send files back and forth between the computer memory and drive B, all of the commands are the same as described, except that you must use the symbol *B:* in front of the filename, inside the quotation marks. The commands are

```
SAVE "B:FILENAME
LOAD "B:FILENAME
```

WHAT IS A FILE?

A file is any collection of information with a filename that is placed on a disk as a single unit. There are two main categories of information stored as files. You've seen that programs are filed with filenames. Programs are created by people, saved by people and loaded by people.

Data files are the other major category. These are created by program statements, sent to the disk by program statements and called from the disk by program statements.

Suppose you have a program with the filename MAILIST that maintains a mailing list of names and addresses. To use that program, the computer operator—whom I'll call *user*—must load MAILIST and run it.

The MAILIST program, when it runs, will organize the names and addresses into a data file and put the names and addresses on the disk. The program will use a filename for the data file, which must be a different filename than the program itself.

When writing the MAILIST program, the programmer supplies the filename and extension for the data file that holds names and addresses. This name is part of the program itself and is written on a program line that creates the data file.

Suppose the programmer uses NAM&ADRS.112 for that file. The filename means NAMES & ADDRESSES. The extension is a code to show the last time the file was updated or revised—in this case the eleventh month of 1982.

If both files are on the same disk, the directory shows MAILIST.BAS and NAM&ADRS.112. The extensions tell you that MAILIST.BAS is a program written in BASIC and that the other file is a data file.

There's more information about filename extensions later in this book.

GETTING OUT OF BASIC

Sometimes you want to return to the Disk Operating System from BASIC. The command is

```
SYSTEM
```

You can enter it from the command mode or from a program line. When it executes, you see the prompt for the operating system. Programs and data that were in memory are gone.

To save a program in memory, save it *before* turning off the computer or returning to the operating system.

VIEWING THE DIRECTORY FROM DOS

When only the operating system is loaded, the command to see the directory is

```
DIR
```

The list of files will be the same, but there is more information about each file. If there are too many files, the display scrolls. Try it and see.

You can stop the scrolling by pressing Ctrl-Num Lock. To resume scrolling, so you can see more of the directory, press ENTER.

You see five columns of information: the filename, extension, a number representing the amount of space on the disk used by that file, the date and time that it was last put on disk.

When you first turn the computer on and bring up DOS, you may check the directory to be sure the program you want is on the disk. Use the DIR command.

To See the Directory for Drive B—The command is

```
DIR B:
```

HOW TO LOAD BASIC AND RUN A PROGRAM WITH A SINGLE COMMAND

When the operating system is loaded and its prompt displayed, you can type a series of commands and they will be executed by the operating system.

Your computer should be at the operating system level now. If so, enter

```
BASIC COWBOY
```

The word *BASIC* asks the Operating System to load the BASIC interpreter. Then the word COWBOY asks it to *load and run* that program. Notice that quotation marks are not needed around the filename when you use this method to call up and run a program.

TESTING YOUR MEMORY

It would be nice if we could put information into our own memories as easily and reliably as we can put it on disks. Because you can't, please review this chapter and repeat any parts that you're unsure of. The finger exercises of entering and running programs are the best way to load this information into your brain. When you have finished, turn off the computer.

I suggested earlier that you should use the IBM book entitled *BASIC* as a reference while working with this book. This is the best time to start doing that.

Read the first three chapters of the IBM book. You will see that some of the explanations are more thorough, and perhaps more complicated, than those in this book. I think you will be pleased at how much you understand.

You will find some subjects that I haven't mentioned yet, and you may not fully understand those discussions. Read them anyway. If you don't understand everything, don't worry about it.

The accompanying table is a list of BASIC words discussed so far in this book. Chapter 4 of the IBM book entitled *BASIC* is a dictionary of BASIC words, arranged alphabetically. Look up all of the words in the accompanying table and read the definitions. You will find more information than I have given you, and you will understand most of it.

BASIC WORDS USED SO FAR

BASIC	GOTO	REM
CLS	IF	RUN
CONT	INPUT	SAVE
DELETE	LET	STOP
DIR	LIST	SYSTEM
ELSE	LOAD	THEN
END	NEW	TROFF
FILES	PRINT	TRON

Here are my answer programs to the exercises mentioned on page 25:

```
10 REM program to print on lines 4, 5 & 6
20 CLS
30 PRINT:PRINT:PRINT
40 PRINT "A"
50 PRINT "B"
60 PRINT "C"
70 PRINT:PRINT:PRINT
```

```
5 REM program to print on lines 4, 6 & 8
10 CLS
20 PRINT:PRINT:PRINT
30 PRINT "A"
35 PRINT
40 PRINT "B"
45 PRINT
50 PRINT "C"
60 PRINT:PRINT:PRINT
```

3 Good Loops

A loop occurs when a program jumps to a preceding line number and repeats an operation. In my opinion, loops that work correctly are the most useful part of computer programming. You've already seen in Chapter 2 that endless loops aren't very helpful.

COUNTERS

Some loops are controlled by a counter that counts the number of executions. When the desired number has been reached, the program leaves the loop and moves to the next part of the program. Here's an example to enter:

```
NEW
10 CLS
20 C = 1: REM set initial value
30 PRINT C: REM perform an operation
40 C = C + 1: REM increment counter
50 STOP
60 GOTO 30: REM loop back and do again
```

List it and check your typing.

Initializing a Variable—The variable C is the Counter. Line 20 sets it equal to one. This is called *initializing* a variable. You have it under control because you established its initial value. Otherwise, the variable may be lurking around in memory with an unknown value. If you use it without initializing it, results are unpredictable.

The Useful Operation—Every loop performs some useful operation and can do it more than once. In this routine, the useful operation is simply to display the value of the loop counter, C.

Line 30 says PRINT C. Because C is not in quotation marks, the computer treats it as a numeric expression and prints the *number represented by C*.

Increment the Counter—The word *increment* means to add something—usually one unit. Each time this loop operates, the loop counter must be incremented because it is counting the number of operations as they are performed.

Line 40 increments the counter. It says: The new value of C is equal to the old value of C, plus one. Line 50 stops execution. Otherwise, the program would run so fast that it would be difficult to see the screen display.

After the program stops, enter CONT to start the program again. Do it the easy way by pressing function key F5.

Jump Back and Do It Again—When the program restarts, line 60 is executed and jumps back to line 30, where the new value of C is printed again. Then the following lines are executed up to the STOP at line 50.

Run the program by pressing F2. You see the first count produced by line 30. The display tells you that it stopped at line 50. Enter CONT or press F5 and it will go through the loop again. Repeat as many times as you wish.

LOOP BOUNDARIES

Every loop has beginning and end statements. Please list the program again. The end of this loop is line 60 because it sends the program back to the beginning of the loop. Obviously, line 30 is the beginning because that's where the program jumps to so it can repeat the operation.

SETTING THE NUMBER OF OPERATIONS

When a loop is controlled by a counter, the usual way to stop looping and move on is to test the value of the counter at each pass through the loop.

When it has executed the desired number of times, the program jumps out of the loop. Please change line 50 as shown below and add line 100.

```
50 IF C = 10 THEN GOTO 100
100 PRINT "End of loop.": PRINT: PRINT: PRINT
```

List it again. Line 50 is now a *decision point,* sometimes called a *branch point.* It tests the value of C, using an IF-THEN statement.

If the value of C is less than 10, the program proceeds to line 60 and then loops back to line 30. When the value of C is 10, the IF condition is met, leading to immediate execution of the THEN statement. The program *jumps out of the loop* and goes to line 100. It executes line 100 and stops.

Run it to see for yourself. The program prints the numbers 1 to 9 in a column and then jumps out of the loop. You may have expected it to print 1 to 10. List it again.

THE ORDER OF EVENTS

Three important events in a loop are the useful operation, incrementing the counter, and the branch point. In this routine, these are lines 30, 40 and 50. *These events can be in a different order.* The order you choose affects loop operation.

In this loop, consider program flow when C = 9. Line 30 prints the number 9. Then line 40 changes C to 10. Line 50 tests C, finds that it is equal to 10, and jumps immediately to line 100. There is no opportunity to print C when its value is 10. Verify that by running the loop with TRON, which is activated by pressing F7.

With a loop structured this way, you can cause the useful operation to happen 10 times by changing line 50 so it does not jump out of the loop until C = 11. Change the line and try it, using TRON to trace program flow. When it stops, enter

```
PRINT C
```

The loop has finished running, leaving the loop counter set at 11.

In the present form, it prints C before incrementing. Try incrementing first, and then printing C. In other words, swap the statements at lines 30 and 40. When you do that, the first number printed will be 2. Try initializing C to equal zero, instead of 1.

Try moving the branch point to different locations. The number of times a line will be executed in a loop depends on its location in reference to the branch point. Lines ahead of the branch point will execute one more time than lines after the branch point.

There is no best order for the events in a loop. The important thing is to write it to do what you want!

DECREMENTING THE COUNTER

Occasionally, you need to count backward. Here's a loop that does it. Please enter

```
NEW
10 CLS
```

(Program continued on next page.)

```
20 C = 33
30 PRINT C
40 IF C = 27 THEN GOTO 90
50 C = C - 1: GOTO 30
90 PRINT: PRINT: PRINT
```

Line 30 is a substitute for some useful operation that would be performed in a real-world program. There's not much demand for loops that merely count and print the number in the counter.

How many times will this loop operate? Run it to find out. I usually use this order of events: The loop performs the useful operation, then tests the counter to see if it should jump out of the loop. If not, it increments or decrements and starts back at the beginning of the loop.

FOR-NEXT LOOPS

This is a more elegant loop that uses a counter *inside the computer* instead of a counter in the program itself. It uses the BASIC words FOR and NEXT. Please enter

```
NEW
10 CLS
20 FOR C = 1 TO 5
30 PRINT C
40 NEXT C
50 PRINT "End of FOR-NEXT loop."
60 PRINT: PRINT: PRINT
```

List it, check it, then run it with TRON operating.

Line 20, the FOR statement, *sets up* the loop by doing several things. It names the loop counter—in this example, C. It initializes the counter to the first number in the FOR statement—in this example, 1. It also sets the number of times the loop will operate. The statement, FOR C = 1 to 5, causes the loop to operate when the count is 1, 2, 3, 4 and 5, but not when the count is 6. When an increment is not defined, the computer assumes that it's 1.

Line 20 is not part of the loop because it is executed only once. Line 30 is the first line of the loop. It merely prints the value of C. Line 40, the NEXT statement, is the last line of the loop. Each time the program reaches NEXT, the loop counter in the computer is incremented and then a decision is made.

If the new value of the counter, *after it is incremented,* is within the range specified by the FOR statement, the program jumps back to the first statement after the FOR statement and goes through the loop again. In this example, if C has any value from 1 to 5, the loop jumps back to line 30.

If the new value of the counter is outside the specified range, then the program flows to the statement that immediately follows the NEXT statement. It does not go through the loop again.

When the loop has operated the desired number of times, the program moves from line 40 to line 50. Some people say that it *falls through* line 40 to reach line 50. It leaves C set to 6. In the command mode, print C to check that.

The boundaries of a FOR-NEXT loop are easy to identify. In this example, only line 30 is inside the loop. It performs the useful operation.

BASIC allows you to omit the name of the counter after the word NEXT. In other words, you can use just NEXT instead of NEXT C or NEXT K or whatever you decide to call the counter. In a simple loop, that's OK. Sometimes it helps to state the counter with the NEXT statement, such as

NEXT C, so you can relate it to the companion FOR statement.

What Should You Call the Counter? — Because the name of the counter is a variable name, you can use any number of characters up to 40, as discussed earlier.

It is conventional to use the letter *I* as the counter in a loop. It is the initial letter of the word *iteration,* which means to repeat. You can use any legal variable name. I have used C so far because mnemonically it's easy to remember that C means *counter.*

FOR-NEXT TRICKS

You don't have to start a FOR-NEXT loop at 1. For example, enter and run

```
20 FOR C = 12 TO 17
```

Counting in STEPS — You don't have to count by ones, either. Try this:

```
20 FOR C = 10 TO 70 STEP 10
```

The STEP statement sets the amount that the counter is incremented at each pass through the loop.
Default STEP Value — Many of the statements in BASIC that allow you to set a number for some operation will work even if you don't set the number. They use a *default value* for that number. Every FOR-NEXT loop can use the STEP statement but, if you don't put it in, it uses the default value — which is 1.
Counting Backward — The FOR-NEXT routine in the interpreter always increments the counter by the number in the STEP statement or the default value. For a backward count, "fool" the incrementer by giving it a negative step value. Enter and run

```
20 FOR C = 100 TO 10 STEP -10
```

Using Variables as Iteration Limits — You don't have to use numbers to set the counter in a FOR-NEXT loop. Sometimes the program itself decides how many executions are needed. Change line 20 to read:

```
20 FOR C = X TO Y
```

Run it. The program doesn't work because it doesn't have any values for X and Y. When you use this form, the program must provide the values for X and Y before it reaches the loop.

You can simulate that by placing values at line 15. Enter and run

```
15 X = 3: Y = 9
```

PLUGGING IN VALUES FROM THE COMMAND MODE

Instead of writing a temporary program line to test or demonstrate a routine, such as line 15, you can assign values to the variables by entering the numbers from the command mode. To see this work, first delete line 15. Now the program needs values for X and Y, just as it did earlier. Enter these assignment statements:

```
X = 22
Y = 28
```

To be sure they are in memory, enter

```
PRINT X
PRINT Y
```

Don't Use RUN — When you run a program using the RUN command, the computer first erases everything in memory except the program itself, so it can begin with a "clean slate." It will erase the values you just plugged into computer memory for X and Y. You can't use the RUN command.

Use GOTO—BASIC allows you to run a program from any line number by the statement GOTO followed by the line number. When you run the program that way, variables in memory *are not erased.* In the command mode, enter

```
GOTO 10
```

The program will execute from the designated line number, and the values you plugged into memory will be used. Try several values for X and Y, and then run the program using a GOTO statement.

FOR AND NEXT STATEMENTS MUST BE IN MATCHED PAIRS

BASIC requires FOR and NEXT statements to be in matched pairs, using the same counter name. If they are not, the computer will stop and display an error message. Try changing the name of the counter in the FOR statement *or* the NEXT statement so they aren't the same. Run the program from line 20 by using a GOTO statement.

REMINDER: TYPE DECLARATION

There are two types of variables: numeric variables—such as 37—that the computer does arithmetic with, and literal expressions—such as "Hello"—that the computer can't calculate with.

Either can be assigned to a variable name. Because there are two types of variables, there are also two types of variable names.

All variable names must have a *type declaration* so the computer knows which kind they are. When you type a variable name, you must tell the computer what type of variable name it is. This can be done by a special symbol that follows the variable name.

If you *omit the symbol* and type just the variable name—such as X—the computer accepts it as a numeric variable name. This is type declaration *by default.* By not using a type-declaration symbol, you actually declare that the variable is of the numeric type.

You must assign a number to a numeric variable name—for example, X = 2. You cannot assign a literal expression to a numeric variable name. X = ABC will not work.

REMINDER: STRINGS

A string is a sequence of one or more characters that is treated as a unit, such as "Hello." Strings are *literal* and are not used to do arithmetic. The type-declaration symbol for a string is $, used at the end of a variable name.

For example, A$ is a variable named *A* that represents a literal string. A$ is pronounced *A string.* Enter

```
A$ = "HELLO"
PRINT A$
```

Placing an expression in quotation marks identifies it as a literal string. The variable A$ can accept "HELLO" because HELLO is inside quotation marks. It cannot accept just HELLO—without the marks. Try it.

The computer objects by displaying *Type mismatch.* The variable name on the left side of = is identified as a string. The characters on the right side are not identified as a string because they are not in quotation marks. The type declarations do not match. This is like saying an apple is an orange.

In addition to being letters and words, strings can be combinations of letters and numbers, or just numbers. Even if a string is all numbers, the computer will treat it literally and refuse to do arithmetic when quotation marks are used.

ASCII

This acronym stands for American Standard Code for Information Interchange and is pronounced *askee.* It's not a BASIC word.

Computers don't store actual letters, numbers and punctuation marks in memory. What they store and process is a *code number* that represents the character. That number is the ASCII code for the character. When computers talk to each other, they send number codes back and forth.

ASC( )

ASC is a BASIC word derived from ASCII. It must be followed by a string expression in parentheses. You can find the ASCII code for any letter or number by asking the computer. Enter this:

```
PRINT ASC("A")
```

The computer tells you that the ASCII code for A is 65. Notice that the character has to be identified as a string and must also be in parentheses.

When you press a key, a code number is generated. The number goes to two places in the computer: The code goes into the computer itself for processing, or to be stored in memory. It also goes to the screen for display. Before being displayed, it is translated back into the character that it represents. When code 65 is sent to the display, the letter *A* is shown.

Confession—Putting a set of empty parentheses after ASC( ) and other BASIC words is not customary in BASIC dictionaries. I write it that way and try to remember it that way because it tells me that what follows must be in parentheses.

CHR$( )

If you want the computer to print the letter *A* on the screen, you can use this form:

```
PRINT "A"
```

and it will. You can also ask the computer to print the code number. The form is

```
PRINT CHR$(65)
```

which also prints *A*. Try it. The expression CHR$ tells the computer that the following number in parentheses is a code. CHR$ is pronounced *character string.*

INKEY$

This is pronounced *inkey string.* It is a character *keyed in* from the keyboard, such as G or 3. The $ at the end of the expression declares the character that is typed to be a literal string. Because it changes when you press different keys, it's a variable.

To use INKEY$ in a program, you must give it a variable name in an assignment statement. This is not as complicated as it seems—after you see it work. Please enter

```
NEW
10 PRINT "Press any key:"
20 V$ = INKEY$: IF V$ = "" THEN GOTO 20
30 PRINT V$: REM display the character
40 PRINT ASC(V$): REM display the code
50 PRINT
60 GOTO 10
```

List the program and check to be sure you've typed it correctly. Here's the program flow: Line 10 asks you for an input from the keyboard. Line 20 sets up a string variable, V$, to receive the INKEY$ from the keyboard. There is no special reason to use V$ as the variable name. It could be any legal variable name ending with the string declaration, $.

The second statement on line 20 causes the program to wait until you press a key. It says, *if V$ is nothing, go back to the beginning of line 20 and wait some more.* The symbol *""* is identified as a string by the quotation marks. Because nothing is inside the quotation marks, it's a string composed of nothing.

Line 30 displays V$, the character that was keystroked. Line 40 displays the code number for V$. Line 50 spaces down. Line 60 loops back so you can do it again.

Run the program and type letters and numbers for a while. The display shows the keystroke you selected on one line and the code number produced by that keystroke on the next line.

Not all keystrokes produce a printable character. For example, press the ENTER key. The resulting code number, 13, is important. I suggest you remember it. Press the space bar at the bottom of the keyboard. Remember its code, too. ENTER is code 13. Space is code 32. If you forget, these codes are in Appendix G of the IBM book entitled *BASIC*.

As you know, function keys are programmed to type a word automatically—replacing your fingers. Press F1. It types the letters of LIST individually, followed by the codes for each letter. The last entry is an invisible character represented by code 32—a space. F2 enters RUN similarly, followed by code 13.

Press lower-case *a* and then upper-case *A*. Subtract the smaller code from the larger. Do the same thing for other letters. To convert upper-case letters to lower case, add 32 to the code. This is how the computer automatically converts lower case to upper case for program statements.

Another Way to Look at It—When you set up an INKEY$ with a variable name such as V$, try thinking of it this way: The variable name V$ is waiting in the computer—waiting for you to press a key. When you do, a character is produced. V$ grabs it and says, "Gotcha!" From then on, every time you ask for V$, you will get the character that was typed—until the program does another INKEY$ routine and V$ represents a new keystroke.

The program you are running is an endless loop. Get out of it by pressing Ctrl-Break. You may have to do it more than once.

CONQUERING THE ENDLESS LOOP
Add these lines to the program in memory:

```
42 IF V$ = CHR$(13) THEN GOTO 70
45 PRINT "TO QUIT, PRESS ENTER."
70 END
```

List the program and check it. Line 45 will execute after the program has displayed the code for the last character that was typed, so it applies to the next keystroke on the next pass through the loop.

In line 42, CHR$(13) represents the ENTER key. Line 42 jumps out of the loop *if the keystroke at line 20 was the ENTER key.*

When you use a GOTO statement, as in line 42, the line that the program jumps to *must exist.* This jump is intended to end the program, so you could put an END statement on line 70. Instead of just END, you could also put in some PRINT statements to move the BASIC prompt symbol downward on the screen.

You can use any keystroke to end the program. For example, it's common to use the letter *Q* in an INKEY$ routine to allow quitting. Run the program to find the code for Q. Rewrite line 45 to use Q instead of ENTER as the *quit* key. Then change line 42 to use code 81 instead of 13. Run it.

A LOOP WITHOUT A COUNTER

A loop doesn't always require a counter, but there must be some way to stop it when it has completed its task. The program you just ran depends on a specified keystroke to jump out of the loop. The loop is controlled from the keyboard.

A LOOP THAT DOES NOTHING

Please enter and run this loop:

```
NEW
10 FOR DL = 1 TO 1000: NEXT DL
```

The FOR and NEXT statements are on the same line, with nothing in between. This provides a time delay while the computer counts from 1 to 1000. You can change the amount of delay by changing how high it counts. Use this loop to slow down a program. In this case, DL means a *DeLay*.

CHARACTERS THAT AREN'T ON THE KEYBOARD

The computer can display characters that aren't available on any key. The only way to make that happen is to call for the character by its code. Try this:

```
PRINT CHR$(3)
```

There's no key for the resulting heart symbol, but you can use it in a display anytime you wish—if you know the secret code. Now try

```
PRINT CHR$(7)
```

The computer doesn't print anything at all. It beeps. The PRINT command actually means *DO IT.* If the code is a printable character, it prints the character. If the code is something else, such as a beep or screen clearing, that's what the computer does.

MODULO ARITHMETIC

This is a strange activity that deals with remainders after division. Enter this statement:

```
PRINT 12 MOD 10
```

That means to divide 12 by 10 until it won't divide evenly any more. Then keep the remainder, which is 2, and throw the rest away. Write and enter a statement to verify that 72 MOD 10 is 2. When you divide 72 by 10, the answer is 7 with a remainder of 2. Throw away the 7 and keep the 2. Here are some more examples: 23 MOD 10 = 3.   9 MOD 2 = 1.   9 MOD 3 = 0.

A SOLUTION TO THE SCROLLING PROBLEM

When a program is printing a long list on the screen, it will scroll if the list is too long. The screen can display 24 lines maximum, not counting the bottom line—which doesn't scroll.

Let's make a program that displays 60 lines so you can become really annoyed at scrolling. Please enter this:

```
10 FOR I = 1 TO 60
20 PRINT "I HAVE ASKED YOU "I" TIMES TO STOP SCROLLING!"
30 NEXT I
```

Run it. Notice that the PRINT statement prints a string in quotation marks, then a numeric that's the value of I, then another string. This is fancy printing. Also notice that the prompt at the bottom forces the rest of the display upward.

Scroll Control — Add this line:

```
25 IF I MOD 20 = 0 THEN STOP
```

List it. Line 25 stops the program *if I divides evenly by 20.* That will happen when I values are equal to 20, 40 and 60. This defines a screen load as 20 lines of text.

To print the next screen load, you must enter CONT or press F5 to resume program operation. Doing it this way is crude, but it demonstrates the principle well.

Run the program. When the first 20 lines are displayed, study them and then display the next screen load.

Instead of crudely stopping the program when the screen is full, you can use an INKEY$ routine. Please change line 25 as shown and add the lines beginning at 100:

```
25 IF I MOD 20 = 0 THEN GOTO 100
100 PRINT "(FOR NEXT SCREEN LOAD, PRESS SPACE BAR.)"
110 V$ = INKEY$: IF V$ = "" THEN GOTO 110
120 IF V$ = CHR$(32) THEN GOTO 30 ELSE GOTO 110
```

List and check your typing. When 20 lines have been printed, line 25 jumps out of the loop for a keyboard routine. Line 100 prints just below the data on the screen and tells the user how to get the next screen load. Line 110 sets up V$ to receive an INKEY$ from the keyboard and wait until one happens.

Line 120 is a decision point. The IF condition is that the keystroke was CHR$(32) — the space bar. When that happens, the THEN statement jumps back to line 30 and the program resumes operation.

In line 120, if a key that is not the space bar is pressed, the IF condition is not met. This leads to execution of the ELSE statement. The program merely returns to line 110 and waits for another keystroke. In effect, this ignores incorrect keystrokes.

Run it and see. There *is* a problem at the end, but we'll fix it later. The program still doesn't stop scrolling. It merely scrolls in batches of 20 lines. The screen should be cleared before each new load.

Here's a way to do that. Enter

```
115 IF V$ = CHR$(32) THEN CLS
```

List it. If the user made the correct keystroke at line 110, line 115 will clear the screen for the next screen load. If the wrong key is pressed, line 115 will not execute. Either way, line 120 will then do what it did before.

Run the modified program. The first screen load displays the command RUN at the top. I forgot to clear the screen at the beginning of the program. Please fix it by using line 5 to clear the screen:

```
5 CLS
```

An Inglorious Conclusion — The program works fine until all 60 lines are displayed. Then, if the user continues to press the space bar, *as instructed,* the program produces an error message.

Please list it and look for the bug. The problem occurs when the program comes out of the loop at line 30 after the FOR-NEXT loop has operated 60 times. This is a *normal termination* of the loop. The computer is finished with the loop and doesn't even remember that it did it.

Then line 100 asks the user to press the space bar again for another screen load. The user doesn't know that there are no more screen loads *and has no other choice anyway.* You and I wish he would just turn off the computer and forget about it. Users are very good at following instructions, especially when the instructions are wrong.

When the space bar is pressed, the screen is cleared and then line 120 jumps to the NEXT statement back at line 30. But that loop is all done. The computer has no use for a NEXT statement that suddenly appears, after all of the FOR statements have been used up. It tells you *NEXT without FOR,* which is exactly what happened.

When the loop has completed all 60 passes, the program falls through line 30 and should end right there. Do that by adding

```
40 PRINT "NO MORE DATA": END
```

List it. Notice that the *only way* the program can reach line 40 is by completing the loop operation. Run it. Run it again with TRON operating. You can see the program waiting at line 110, as it should, until you press the space bar to get the next screen load. Disable TRON.

Here's a tip for programmers from a leading software house—a company that distributes ready-made programs. It says that new screen loads should always be produced by pressing the space bar. You can now do that.

WOULD YOU LIKE TO SLOW DOWN A LITTLE?

Programming is so much fun that I am anxious to get you started so you can enjoy it, too. There isn't any way to do a little bit of programming. After you display *HELLO* a few times, you either get into it or get out of it.

When you learn one thing, you're ready for the next. The problem is knowing when you've learned something. Learning takes time, repetition and sometimes quiet thought. I hope you are pacing yourself and not trying to gobble up everything at one sitting. Because you know how to save the program you're working on, you can stop anytime and load it later to resume.

I suggest that you back up occasionally to review what you have read and entered into the computer. Do the programs again, if you wish. A good exercise is to write similar programs—but you know that. You may need a mental delay loop once in a while, as I do. Take a break when you want one.

USING ONE STATEMENT TO PRINT MORE THAN ONE ITEM

With one PRINT statement, you can print more than one item. The form is: PRINT followed by *the list of items you want to display.* Some specific examples follow.

PRINTING WITH AUTOMATIC TABS

The screen is divided by the computer into six vertical columns. The first five are 14 spaces wide. The last one gets what's left—10 spaces. If you put commas between items on a list to be printed, each comma will automatically tab over to the next column. Enter

```
PRINT "A", "B", "C", "D", "E", "F"
```

Notice that no comma is needed after the sixth item.

OR

This is a BASIC word that can be used in IF statements. The idea is: IF it is Saturday OR Sunday THEN don't go to the office.

PRINTING SOME OF THE CODES

With only a few deft keystrokes, you can convert the scroll-control program into something useful. Please change line 10 so it counts from 1 to 255. Change line 20 like this:

```
20 PRINT I, CHR$(I)
```

Run it. CHR$(12) clears the screen and prevents displaying the first 11 codes. We'll fix that soon.

Three Kinds of Codes—Some codes print, some do other things. There are three kinds. *Character codes* print characters on the screen. *Control codes* cause something else to happen, such as an audible tone or screen clearing. *Extended codes* are produced by combinations of keys, such as Ctrl-Break, function keys and other special keys.

Please refer to the IBM book entitled *BASIC*. Find the first page of code listings in Appendix G. The first 31 code numbers are listed at the left. The next two columns show two meanings for each of these 31 numbers. As character codes, they print the character shown or produce the event described.

As control codes, they generate standard messages that are used from computer to printer or from one computer to another. Code 10 performs a *line feed* on the screen, on your printer if you have one, and on a distant teletype machine or another computer if you send it over a telephone line. Line feed means to move down to the following line.

As control codes, the 31 numbers have standard meanings. You don't need to understand all of them—at least not now.

As character codes, the meanings are standard if they agree with the control codes. Otherwise a computer manufacturer can use them as he pleases. For example, IBM gives you a smiling face for code 1. Other computers may not do that.

How does the computer know if you want a control code or a character code? It does both. The same code can print a character on the display and send a message to another device.

Starting with 32, the codes have only one use. They are character codes. Codes are standardized from 32 through 128. Larger numbers can be used for whatever the manufacturer wants. IBM gives you a lot of unusual characters and graphics symbols.

PRINTING NEARLY ALL OF THE CODES THIS TIME

Code 12 is a problem because it clears the screen and prevents displaying the first 11 codes and their effects. Code 11 is also a problem. It sends the cursor home and makes following lines overprint.

What we must do is change the program so line 20 does not operate if I = 11 or I = 12. Here's one way:

```
15 IF I = 11 OR I = 12 THEN GOTO 25
```

Run the program with that line. Notice the space after line 10. It is produced by CHR$(10), which is a *line feed*. CHR$(13) is produced by the ENTER key. On the display, it causes the cursor to move to the left and also produces a line feed.

PRINTING MORE CODES

This program would be more satisfying if codes 11 and 12 were not just omitted. Try this:

```
15 IF I = 11 THEN PRINT " 11", "HOMES CURSOR": GOTO 25
18 IF I = 12 THEN PRINT " 12", "FORM FEED AND CLS": GOTO 25
```

If you want to be meticulous about it, you can write program lines to say what code 7 does and also explain the blanks starting at code 28. Can you figure out why code 30 isn't listed?

What About Code Zero?—Evidently, you peeked in Appendix G of the IBM book entitled *BASIC* and noticed that there is a code zero. You can display it by changing line 10 to count from 0 to 255 instead of 1 to 255. Run the program. The first screen load is only one line. Obviously, line 25 executed immediately. To see the reason, ask the computer to print the value of 0 MOD 20.

We've finished using this program. If you think you may want to refer to it again later, save it by giving it a name such as CODES.

RENUM

When you add some lines between existing lines in a program, the result looks untidy because the lines aren't multiples of 10. BASIC has the command RENUM, for renumbering program lines. The form is RENUM *new line number, old line number, increment.*

The computer will assign the new line number to the old line number, then it will renumber all following lines using the increment you selected, such as 10.

If you merely enter RENUM, the rest of it takes default values. It will start at line 10 and renumber the whole program with increments of 10. Usually, this is what you want to do.

List the program now in memory. Renumber it and list again. When you add lines to a program, RENUM is sometimes necessary to make room for new lines.

SETTING FLAGS

Suppose you're in a business meeting and receive a phone call asking you to do something. You will probably just make a note to remind yourself to do it after the meeting. In the computer, one way of making a note is called *setting a flag.*

I use a variable named *FG* for the flag. Initialize it to 0. To make a note, set it to 1. Use a REMark to explain what the note or reminder is.

Later, the program tests the flag to see if it is set and uses the information carried by the flag to make a decision. Then the program resets the flag to 0—which is like tearing off the top sheet of the scratch pad and throwing it away.

In BASIC, a flag can have lots of values. It can be 0 when initialized, 1 for apples, 2 for oranges, 3 for bananas and so forth. You must assign a meaning to each value of the flag and not forget it. REMarks will help.

GOING OUT THE SIDE DOOR

I imagine that a loop has a front door, a back door and one or more side doors. To see what I mean, enter and run

```
NEW
90 CLS
100 FOR J = 1 TO 10
110 PRINT J
120 NEXT J
130 PRINT: PRINT "Loop ended. J = "J
```

All it does is print the numbers 1 to 10. It goes out the back door of the loop—meaning through line 120. This is a normal termination of a FOR-NEXT loop. At line 130, the print list has two items—a string followed by a numeric variable.

Now, put in an exit at a side door:

```
115 IF J = 5 THEN GOTO 130
```

Sometimes you will use a loop to look through a list of some kind and tell you if it finds what you are looking for. In this example, that occurs when line 115 recognizes that J is 5 and jumps out of the loop through a side door. Run it and see.

In a FOR-NEXT loop, the FOR statement names the counter and sets the number of times the loop will operate. These specifications are saved at a special location in computer memory. When the NEXT statement increments the counter, it refers to the loop specifications in memory to decide whether or not to run the loop again.

When a loop makes the set number of executions, the specifications for that loop are erased from memory. This is a normal termination of the loop.

However, a side-door exit leaves the loop specifications in memory because the loop never makes a normal termination. You can do this a few times with no problem. Eventually that location in memory gets filled with residue from unfinished loops and the program will stop. An error message tells you the problem: *Out of memory.*

There are a couple of ways to run a FOR-NEXT loop to a normal termination and still do the equivalent of a side-door exit. These methods are useful for other reasons, also. Here is one way. Change lines 90, 115 and 130 as shown.

```
90 CLS: FG = 0: REM initialize flag
115 IF J = 5 THEN FG = 1
130 PRINT: PRINT "Loop ended. J = "J" FG = "FG
```

In line 115, when J = 5 the program will make note of it by setting the flag FG to 1. After setting the flag, the loop runs to the full count and makes a normal exit out the back door. The loop specifications in computer memory are deleted.

Later in the program, you can test the flag to see what its value is and do whatever is appropriate. Set the flag back to 0 as soon as you have used the information.

Doing More than One Thing in a Loop—Sometimes you may want a loop to do more than one thing while it is running. This is the best reason not to jump out the side door of a loop. Please change line 90, add line 118 and change line 130:

```
90 CLS: FG = 0: FG1 = 0: REM initialize flags
100 FOR J = 1 TO 10
110 PRINT J
115 IF J = 5 THEN FG = 1
118 IF J = 7 THEN FG1 = 1
120 NEXT J
130 PRINT: PRINT "Loop ended. J = "J" FG = "FG" FG1 = "FG1
```

This routine sets two flags with different names. Run it.

Saving a Little Time—In a complicated program, with complicated loops, you will sometimes want to make the loops run faster. In this program, all of the useful work is completed when the counter reaches 8. If you let the loop run its full course, the executions from 8 through 10 are wasted time. Add line 105 to prevent those executions.

```
105 IF J = 8 THEN J = 10: GOTO 120
```

Run and list. When J = 8, line 105 changes J to 10. The second statement on that line jumps to line 120. The counter is now 10. The computer increments it to 11, decides that the job is done and makes a normal termination of the loop by erasing the loop specs in memory and moving on to line 130. As you can see in the display, the loop made only 7 passes and then stopped.

I think it's good programming practice to set flags and run a FOR-NEXT loop to a normal termination, one way or another. In addition, it's always OK to leave a loop by the side door, do something else for a while and then return to the loop to finish running it.

RELATIONAL OPERATORS

Relational operators are used to compare two quantities and make a decision depending on the result.

```
IF X = Y   says   IF X IS EQUAL TO Y
IF X < Y   says   IF X IS LESS THAN Y
IF X > Y   says   IF X IS GREATER THAN Y
IF X <= Y   says   IF X IS LESS THAN OR EQUAL TO Y
IF X >= Y   says   IF X IS GREATER THAN OR EQUAL TO Y
IF X <> Y   says   IF X IS NOT EQUAL TO Y
```

You now have two uses for an equals (=) sign. You can use it to declare that one thing is equal to another, such as X = 5. Or, you can use it as a relational operator to *test the relationship* between two quantities. IF X = 5 and IF X = Y are examples.

These operators can be combined in a more complicated statement using the BASIC words AND and OR, which mean the same thing in BASIC as in English. Here are some examples:

```
IF X = Y AND P = Q THEN GOTO 500
IF X = Y AND P <> Q THEN GOTO 500
IF X = Y OR X = 12 THEN GOTO 500
```

USING RELATIONAL OPERATORS IN A LOOP

This loop uses I as the loop counter and sets the value of a variable, J, by operations inside the loop. It uses the asterisk, *, which in BASIC means to multiply. Please enter

```
NEW
10 CLS
20 FOR I = 1 TO 10
30 J = 2*I
50 PRINT "J = "J
60 NEXT I
70 PRINT: PRINT "I = "I
```

List it, check it and run it. Line 30 sets the variable J equal to 2 times the value of the loop counter, I. Line 40 is not used yet. Line 50 prints J. Line 70 prints a blank line and then prints the value of I after the program has left the loop.

Line 40 will use some relational operators to control program flow. Try each of the following lines and run the program. List the program and be sure you understand what happened.

```
40 IF J = 14 THEN GOTO 70
40 IF J < 7 THEN GOTO 60
40 IF J < 10 OR J > 10 THEN GOTO 60
40 IF J = 10 THEN GOTO 60
40 IF J > 10 THEN GOTO 60
40 IF I = 5 THEN J = 777
40 IF J > 4 THEN I = 10
```

Try other statements in line 40 until relational operators seem simple to use.

WHILE-WEND

Recent versions of BASIC have this loop. It begins with a WHILE statement such as

```
100 WHILE (X = Y)
```

It ends with the word *WEND,* all by itself. Think of WEND as a contraction of WHILE END, meaning the end of the WHILE loop.

Following WHILE is an expression in parentheses that I call the *proposition.* The proposition is tested at the WHILE statement. If it is true, the program proceeds through the loop to the WEND statement. At this point it jumps back to the WHILE statement, and the proposition is tested again.

When the proposition is found to be false, the program jumps from the WHILE statement to the line immediately below the WEND statement. The operation is similar to a FOR-NEXT loop except that the jump test is different. There is no line counter in a WHILE-WEND loop.

A WHILE-WEND Example—This is the last type of loop discussed in this book. Let's celebrate by writing a simple two-person game called *Guess The Secret Number.* Enter

```
NEW
10 CLS: PRINT: PRINT: PRINT: PRINT
20 PRINT "PLAYER #1, TYPE A SECRET NUMBER FROM 0 TO 9"
30 N1$ = INKEY$: IF N1$ = "" THEN GOTO 30
40 CLS: PRINT: PRINT: PRINT: PRINT
100 PRINT "PLAYER #2, GUESS THE SECRET NUMBER FROM 0 TO 9"
110 WHILE (N1$ <> N2$)
120 N2$ = INKEY$: IF N2$ = "" THEN GOTO 120
130 PRINT: PRINT N2$;
140 IF N2$ > N1$ THEN PRINT " IS TOO LARGE. TRY AGAIN."
150 IF N2$ < N1$ THEN PRINT " IS TOO SMALL. TRY AGAIN."
160 WEND
200 PRINT: PRINT: PRINT "CONGRATULATIONS! "N2$" IS CORRECT."
```

List it and check your typing. At line 30, Player #1 keystrokes a number that is received by N1$. Then instructions are displayed for Player #2. The WHILE-WEND loop is set up by line 110. The proposition is that the secret number and the player's guess are not equal. As long as that is true, the loop keeps looping.

Inside the loop, Player #2 keystrokes his guess as N2$ and gets some clues. The semicolon at the end of line 130 causes the next thing printed to print on the same line as N2$, rather than on the following screen line. A semicolon at the end of a PRINT statement suppresses the normal line feed and carriage return. If the guess is correct, the program jumps to line 200. Play this game until the thrill is gone or you understand the WHILE-WEND loop.

An INKEY$ routine is often used in games and general-purpose programs because it doesn't require pressing the ENTER key. It speeds things up and makes keyboard operation more simple. The disadvantage is that it can receive only one keystroke at a time. This limits the number selections to single digits.

Notice that the WHILE proposition is comparing two strings. The computer does this by comparing the ASCII codes for the strings. If one number is larger than the other, its ASCII code is also larger, so this works.

However, the game can also be played with letters. Line 20 says to type a number, but the

INKEY$ routine doesn't care what you type. It works just fine with letters if you remember that the program is actually comparing ASCII codes. Try it.

This game could be scored by counting the errors. As an exercise, zero a counter ahead of the loop and then increment it inside the loop. When a player guesses correctly, display the number of guesses. Low score wins, of course.

Try putting a title on the screen when the program runs. Try putting some program lines at the end to allow playing again without entering RUN.

To play the game with larger numbers, use INPUT statements with numeric variables. Then players will have to press ENTER after typing a number. That game will not accept letters as an input. My version, GAME5, does all of these things. It's at the end of this chapter, page 65.

GOSUB-RETURN

Often, you will write a section of a program, called a *routine,* that you need to use several times in the same program. It's tedious to write the routine into the program at several places when it's needed several times.

Instead, you can treat it as a *subroutine,* placing it perhaps at the end of the program. Then, when you need to use it, you can jump to it. When it has finished, you return to the next operation in the main stream of the program. Do this with the GOSUB statement.
Here's the basic idea:

```
100 (main program line)
110 GOSUB 1000 (executes subroutine)
120 (returns to next statement)
1000 (subroutine to do something)
1010 (subroutine statement)
1020 (subroutine statement)
1030 RETURN (causes jump back to main program at
             statement following GOSUB statement)
```

The main program calls the subroutine with the GOSUB statement at line 110. The GOSUB statement designates the first line number of the subroutine. The program jumps to that line, and the subroutine executes. The last statement of the subroutine must be the word *RETURN.* This sends the program back to the next statement *after* the GOSUB call—which may be on the same line. If it isn't, the program returns to the following line, in this example line 120.

When you have a subroutine, you can call it as many times as you wish from different parts of the main program.

Your program has to *execute* the same number of GOSUBs as it does RETURNs. If the computer ends up with a surplus of either one, it will stop and tell you about it. In this case it sometimes takes a while to figure out what's wrong.

USING A DELAY LOOP

Occasionally, it may be effective to replace an item on the screen with another item at the same location, perhaps in a box. You must leave each item in view long enough for it to be read.

Here's a simplified program for crossword-puzzle addicts. Enter it.

```
NEW
10 CLS
```

(Program continued on next page.)

```
20 A$ = "BO"
30 B$ = "E"
40 FOR I = 1 TO 26
50 CLS: PRINT: PRINT: PRINT
60 PRINT A$ CHR$(64 + I) B$
70 GOSUB 1000: REM delay
80 NEXT I
100 END
1000 FOR DL = 1 TO 1000: NEXT DL
1010 RETURN
```

This program starts with a four-letter word— *BO E*—with the third letter blank. It fills the blank with each letter of the alphabet, in sequence, so the crossword puzzler can pick the right one. List it, check it and run it. List it again.

The loop is from line 50 to line 80. Line 50 clears the screen and locates the cursor. Line 60 prints the first two letters of the word, then the variable letter, then the last letter. The computer will evaluate the expression in the parentheses after CHR$. It prints CHR$(65), then CHR$(66) and so forth.

Each new word is left on display for a short time. This is done by line 70, which jumps out to a subroutine at line 1000. Counting from 1 to 1000 takes a short time. On return from the subroutine to line 80, the loop operates again, printing the next word at the same location. Line 100 prevents the program from running into the subroutine after the loop operation is completed. That would produce an error message: *RETURN without GOSUB*.

You can change the delay at line 1000. Try it. By changing A$ and B$, perhaps as a keyboard input, this program will work with different sets of letters. Try it.

With a more sophisticated program, you could plug in more than one variable letter, at more than one location in the word. That requires nested loops.

NESTED LOOPS

A nested loop is one loop operating inside another loop. Some people are intimidated by nested loops. Hoping not to intimidate you, I sneaked one into the last program. The delay subroutine is a loop. Even though it is called up as a subroutine, it operates inside the main FOR-NEXT loop of the program. It would work just the same if the delay loop were typed inside the main loop.

Please change line 70 so it reads the same as line 1000. Then delete lines 1000 and 1010. List it. Run it. It works exactly the same way. List it again. Observe that during each pass through the main loop, the program must enter the delay loop at line 70 and execute it completely before it can return to the main loop and finish executing it. Save this program, using the name CROSWORD.

The rules for nested loops are illustrated by this outline:

```
NEW
10 FOR I = 1 TO 100:' (I loop is the main loop)
20 FOR J = 1 TO 100:' (J loop is nested inside I loop)
30 FOR K = 1 TO 100:' (K loop is nested inside J loop)
40 '
50 '(lines for operations performed by the loops)
60 '
```

(Program continued on next page.)

```
100 NEXT K
110 NEXT J
120 NEXT I
```

Notice the structure. The order of the FOR lines is I, J, K. The order of the NEXT lines is K, J, I. The NEXT lines are in *reverse order,* as follows.

```
NEW
10 CLS
20 FOR I = 1 TO 2
30 PRINT "PASS "I" THROUGH I LOOP"
40      FOR J = 1 TO 2
50      PRINT "     PASS "J" THROUGH J LOOP"
60          FOR K = 1 TO 2
70          PRINT "         PASS "K" THROUGH K LOOP"
80          NEXT K
90      NEXT J
100 NEXT I
```

List it and check your typing. The purpose of the indentation is to show the lines that are part of each loop on the same indentation.

Follow the program in your mind: Line 20 starts the I loop. Line 30 is part of the I loop and is controlled by the I counter. The program executes line 30.

Then it encounters line 40, which starts the J loop. Line 50 is part of the J loop. Line 50 executes.

The program arrives at line 60, which starts the innermost loop with K as the counter. Line 70 executes. Line 80 is the end of the K loop, so the program jumps back to 60 and executes again. The K loop will run to a normal termination.

Then the program reaches line 90, which is the end of the J loop. One pass of the J loop has been completed—with a detour through the K loop. The program jumps back to line 50 and begins the second pass through the J loop.

At line 60, it finds the starting point for the K loop again, so the program must execute the entire K loop once more before it can return to the J loop to finish it.

When the K loop has completely executed, line 90 is reached. That was the second pass through the J loop, so the program falls through line 90 to line 100, which has been waiting a long time.

The I loop has just completed its first pass. The program jumps back to line 30 to begin the second pass through the I loop. Everything that happened on the first pass happens again during the second pass.

Run the program. Look at the program in this book and the display on the screen. The display shows what I have just described. I hope that one display is worth a thousand words. Then run the program again with TRON operating. It prints the line numbers as they execute. Compare what TRON shows to the program itself.

Try changing the number of times the loops operate and run again. Nested loops add horsepower to your programs. If you want to refer to this program again, save it using the name LOOPDEMO

IMPROVING YOUR MEMORY

Programming requires you to remember a lot of things. Some of them become habits, which is both good and bad. It's good when it works. Occasionally, something you write by habit won't work because of some special circumstance or situation.

Those bugs are very difficult to recognize because it's hard to turn your brain on and challenge something you do out of habit. Because we all feel secure in our habits, it's best to think about each statement and routine as though you are writing it for the very first time.

Please refer to the IBM book entitled *BASIC*. Read Appendix A, *Messages*. This is a list of error messages that the computer can display. You'll understand most of them. Look again at Appendix G, if you wish. It should be friendly territory by now.

Look through Appendix I and carefully read the section entitled *Tips and Techniques*. You'll find a couple of suggestions that don't agree exactly with recommendations I have made. Take your choice. Neither is wrong. You'll find some advice that I haven't given yet.

Read Appendix J, the *Glossary*. It's like reading a dictionary, but it's short and good for your mind.

Please look through this chapter from the beginning. Go over any parts that you're unsure of.

Following is a list of BASIC words that were introduced in this chapter. Please look the words up in section 4 of the IBM Personal Computer book *BASIC*. Refer to the list, below, of all BASIC words used in this book so far. Review them, too, and look up any that are strangers.

BASIC WORDS INTRODUCED IN THIS CHAPTER

AND	NEXT
ASC( )	OR
CHR$( )	RENUM
FOR	RETURN
GOSUB	WEND
INKEY$	WHILE
MOD	

BASIC WORDS USED SO FAR

AND	GOTO	REM
ASC ( )	IF	RENUM
BASIC	INKEY$	RETURN
CHR$( )	INPUT	RUN
CLS	LET	SAVE
CONT	LIST	STOP
DELETE	LOAD	SYSTEM
DIR	MOD	THEN
ELSE	NEW	TROFF
END	NEXT	TRON
FILES	OR	WEND
FOR	PRINT	WHILE
GOSUB		

This is the exercise program mentioned on page 61:

```
5 'SECRET NUMBER accepts any number. filename "GAME5"
6 ' with score, title and redo
10 CLS: PRINT: PRINT: PRINT: PRINT
15 PRINT"                        GUESS THE SECRET NUMBER"
18 PRINT: PRINT: PRINT
20 PRINT "PLAYER #1, TYPE AND ENTER A SECRET NUMBER"
30 INPUT N1
40 CLS: PRINT: PRINT: PRINT: PRINT
100 PRINT "PLAYER #2, TYPE AND ENTER YOUR GUESS"
105 SCORE = 0
110 WHILE (N1 <> N2)
120 INPUT N2
125 SCORE = SCORE + 1
130 PRINT
140 IF N2 > N1 THEN PRINT N2 " IS TOO LARGE. GUESS #"SCORE
150 IF N2 < N1 THEN PRINT N2 " IS TOO SMALL. GUESS #"SCORE
160 WEND
200 PRINT: PRINT: PRINT "CONGRATULATIONS! "N2" IS CORRECT, ";
210 IF SCORE = 1 THEN PRINT "WITH ONLY "SCORE" GUESS!"
220 IF SCORE > 1 THEN PRINT "WITH "SCORE" GUESSES."
230 PRINT: PRINT: PRINT:
240 PRINT "PLAY AGAIN, Y/N? ...... Press Y for Yes, N for No."
250 ANSR$=INKEY$: IF ANSR$ = "" THEN GOTO 250
260 IF ANSR$ = "Y" OR ANSR$ = "y" THEN GOTO 10
270 CLS: PRINT: PRINT: PRINT"END OF GAME"
280 PRINT: PRINT: PRINT
```

4 Arrays

This chapter includes the fundamentals of arrays and a little more about printing on the screen.

MANAGING SPACES WHEN PRINTING

Sometimes, items that you print have spaces where you don't want them—or don't have spaces where you need them. Usually, these problems are easy to fix.

In a program with *two separate* PRINT statements, the second item normally prints on the line below the first item. Enter and run this:

```
NEW
10 CLS
20 PRINT "Item 1";
30 PRINT "Item 2"
```

The semicolon at the end of line 20 causes the next item to be printed on the same line, *immediately* behind the first item.

Usually you don't want the letters to run together like that. You can fix it by putting one or more spaces inside the quotation marks, either behind the *1* of *Item 1* or before the *I* of *Item 2*. Any character inside quotation marks will print, even if it is a space. Do one or the other and run it again. Spaces outside of parentheses do not print.

Now enter

```
NEW
10 CLS
20 A$ = "TODAY AND"
30 B$ = "TOMORROW"
40 PRINT A$ B$
```

Line 40 has a single PRINT statement followed by a list of two items to be printed. Because both items are in the same PRINT statement, without a semicolon after the first item, one will follow the other on the same line. Run it and you have the space problem again.

The two items that were printed are strings, rather than characters enclosed in quotation marks. There is no way to "open up" one of the *string names* to insert the needed space.

You could go back to line 30 and insert a space in front of the *T,* inside the quotation marks. It would work, but sometimes it isn't convenient to do that in real-life programming.

Here's a better way to add a space between the two items on line 40. Enter this line and then list the program.

```
40 PRINT A$ " " B$
```

Now there are three items to be printed. The first is a string variable. The second—the space—is treated as a string because it is in quotation marks. The third is another string variable. Run the program.

Automatic Tabs—In a single PRINT statement that prints more than one item, or with a series of PRINT statements, you can put the items into columns automatically by placing commas at the end of each item except the last one. If the items are in quotation marks, the commas must be outside of the quotation marks so they don't print as commas.

Commas have more than one meaning. Inside quotation marks, they are commas. Outside of quotation marks, or between variable names, they are automatic tabs. Enter a line that looks exactly like this:

```
PRINT "A", "B", "C," "D"
```

Notice what happens when you get a comma inside the quotation marks.

ARRAYS

An array is a list or table of data items as well as a way of managing the data. It's the *management method* that makes an array. Arrays are stored in memory.

The management plan is simple. If an array is a list, an item is sent to the array in memory by specifying its position in the list—such as the fifth item from the top. A data item is retrieved from the array by specifying its position—such as the fifth item from the top.

Imagine a hotel with 10 rooms. Behind the desk is the usual set of boxes to hold room keys and messages. The boxes are in a vertical column. Number 1 is at the top and number 10 is at the bottom.

A stranger enters the lobby and hands the desk clerk an envelope. "Give this to the person in room 3," says he. You know what the clerk does with it. He puts it in Box 3.

Later, a gentleman strolls up to the counter and asks if there are any messages for room 3. The clerk takes the envelope out of box 3 and hands it to the gentleman.

The vertical column of boxes is similar to an array in your computer's memory. What the desk clerk does is similar to what the computer does when it puts data into an array and then gets the data back out.

ARRAY NOTATION

A special way of writing something is called a *notation*. In the hotel business, boxes for messages are called Box 1, Box 2 and so forth. To identify individual boxes or locations in an array, a certain notation is used to tell the computer that you are referring to an array.

X is the name of a numeric variable. Its value could be 5, 6.89, 32 and so on. X( ) is a name for a *numeric array*—which can hold several numbers at different locations. X( ) is pronounced *X array*. The empty parentheses are symbolic, used as a reminder that this is the name of an array.

To identify a specific location or box in the array, a number is placed inside the parentheses. X(1) identifies the first box in the array X( )—and also the contents of that box. X(7) is the seventh box. You can put one number in X(1), such as 123.45, and a different number in X(7). When you want the numbers, ask for the box. What you get is the *content* of the box—meaning whatever you have stored at that location in the array. PRINT X(1) will print the number at location 1 in X( ).

X$ is a name for a *single* string, such as "HELLO". X$( ) is a name for an array that can store one or more strings. It is pronounced *X string array*. A number is placed inside the parentheses to identify a location in the array. X$(3) is the third box or location in the array X$( ).

If you put *"Now"* in X$(1), *"is"* in X$(2) and *"the"* in X$(3), the statement PRINT X$(1), X$(2), X$(3) makes the computer display

Now   is   the

Even though the names X, X( ), X$ and X$( ) all begin the same, they are all different and mean different things to the computer. If you use all four of these names in the same program, the computer will not become confused.

When you type a variable name followed by a number in parentheses, the computer knows *automatically* that you are referring to an array. There is a visual clue in array notation. Notice that the ( ) in A( ) looks like a box. The expression A(7) is box 7 in array A( ).

LOOPS WITH ARRAYS

This is the most important subject in this book. I will give detailed explanations of loops used with arrays, repeat everything four or five times and probably bore you eventually.

If you have an array in computer memory with the name ARRAY( ) and it has 50 locations, you can print all 50 data items in the array by writing 50 statements:

```
PRINT ARRAY(1)
PRINT ARRAY(2)
```

and so forth. Of course this is tedious. Use a loop instead. The loop *supplies and changes* the number in the parentheses. With a loop, you can print all 50 items in the array with only three statements:

```
100 FOR I = 1 TO 50
110 PRINT ARRAY(I)
120 NEXT I
```

Each time the loop operates, the loop counter, I, has a new value starting with 1. At line 110 in this program, the value of I is *captured* inside the parentheses and used to designate a location in the array. As the loop operates, line 110 will print the contents of ARRAY(1), the contents of ARRAY (2), the contents of ARRAY(3) and so forth.

Using loops to read and write arrays in an orderly fashion is the secret of handling data in a computer. It's the most powerful and useful technique we have to handle large amounts of data—either numeric or string.

The expression ARRAY(5) is sometimes called the *address* of item 5 in the array. Using that expression is sometimes called *addressing* a location in the array.

The number in parentheses is called a *subscript*. If you see the term *subscripted variable* in a computer book, it means that the variable has a subscript and is therefore the name of a location in an array.

The next program acts like the desk clerk. It has 10 boxes in computer memory to receive data items. The loop will ask you for messages—data items—in order, 1 through 10. You type each one on request, and the program immediately puts it in the correct box in the array.

Each of the data items you supply must be only a single keystroke. That's because this program uses the INKEY$ method of accepting a keystroke from the keyboard. Later, you will see other ways of inputting data from the keyboard that allow you to type longer messages.

For the data items, type letters starting with A. Then you can check later to see if the program filed them correctly. Please enter

```
NEW
10 CLS
20 FOR I = 1 TO 10: REM loop to fill an array
```

(Program continued on next page.)

```
30 PRINT "Please type a data item now: ";
40 M$ = INKEY$: IF M$ = "" THEN GOTO 40
50 PRINT M$
60 A$(I) = M$: REM Assign M$ to array location A$(I)
70 NEXT I
   PRINT: PRINT "Thank you. A$() is full.": PRINT
```

List and check to be sure you typed it correctly. Run it and input the letters A through J from the keyboard.

In line 30, notice the space after the colon and the semicolon at the very end. You can see their effects in the display. Now that you have seen the program operate, list it again so you can look at it on the screen while reading the following discussion.

Each time the program goes through the loop, M$ will be different because you input a new value for it at line 40. There is no special reason to use M$ other than thinking of it as a *Message string* from the keyboard. Line 50 prints M$ so you can see what you typed, but the keyboard input would go into the array without line 50.

The array is given its name in the first part of line 60. Because of the parentheses, the computer knows that you are building an array with the name A$( ). The location in the array is specified by the number in parentheses, which is the value of I. As the loop operates, it changes the number in the parentheses from 1 to 10.

Line 60 assigns the data item, M$, to the array location A$(I). When I is 3, the data that you type goes to location A$(3). On the next pass through the loop, location A$(4) is filled with the next data item that you type.

Line 60 appears to say that A$(I) is equal to M$. What it really means is: Put M$ into location A$(I) of the array A$( ).

If you send data to a small array that does not already exist, the computer will create it automatically. This program *creates* an array, A$( ), with 10 locations because that's how many times the loop will operate. It fills the 10 array locations with 10 different data items because you type in a different data item each time.

What you have done is created an array and then filled it with data items. If the loop operated 20 times, it would build an array with 20 locations.

From the command mode, you can PRINT the contents of any array location in memory. You must specify both the name of the array and the location of the item you want to see. Enter

```
PRINT A$(1)
```

If you typed the letter A as the first data item, you see an A on the screen. Print the contents of other locations in this array until you see that the program works correctly. Enter

```
PRINT A(5)
```

You get a 0 because you addressed the wrong array. A(5) is not the same as A$(5).

HOW KEYBOARD INPUTS BECOME STRINGS

When you use the INKEY$ routine, it is not necessary to type quotation marks around the character that you wish to place into memory. When a character is typed, the computer assigns it to a string variable—in this example M$—which *automatically* makes it a string.

READING AND PRINTING AN ARRAY

You have a program in memory that builds and fills a simple array. Please clear the screen and list the program. Add these lines:

```
90 STOP
100 CLS
110 FOR I = 1 TO 10
120 PRINT A$(I)
130 NEXT I
```

The STOP at line 90 divides the program into two routines that you can execute separately. Lines 110—130 print the array on the screen. Line 120 prints whatever is stored in memory under the name A$(I).

On each pass through this loop, A$(I) will be printed. During the 10 operations of the loop, the value of I will change from 1 to 10, so A$(1) to A$(10) will be printed.

Run the program from the beginning again and input the letters A through J, as before. When the program stops at line 90, continue by pressing F5 to execute the second part of the program and print out the data. If you do everything correctly, you should see the letters A through J in a column as printed by the second loop. Run the second part of the program again by typing

```
GOTO 100
```

The command GOTO does not erase anything in memory, so the data should still be in the array. The program will print it again. Now enter

```
RUN 100
```

The RUN command erases everything in memory except the program. The routine starting at line 100 executes, but it won't print anything because the array A$( ) is empty. Now run the program again from the beginning and put the letters back into the array.

DOING SOMETHING USEFUL

Except as a learning exercise, using a loop to fill an array with letters and then using another loop to print it out is not useful. Here are some useful things you can do with an array:

1) If you have data stored on a disk and you want to use it in a program, you must run the disk and transfer the data into memory. An array is a very handy way to receive data in memory. It neatly puts everything where you can find it.

2) If you input data from the keyboard, an array is often the best way to receive it and store it in memory.

3) When you have an array in memory, you can read and use the items in any order, forward, backward, every third one or any way you choose. For example, try this:

```
PRINT "Get me a "A$(3)A$(1)A$(2)"!"
```

You can change items in an array. Try this:

```
A$(10) = "X"
PRINT A$(10)
GOTO 100
```

A$(10) used to be "J". You changed it permanently in the computer memory. Please change it back to "J" again.

ONE-DIMENSIONAL ARRAYS

The program you have been running accepts and displays a single column of data. Array A$( ) is a *one-dimensional* array because it has only a single column of data.

HOW THE COMPUTER STORES SMALL ONE-DIMENSIONAL ARRAYS

Your computer handles one-dimensional arrays of up to 11 items automatically. It merely finds some empty space in memory and stores the array, remembering where it is. You have already filled 10 of the 11 spaces in array A$( ). Enter this:

```
A$(11) = "K"
```

The error message, *Subscript out of range,* means that the array doesn't have a location A$(11). Try this:

```
A$(0) = "K"
PRINT A$(0)
```

That works because the array has a location A$(0).

Few of us remember that 0 is the first number in the decimal system. This array has 11 locations, but they are numbered 0 through 10. Most people ignore the zero slot in an array and never use it.

You just put the letter K into A$(0). Execute the program from line 100 by typing and entering

```
GOTO 100
```

It didn't print A$(0) because line 110 supplies values of I from 1 to 10. It didn't ask for A$(0). To enter and then print out all 11 items in this array, change both loops so they count from 0 to 10 instead of 1 to 10. Then enter the data items again while running the program from the beginning. You can start with A, rather than K, if you wish.

WHAT HAPPENS TO MEMORY WHEN YOU CHANGE A PROGRAM LINE

If you stop a program, change a program line and then enter it, you lose everything in memory except the program itself. All variables disappear, including arrays. This is true no matter how the program is stopped. It applies when you stop execution by pressing Ctrl-Break, by a STOP statement in the program or by letting the program run to completion.

DIM STATEMENTS

Arrays with subscripts greater than 10 require a DIMension statement in the program. This statement gives the name of the array and the *largest subscript number* that can be used.

A DIM statement can be anywhere in the program, but it must be executed *before* the array is addressed. It's customary to put DIM statements near the beginning. When the computer executes the DIM statement, it reserves space in memory for the array. It also clears memory in that reserved space, so a newly dimensioned array is always empty. List the program in memory and DIMension it to allow a longer array by adding line 15.

```
15 DIM A$(25)
```

A DIM statement *creates* an array. The array exists in memory even if it is empty. This allows the program to fill it with items of data.

Line 15 says *the largest allowable subscript in the array A$( ) is 25.* Change both loops in the program to count from 0 to 25. List it again. Now A$( ) will hold all 26 letters of the alphabet, even though you may be mentally uncomfortable with A$(0) holding "A".

Run it anyway, and type in the letters of the alphabet. When the program stops, enter CONT or press F5 to continue. The screen will display all 26 letters, but they will scroll off the screen at the top.

Clear the screen and execute the program segment starting at line 100 by entering

```
GOTO 100
```

That simply runs the second loop and prints the letters again, still scrolling. You know how to stop the scroll, but I suggest you don't bother with it now.

OPTION BASE

This command allows you to eliminate location 0 of an array if you don't intend to use it. It saves a little space in memory, but you can no longer address that location. Make the following lines look like this:

```
12 OPTION BASE 1
15 DIM A$ (26)
20 FOR I = 1 TO 26
110 FOR I = 1 TO 26
```

List it. Line 12 eliminates the zero location in all arrays used in this program. In effect, it says that the smallest location number in all arrays is 1, not zero. Line 15 dimensions A$( ) accordingly. Lines 20 and 110 change the loops to run from 1 to 26 so they can accommodate all 26 letters of the alphabet. Try it. When you have finished running it, save this program under the name ARAYDEM1, meaning *demonstration of a one-dimensional array*. When you want to fix the scrolling problem, load it again.

The only allowable numbers that can be specified by OPTION BASE are 1 or 0. The default value is 0 so, if that's what you want, you don't have to use an OPTION BASE statement. With OPTION BASE 0, an *undimensioned* array can hold 11 items, 0 through 10. With OPTION BASE 1, the array can hold only 10 items.

ARRAYS WITH MORE THAN ONE DIMENSION

Printed tables of data often have several columns. Columns are vertical, like the columns of a Greek temple. *Rows* are horizontal. Arrays are exactly like printed tables of data, except that they are stored in the memory of your computer.

Two-dimensional arrays have two columns. Three-dimensional arrays have three columns, and so forth up to the limit. For the IBM Personal Computer, the limit of columns is 255. Whether or not you can actually use an array that large depends on the amount of memory available. When memory is full, the computer will tell you so by printing an error message on the screen.

ADDRESSING MULTI-DIMENSIONAL ARRAYS

Using multi-dimensional arrays in a program seems complicated at first. But it will be easier if you think about it in small pieces.

Please imagine a hotel with 100 rooms. The boxes in the lobby are arranged in 10 rows and 10 columns. You would have no difficulty finding the box that is four rows down from the top and three columns over from the left. In array notation, that's box (4,3), meaning four down and three over.

To address a location in a multi-dimensional array, two numbers are used in the parentheses. The first specifies the row number, counting down from the top. The second is the column number, counting from the left. The form is B$(R,C) in which B$( ) is the name of the array, R is row and C is column. You must remember which is which.

I use mnemonic tricks to put things into my brain. When using a multi-dimensional array, I think I am Really Clever. It helps me remember that Row comes before Column. The statement

```
PRINT B$(4,3)
```

will print the data in row 4, column 3 of the array B$( ). In other words, *four down and three over*.

DIM STATEMENTS FOR MULTI-DIMENSIONAL ARRAYS

All multi-dimensional arrays should have a DIM statement. If no subscript will be greater than 10, a DIM statement is not essential, but you should use one anyway. DIM statements help the programmer and anyone else who reads the program understand what's to come.

For multi-dimensional arrays, the form is DIM(R,C). R is the number of rows, C is the number of columns. For example

```
DIM B$(5,4)
```

creates an array with five rows and four columns. When the computer executes a DIM statement, it reserves and clears space for the specified array. Multi-dimensional arrays are *created* by a DIM statement and then *filled* by the program.

You could fill a multi-dimensional array by a series of statements such as:

```
B$(1,1) = "A"
B$(1,2) = "B"
B$(1,3) = "C"
```

and so on. Each of these statements puts data in row 1 of the array B$( ) because the first number in each set of parentheses is 1. The *second* number changes from 1 to 2 to 3, moving from left to right along row 1. The letter *A* is at the top of column 1, *B* is at the top of column 2, *C* is at the top of column 3.

Of course it is better to use loops. Because there are two numbers to be plugged into the parentheses, you must use two. Use one loop to set the row number and another loop to set the column number. When row and column are set, then a data item can be entered for that location.

The following program uses two loops to build an array with five rows and four columns. R is the counter for the loop that sets row numbers. When the R loop has selected a row number, the nested C loop then sets column numbers, one at a time, moving from left to right across the data table. A data item is entered in each column. An entire row is filled by one complete operation of the inner, C, loop.

Then the R loop selects the next row number, and the C loop generates all of the column numbers again, to fill the second row—and so forth until the bottom row is filled. Enter

```
NEW
10 CLS
20 DIM B$(5,4): REM creates array B$()
30 FOR R = 1 TO 5: REM sets Row number
40 FOR C = 1 TO 4: REM sets Column number
50 PRINT "Please type data item for Row "R", Column "C": ";
60 M$ = INKEY$: IF M$ = "" THEN GOTO 60
70 PRINT M$
80 B$(R,C) = M$: REM fills array B$()
90 NEXT C
100 NEXT R
```

List and see that it is typed correctly. Notice that line 50 prints a string in quotation marks, the value of R, another string that begins with a comma and a space, the value of C, then another string that is just a colon and a space.

What the nested loops do is change the array address in line 80. The loop using R as its counter selects row numbers. When a row number has been selected, the C loop selects column numbers until a complete row is formed across the table. For the first row, the array address will change like this: B$(1,1), B$(1,2), B$(1,3), B$(1,4). For the second row, the addresses are B$(2,1), B$(2,2), B$(2,3) B$(2,4). The box in the lower right corner is B$(5,4).

For each B$(R,C) address, as it is produced by the program, the M$ that you type is plugged into the array at that address. The loops don't have much to do with the array itself. They just figure out addresses in an orderly manner. Don't confuse the loops with the array.

The useful work is done by lines 60 and 80. Line 60 accepts a keystroke and names it M$. Line 80 then plugs that keystroke into a location of the array.

Now add a routine to print out the array:

```
190 CLS
200 FOR R = 1 TO 5
210 FOR C = 1 TO 4
220 PRINT B$(R,C),
230 NEXT C
240 PRINT: REM drop down one line for next row
250 NEXT R
260 PRINT
```

The comma at the end of line 220 causes automatic tabs inside the C loop. The PRINT command at line 240 is encountered each time the program leaves the C loop, after printing one complete row. It moves the cursor down one line so the next row is printed on the next line.

Run the program. For data items, enter letters. The array is 5 rows by 4 columns, as expected. Display some of the array items by typing

```
PRINT B$(1,1)
PRINT B$(3,2)
```

and so forth. Compare what is printed with its location in the array at the top of the screen. Continue until you are sure you understand how this array is addressed. Save this program using the name MULTARAY.

NUMERIC OR STRING ARRAYS

The data items at each location of an array are called *elements*. An array can hold numeric elements or string elements. You must choose one or the other when you create the array with a DIM statement. Here are some examples:

DIM PARTNUM (50,3) creates an array of part numbers with 50 rows and 3 columns.

DIM PEOPLE$ (100,3) is an address book. The $ symbol means it holds string expressions. It has 100 rows of three elements. The elements could be: Name, Address, Phone Number.

Numeric elements and string elements are incompatible. Enter this to prove it:

```
DIM TEST$(12,2)
TEST$(1,1) = "Bill Jones"
PRINT TEST$ (1,1)
TEST$(2,2) = 12345
```

ANATOMY OF AN ARRAY

Think of an array as an orderly arrangement of boxes or *locations.* Each location has a name that is used to put data into the array and get it back from the array.

A location in an array is specified by stating *the name* of the array, followed in parentheses by *the row number,* then *the column number.* The numbers are separated by a comma. Example:

```
ARRAYNAME (R,C)
```

In this example, *ARRAYNAME* represents the name of the array. *R* is the row number. *C* is the column number. Location (5,3) is marked in this illustration of an array.

The number of columns in an array is called its *dimension.* This is a five-dimensional array because it has 5 columns. If an array has only one column, it is a one-dimensional array, which is exactly like a numbered list. If there is only one column, the column number is omitted when specifying a location. ARRAYNAME(12) is the twelfth item from the top of an array that has only one column.

In this book, the notation X( ) refers to an array named X. The empty parentheses are used to show that it is an array and that items in the array are designated by putting numbers inside the parentheses. X( ) is not the same as the variable X. X( ) can hold many items of data. X can hold only one item.

Array names are variable names. They are either *numeric* variables or string variables. An array with the name X( ) is a numeric array that can hold only numbers. An array with the name X$( ) is a string array that holds only strings.

The number in parentheses, Z$(3) for example, is called a *subscript.* Therefore, Z$ is a *subscripted variable.* That means it's the *name* of an array. Without the subscript, it would be the name of an ordinary variable, not an array.

Numbers or strings are *placed in an array* by assignment statements. X(5,3) = 7 puts the number 7 in location (5,3) of the array X( ). Locations in arrays are sometimes called *elements.* In this example, the value of *element* (5,3) in the array X( ) is 7.

Numbers or strings are *retrieved from an array* by assignment statements. Y = X(5,3) gives Y the value of whatever is at X(5,3). If the value in that array location is 7, then Y = 7. "Getting" a value from an array does not remove it from the array. It is still there and you can "get" it again, anytime you need it.

Changing the value of an array element is done by an assignment statement. In this example, X(5,3) was set to 7. The statement X(5,3) = 9 will change the content of that location in the array. Now, it is 9. If you set Y equal to X(5,3) again, by the statement Y=X(5,3), Y will take the number 9 as its value.

THIS ARRAY HAS 5 COLUMNS

A ROW

A COLUMN

THIS ARRAY HAS 7 ROWS

LOCATION (5,3)

The error message resulted because you tried to put a numeric expression into an array that was created to hold string expressions. You can put 12345 into the array if you *declare* it to be a string by putting it in quotation marks. Try it this way:

```
TEST$(2,2) = "12345"
PRINT TEST$ (2,2)
```

Create an array with the array name N( ) to hold numeric elements. Put a number in it and print that element. Then put a letter in it.

Remember the rules about type declaration. They also apply to arrays. Anything that you put into a numeric array will be treated as a number. You can put both numbers and letters into a string array, but you must put numeric expressions in quotation marks or use another method of making them into a string.

MAKING STRINGS

So far, you've seen three ways to make characters into strings. You can put a string directly into a program line by typing it in quotation marks. Enter

```
X$ = "12345"
PRINT X$
```

You can do it indirectly, using two statements:

```
X$ = "12345"
Y$ = X$
PRINT X$
PRINT Y$
```

Or, you can do it from the keyboard by inputting keystrokes into a string variable name. The INKEY$ method accepts only a single keystroke and gives it a string name that you've created, such as V$ or M$. To input more than one character at a time, use an INPUT statement. When you do, it accepts characters until you press ENTER to tell the computer to accept what you've typed. Enter

```
INPUT Z$
```

Then type some letters and numbers. Enter

```
PRINT Z$
```

When you input characters from the keyboard into a string variable, those characters automatically become a string. The variable's type declaration does that. You don't need to use quotation marks.

WHICH TYPE IS BETTER?

For pure mathematics dealing only with numbers, a numeric array is obviously the better choice.

For most other applications, a string array is better because you can store both letters and numbers as strings. In an accounting program, for example, you would store names of accounts or customers and dollar amounts that must be treated as numbers. Putting both types of data items into the same array is a convenient way to handle the data.

Storing a number as a string is convenient, but you have to convert numbers into strings before you can put them into a string array. One way is to put the number in quotation marks, as you have seen. Later, when you want to use it as a number, you must convert it from a string back into a number. The computer will not do arithmetic with strings.

STR$( )

STR$( ) is a BASIC word that converts numbers to strings. I pronounce STR$ as *string value of*. Enter

```
X$ = STR$(12345)
PRINT X$
```

Notice that there is a blank space ahead of the number when it's displayed on the screen. Enter

```
X$ = STR$(-12345)
PRINT X$
```

The blank space is for the sign. If the number is positive, the sign is not displayed; if negative, it is.

Sometimes, a program has numeric variables that result either from a calculation or from a keyboard entry. These numbers have been assigned to a variable name, such as Y. You can convert them to a string by using the variable name instead of the actual number. Enter

```
Y = 2*9
Y$ = STR$(Y)
PRINT Y
PRINT Y$
```

Now you have the same number stored in two ways—as a numeric variable Y, and as a string variable Y$. You can use either one, depending on your purpose.

Reminder—Putting a set of empty parentheses after STR$( ) and other BASIC words is not customary in BASIC dictionaries. I write it this way as a memory aid. It reminds me that what follows must be in parentheses.

VAL( )

This does the opposite of STR$( ). Feed VAL( ) a string and it gives you back the number contained in the string—in other words, the VALue of the string. Suppose your program files Y$ in a string array. Later, it brings Y$ back from memory to calculate an amount due, or the profit for last month. Use VAL( ) to convert back to numeric. For example, enter

```
PRINT VAL(Y$)
```

and you get back the number 18. Try this:

```
X = VAL(Y$)
PRINT X
```

It's handy to store numbers as strings in a string array. With VAL( ) it's easy to convert them back to numbers when you need to do arithmetic with them.

Function and Return—Many computer books use the word *function* to describe the kind of word that VAL is. Defining a function is difficult, especially for non-mathematical folks, but here goes. A function is a procedure or operator that changes a number in some way without losing its fundamental meaning, or that derives one number from another.

In this example, the function VAL changes a number from its string representation to its numeric representation. You may be glad to know that you can use the word VAL liberally and successfully without ever knowing what *function* means.

A computer book may tell you that "The *function* VAL *returns* the numeric value of a string." The word *returns* means this: When you feed VAL a string it returns a number.

CLEARING AN ARRAY

Sometimes you need to remove all data from an array or part of an array so you can put other data in without worrying that an element may be left over from the earlier array. This is called *clearing*. One way to do that is to go through the array and put nothing at every location you want to clear.

What is Nothing?—Nothing in a numeric expression is 0, called *zero*. Nothing in a string expression is a set of quotation marks *not* separated by a space, *""*, which is called *null*. Zero and null are *not* interchangeable.

Putting in Nothing—To null or zero one row or column of an array requires one loop. This routine clears row 5 of a 10x10 string array with the name AR$( ). Read through these program lines, but don't enter them.

```
50 FOR C = 1 TO 10
60 AR$(5,C) = ""
70 NEXT C
```

The row number is set at 5 and will not change. It is always 5. As the C loop operates, the value of C changes. A null is placed in AR$(5,1), AR$(5,2), AR$(5,3) and so forth until all 10 columns of row 5 are nulled.

The following routine clears column 7 of a 10x10 numeric array with the name AR( ). Don't bother entering it.

```
230 FOR R = 1 TO 10
240 AR(R,7) = 0
250 NEXT R
```

To null a *single* array location, do it with program statements like these. Don't enter them.

```
450 A$(5,4) = ""
460 X(3,2) = 0
```

The first statement *nulls* one element of a string array. The second statement *zeroes* one element of a numeric array.

ADDING IT UP

You can scan an array for other reasons, such as adding up the columns, multiplying the number at one location by the number at another or whatever you need to do.

You should have the MULTARAY program on disk, or it may still be in memory. List it to remind yourself of what it does. Then add this routine to the program. It adds numeric values of every item in column 1 of the array and prints the total.

```
500 T = 0
510 FOR R = 1 TO 5
520 T = T + VAL(B$(R,1))
530 NEXT R
540 PRINT "TOTAL OF COLUMN 1 IS: "T
```

Run it and enter numbers instead of letters. See if it prints the correct result. List it. It scrolls a little bit.

Line 500 initializes the variable T to zero. T will be used to accumulate the total of column 1.

Line 520 has nested parentheses. To specify the array location, it is necessary to use the form

B$( ). To use the VAL( ) function, it is necessary to place the string that will be evaluated inside the parentheses used with VAL( ). This results in the form VAL(B$( )). In other words, B$( ) itself is enclosed in parentheses because VAL( ) requires it.

During each pass through the loop, line 520 makes T equal to its previous value plus an added amount, which is VAL(B$(R,1)).

Row numbers will change as the loop counter R changes from 1 to 5. The column number will not change because it is not a variable. It is a constant and remains at 1. This adds up column 1 of the array.

On the first pass, T is equal to zero plus VAL(B$(1,1)). On the second pass, VAL(B$(2,1))is added and so forth. On the last pass, VAL(B$(5,1)) is added. Then the total is printed.

What is The Value of a Letter? —Run the program and input one or more letters in column 1. See what happens. You know enough BASIC now to do some high-class experimental programming— trying things to see what happens, or just messing around. Things you teach yourself are seldom forgotten, so feel free to try your own ideas as you do the programs in this book.

Scroll Control When LISTing a Program—This is the first program in this book that you can't display in one screen load. The method demonstrated earlier on page 54 controls the scroll when you are printing a list from a program you wrote.

You can't get into the computer's internal routine that lists a program when you enter LIST, so you must stop the scroll another way. You know that you can specify the range of lines to be listed, such as LIST 10—100. You can stop scrolling by pressing Ctrl-Break, which returns to the command mode. In the command mode, you can change program lines, if you wish. To see more program, you must enter LIST again and stop it again.

If you merely want to look at a program that scrolls, you can pause by pressing Ctrl-Num Lock. This does not return to the command mode, and you cannot change program lines. To resume scrolling, press ENTER. You can stop and go as much as you wish until you reach the end of the program. Try it with the program now in memory.

Practice—In its last appearance, the program in memory added up the values in column 1 of the array. Please delete lines 500—540. Then write a new routine starting at line 500 that adds the items in column 3.

Please delete everything from 500 to the end of your program. Then write a routine starting at line 500 that adds horizontally across the array. Add up all the numbers in row 4. This means the row number remains fixed while the column number changes.

One way to do each of these things is shown at the end of this chapter.

ERASE

This BASIC statement is used to erase a single array, or a list of arrays, from the program and also from memory. It leaves everything else in memory intact.

The statement is ERASE X. In this statement, X is the name of a numeric array *without parentheses*. Or you can use ERASE Z$ in which Z$ is the name of a string array *without parentheses*. The statement ERASE X, Z$ will get them both.

If you have both the variable name X and the array X( ) in memory, ERASE X will zap only the array. If you have both Z$ and Z( ) in memory, ERASE Z$ will zap only the array.

After erasing, the same array name can be redimensioned and used again.

The program in memory created an array B$( ), which is stored separately from the program itself. Use the ERASE command to erase the array. Then test to see if it is really gone.

CLEAR

The CLEAR command erases everything in memory, including arrays, *but not the program.* It erases all DIM statements. CLEAR can be entered from the command mode or as a program statement.

RUN

This command automatically executes a CLEAR before running the program. RUN is versatile. If entered alone, it runs the program in memory from the first line. If followed by a line number, it runs the program starting at that line. If followed by a filename, it clears memory, loads the specified program and runs it from the beginning.

You should have the program MULTARAY on disk. Enter

NEW

Now, nothing is in memory. Enter

RUN "MULTARAY

The disk drive should run to load the program. Then the program will run without a separate RUN command.

NEW

As mentioned and used earlier, this command erases everything in memory, including the program.

USING MULTI-DIMENSIONAL ARRAYS

You've seen that a multi-dimensional array is equivalent to a printed table with several columns. Arrays are used for the same purposes as tables, too.

You should consider arrays as more than a repository of data or a look-up table because the computer can operate on the elements of an array, make decisions, give you reports and do other useful deeds. An array can be used as a data bank. Here are a few sketchy examples:

Put your checkbook register in an array and save it on disk. Include a note about how the money was spent. Then you can scan the array to make totals of the amounts spent for food, clothing, frivolity and other items in your budget. You can print out tax deductions at the end of the year. You can balance your checkbook.

Put personnel information in an array. You can scan it to see who is overdue for a raise. Who has the most absences. How many are male Lithuanians, how many are not. How many are under 30, who will retire in the next five years and so forth.

Put names, addresses and birthdays in an array. You'll become known as a person who never forgets—provided you remember to run your program.

MATRIX ALGEBRA

In mathematics, an array of numbers is called a *matrix,* plural is *matrices.* Using matrices is powerful. For example, you use them to solve a bunch of equations simultaneously. If you understand this kind of math, you will have already surmised that you can use arrays and BASIC statements to manipulate matrices.

MEMORY IMPROVEMENT

Please review this chapter. Before going on, you should understand arrays and how to use loops to fill and read them. If you don't, and reviewing this chapter doesn't help, I suggest that you either find someone to answer your questions face-to-face or try another book. Being able to use arrays is essential to efficient programming.

Load ARAYDEM1 and put in a routine that displays screen loads of 8 lines at a time. If you want to review how we did it before, it's in Chapter 3.

Following is a list of BASIC words used in this chapter, some for the first time. Please look them up in the IBM book entitled *BASIC.* You'll learn some things that I didn't tell you.

BASIC WORDS USED IN THIS CHAPTER

CLEAR   OPTION BASE
DIM   RUN
ERASE   STR$( )
GOTO   VAL( )
NEW

ADDING UP ROW 4 IN MULTARAY

You also wrote a routine to add horizontally across row 4. Here's my version:

```
500 T = 0
510 FOR C = 1 TO 4
520 T = T + VAL(B$(4,C))
530 NEXT C
540 PRINT "TOTAL OF ROW 4 IS: "T
```

ADDING UP COLUMN 3 IN MULTARAY

Earlier in this chapter, you wrote a routine to add up column 3 in the array created by the program MULTARAY. Here's how I did it.

```
500 T = 0
510 FOR R = 1 TO 5
520 T = T + VAL(B$(R,3))
530 NEXT R
540 PRINT "TOTAL OF COLUMN 3 IS: "T
```

5 How To Edit Program Lines

At the beginning of this book, I suggested that you retype entered program lines to change them. I let you do it that way for four chapters, even though there is an easier method. I did it because the best way to learn BASIC is through your fingers. The way to learn the keyboard is also through your fingers. Type more to learn more.

The program-editing methods provided by the IBM Personal Computer are powerful and versatile but, if you do something wrong, the results can be confusing. I don't think a beginner should try to learn to write BASIC program lines and edit them at the same time.

By now you know enough about the language and syntax of BASIC to see and understand the effects of the editing commands. If something goes wrong, you can see what is happening and cope with it.

EDITING A PROGRAM LINE BEFORE IT IS ENTERED

Please clear both memory and the screen. Type this line, but do not press ENTER at the end:

```
100 FOR I = 1 TO 30: PRINT "Please enter data
```

The cursor is sitting at the end of the word *data,* winking and blinking. Assume that you notice an error earlier in the line—the number *30* should have been *50.*

If you do what I suggested earlier, you would fix that by backspacing all the way back to *30* and changing it to *50.* Because backspacing erases characters as you backspace past them, it would be necessary to type the rest of the line again. There is an easier way.

Set the Keypad to the Edit Mode—The keypad has two modes, selected by pressing the Num Lock key. To see how it's set, press the keypad key labeled *4.* If it displays a *4,* the keypad is in the *numeric mode.* That means it will produce the numbers engraved on the keys. If the key did print a *4,* press the backspace key once. The *4* disappears and the cursor is where it was before.

If the cursor moves to the left, the keypad is in the *edit mode.* To edit program lines, you want the keypad to be in the edit mode. Put it in the edit mode now.

In this mode, the keys on the keypad do what is indicated by the symbols engraved below the numbers. However, keys labeled *PgUp* and *PgDn* don't do anything in this mode. Key 4 is Cursor Left, key 8 is Cursor Up, key 6 is Cursor Right, and key 2 is Cursor Down.

Change a Character—Press Cursor Left with the index finger of your right hand, and move the cursor under the *3* in *30.* Notice that nothing was erased. Press the number *5* at the top of the keyboard. That fixes the error by changing the character from *3* to *5.*

There are two ways to move the cursor back to the end of the line so you can continue typing. Try doing it with Cursor Right, using the third finger of your right hand. If you hold any of these keys down, the cursor will move continuously until you release the key.

Use Cursor Left to place the cursor again under the *5* in *50.* Now press key 1 on the keypad, which is *End* in this mode. The cursor jumps immediately to the end of the line.

Making More Than One Change in the Line—Suppose you are typing this line and you notice two errors. *I* should be *J,* and *50* should be *10.* Use Cursor Left to place the cursor under *I.* Change it to *J.* Use Cursor Right to place the cursor under the *5* in *50.* Change it to *1.* Then move the cursor to the end of the line.

Delete One Character—The Delete key is labeled *Del.* Put the cursor under the *l* in *Please.* Press the Delete key and release it quickly so it doesn't repeat. The letter disappears and the space where it was is closed up. Move the cursor to the end of the line.

Insert One Character—The Insert key is labeled *Ins.* You can use it to fix the error in *Pease.* Put the cursor under the first *e.* Press the Insert key. Notice that the cursor changes to a rectangle—a visual clue that the computer is set to insert whatever you type.

Press the letter *l* and release it quickly so it doesn't repeat. The letter *l* is inserted. The rectangular cursor remains over the *e* and indicates that the computer is still in the insert mode. Move the cursor to the end of the line. When you move the cursor, the insert mode is cancelled, and the cursor reverts to its normal appearance.

When you insert something, the character above the cursor and everything behind it moves to the right to make room for whatever you're inserting.

Delete a Word—Using the Delete key, delete the word *Please* and the space behind it. Return the cursor to the end of the line. The word *enter* doesn't look right. Change it to *Enter.*

You can also use the Delete key to delete more than one word.

Insert a Word—Put the cursor between the words *Enter* and *data.* Press the Insert key. Type the word *the.* Move the cursor to the end of the line. If you forgot to put a space ahead of the word *the,* fix it.

You can also use this method to insert more than one word.

Delete to the End—Suppose you decide to put the PRINT statement on a separate line, instead of on line 100. Move the cursor under the colon. Press Ctrl-End, press ENTER and say goodbye.

Putting the Line in Memory—Now LIST line 100 using the F1 key. The line placed in memory is the line as it looks *when you press ENTER.* While typing a line, you can make as many changes as you wish. The changes affect only what appears on the screen. *Nothing happens* in computer memory until you press ENTER.

Practice—Type program lines and practice using these editing techniques.

EDITING A LINE THAT HAS BEEN ENTERED

Enter the command FILES to see what is on disk A. One of the files should be MULTARAY.BAS. Load and list it. It should scroll off the screen.

Suppose the line you want to edit is not on the screen, such as line 10 in this case. Display it by entering

```
EDIT 10
```

If there is a program in memory with that line number, entering EDIT followed by the line number will display that line and put the computer in the edit mode. It places the cursor all the way to the left, so you can begin editing there.

From this point, the editing techniques are the same as already discussed. The changes you make affect only the screen, *until you press ENTER while the cursor is still on that line.*

Add a remark at the end of line 10, so the screen looks like this, then press ENTER:

```
EDIT 10
10 CLS: REM DO NOT SAVE THIS PROGRAM
```

You are going to use this program to practice editing. When you are through, it will be changed. Don't put it back on the disk. The version now on disk is correct.

The cursor is on the blank line below line 10. Even though you don't see the BASIC prompt symbol, the computer is now in the command mode, ready to accept a command or to enter another program line. List lines 10—100 of the program. Notice that the change you made to line 10 is in memory.

THE SCREEN-LINE EDITING MODE

When more than one program line is displayed on the screen, you can edit any of them by moving the cursor to that line. When the cursor is in the line, the editing technique is the same as already discussed. This is a great timesaver and very easy to do, but there are some traps for the unwary.

When you move the cursor up into the program lines, the computer is automatically in the edit mode. *Anything you do with the cursor in the program lines will be accepted as some kind of editing—even if it's wrong!*

Using the arrow keys on the keypad, move the cursor to line 30 and position it under the number *5.* Insert a number *1,* so it reads *15.* Using the Down Arrow, move the cursor to the bottom of the screen. Look at line 30. Now list lines 10—100 again. Look at line 30.

You made a change on the screen, but it didn't go into memory because you didn't press ENTER while the cursor was still on that line.

Do it again and press ENTER this time. You can press ENTER when you finish editing the line, no matter where the cursor is, as long as the cursor is still in that program line. When you press ENTER, the cursor drops down to the beginning of line 40. Everything looks OK.

Let's check to see if the change went into memory. Press the F1 key to type LIST and then press ENTER.

Look where line 50 used to begin and you see *Syntax error.* What happened? *Any time* the cursor is in the program lines, the computer is *in the edit mode.* The computer thought you wanted to begin line 40 with the word *LIST,* which is a syntax error.

To avoid getting deeper into trouble, move the cursor down below the program lines. Now list the program. Line 30 accepted the change you made because you pressed ENTER before moving the cursor out of that line. You edited that line correctly. The other lines were not affected by the syntax error.

Making a Really Big Mistake—When you're making changes to program lines, you're usually in a hurry to see the result. Let's get in a hurry and make another mistake. Move the cursor up to line 40. Put it under the *4* and change it to *9* by pressing the key labeled *9* at the top of the keyboard. Leave the cursor under the colon. I do hope that fixes the program. Press the F2 key to run it and see.

Oh my. Move the cursor down below the program lines. Look at the display at the bottom of the screen to remind yourself that pressing F2 types both RUN and ENTER. Look at line 40. The computer thinks that you edited line 40 to put the word RUN right in the middle.

With the cursor *below* the program lines, press F2 again.

Syntax Error—When a program is running and finds a syntax error in a program line, it stops, prints an error message with the line number where the error occurred, displays the BASIC prompt symbol, displays the line with the error, positions the cursor at the extreme left of that line and enters the edit mode so you can fix it. The display now looks like this:

```
Syntax error in 40
Ok
40 FOR C = 1 TO 9RUNEM SETS COLUMN NUMBER
```

Look at line 40 again. Sure enough, RUN is right there in the middle. Because the colon and REM were removed, the BASIC interpreter changed all lower-case letters to upper case in memory. When you listed the line, it appears as it actually is in memory. Move the cursor over, replace the *R* with a colon, replace the *U* with a space, change the *N* to an *R*, press ENTER. That should make the change you originally intended.

List lines 10—100 again to check. If you did everything correctly, the line looks like this:

```
40 FOR C = 1 TO 9: REM SETS COLUMN NUMBER
```

Don't run the program. The changes you made were for practice only. The program is useless. If you wish, you can change the remark back to lower case.

RULES TO LIVE BY

1) When you edit a line, press ENTER before leaving that line.

2) When you've finished editing, move the cursor down below the program lines before entering any command.

DELETING AN ENTIRE LINE

There are several ways to delete a line:

Before It is Entered—If you are typing a line but have not yet entered it, and you decide to redo the whole thing, press and hold down the Backspace key until the cursor reaches the left margin. It won't go any farther. Then retype the line, including the line number.

After It is Entered—Once entered, the line is in memory. To delete it, type the line number and then press ENTER. That replaces the previous line in memory with a new blank line. The BASIC interpreter deletes blank lines.

If you intend to delete the old line and replace it with another, enter the line number followed by the new line. When you press ENTER, the new line replaces the old one in memory.

Not Using the Escape Key—If you're typing a line that *hasn't been entered,* pressing the Escape Key—labeled *Esc*—will delete it on the screen. Because the line was never entered, it is not in memory.

If you list a program in memory, move the cursor into one of the lines and then press Esc, the line disappears from the screen but *not from memory.* If you press Esc and then ENTER, nothing happens because you entered a line that is both blank and without a line number. That still does not delete the numbered line from memory. Try it if you wish.

I suggest that you don't use the Esc key. You can do the same thing with the editing techniques already discussed.

CONTROLLING WRAP-AROUND

As you know, a program line can be longer than one line on the screen. If you allow the computer to perform a *wrap-around* at the end of a screen line, the result is often visually unattractive and hard to read, especially if it happens in the middle of a word.

It's better to control wrap-around by putting it where you want it, such as between statements or between the last statement and a remark. When you reach a place where you would like to drop down a line, insert a line feed by pressing Ctrl-ENTER. This produces the control code CHR$(10).

Depending on the device that receives it, a line feed is executed in different ways. On a printer, it advances the paper one line. On the display screen, it automatically inserts blanks to cause the desired wrap-around. This makes the program lines longer, which requires more memory to store them, but it is usually worth it. Please type the following words. At the end of the word *men,* press Ctrl-ENTER and then type the second line.

```
500 PRINT "Now is the time for all good men
    to come to the aid of their country."
```

When you have typed the second line, press ENTER. List the program. Notice that the words *to come* are underneath the line numbers. When I go to the trouble of controlling wrap-around, I usually put spaces in front of the second line so it lines up with the text portion of the first line rather than the line number. Insert four spaces before the word *to*.

Please clear the screen. Sometimes I think it makes a program easier to read if remarks are on separate screen lines. Use the EDIT command to bring line 80 onto the screen, ready for editing.

Move the cursor to the blank space following the colon. Press the Ins key. Then press Ctrl-ENTER to put in a line feed. You can see the computer automatically inserting spaces to produce the line feed. Notice that the cursor still indicates insert mode. Move it to the beginning of the second line. That cancels the insert mode. Get back into it and insert two more spaces. Press ENTER. Now the line looks like this:

```
80 B$(R,C) = M$:
   REM fills array
```

List the program again and look at line 80.

Suppose you're worried about all of those spaces going into memory and decide to take them back out. Move the cursor to the end of the first line, after the colon. Press the Delete key intermittently and watch the computer unwrap the wrap-around. If you hold the Delete key down too long, the computer will beep. That means the keyboard is sending deletes faster than they can be executed. No harm is done, except that you may enter more deletes than you intend to.

LET YOUR FINGERS DO THE EDITING

I suggest that you practice editing the program now in memory, using all of the techniques discussed in this chapter. Practice until your fingers can do it without your thinking about the mechanics of program editing.

Don't worry about what you're doing to the program. When you have finished, enter NEW to delete it from memory.

Then refer to Chapter 2 of the IBM book *BASIC*. Find the section called *The BASIC Program Editor*. Read carefully from there to the end of the chapter. You will see a couple of editing methods that I haven't discussed.

6 How To Input Data From The Keyboard

Most programs can't do anything useful without data from the outside world. I am using the word *data* to mean anything you want to put in—numbers, letters, words, poetry, astrological truths, even long and preachy book manuscripts.

Your computer can receive data over a phone line from a databank or another computer. You can obtain data on a disk and play it into your computer. But the most common way to *input* data is from the keyboard.

The only data that a computer program can use is data in memory. You can input it from the keyboard, input it from a disk or put it on program lines in the program itself. But for data to be useful, it must be assigned a name and placed in memory. When the program needs the data, it calls for it by name.

INPUT

This is a BASIC word that tells the computer to *get ready* to receive data from the keyboard. The word *INPUT* alone is not enough. The second part of the statement *names* the variable that will receive the data and tells the computer that it will be either numeric or string data.

As data is typed, it appears on the screen but does not go into memory. If a typing error occurs, it can be corrected on the screen. When the data has been typed, the user must press ENTER to signal the computer to accept what is displayed on the screen and place it in memory.

The statement INPUT X prepares the computer to receive *numeric* data from the keyboard because X is a numeric variable. It assigns the variable name *X* to the data. When you end the input by pressing ENTER, the computer puts the data in memory, under the name *X*.

The statement INPUT X$ is similar, except that it accepts string data and the computer will not accept a numeric input. From the command mode, enter

```
INPUT X
```

Notice that a question mark is displayed, followed by the cursor. The question mark is produced by the INPUT statement. It is a *prompt* to tell the user that the computer is waiting for data to be typed. Type and enter

```
12345
```

Computer says *Ok,* which means that the INPUT statement has been executed. The number 12345 should be in memory under the name *X.* Enter

```
PRINT X
```

to see if it is there.

It will be interesting to input a variety of data items from the keyboard in response to an INPUT statement. To make it easy, enter this program:

```
NEW
10 CLS
```

(Program continued on next page.)

```
20 PRINT "Please type and enter a number."
30 INPUT X: REM enter a number and put into memory
40 PRINT X: REM get from memory and display
50 IF X = 99 THEN GOTO 100: REM jump out of loop
60 PRINT: GOTO 20
100 PRINT: PRINT
```

Line 50 provides a way to get out of the loop. The computer will accept 99 as a valid input and display it. Then it will jump to line 100. List it, check your typing and run it.

The question mark used as a prompt indicates that the computer is waiting for data from the keyboard. Enter

```
7
```

The computer accepts 7 and names it X. Enter

```
12345.00
```

On this pass through the loop, you gave X a different value. The computer doesn't display zeros after the decimal point unless you use a special technique discussed in Chapter 10. Enter

```
1.2345
```

Decimals are displayed if they are significant. Try entering a number with a comma. The computer balks because of the comma. It is standard in BASIC not to allow commas in numbers. Most people are accustomed to putting commas in large numbers.

Telling a keyboard operator to type 12345 when the number is 12,345 is not a good way to handle the comma problem. Even if you put a sign on the wall, people are going to put commas in large numbers. This makes life difficult for beginning computer users. Later, I'll show you a couple of ways to solve this problem. Enter

```
123:456
ABC
123ABC
123$
```

When you have promised the computer a numeric expression, such as X, you must input a number. Decimal points are allowed. Commas are not allowed. Enter 99 to get out of the loop.

Now use Edit commands to change lines 20, 30 and 40 so the program expects a string input, and change line 50 to get out of the loop when ZZ is input.

```
20 PRINT "Please type and enter a string."
30 INPUT X$: REM enter a string and put into memory
40 PRINT X$: REM get from memory and display
50 IF X$ = "ZZ" THEN GOTO 100: REM jump out of loop
```

List it, admire it and run it. Enter

```
12345
```

Even though you entered a number, the computer accepted it as a string. That's because line 30 says *Whatever is input from the keyboard will be given the name X$*. Any combination of characters that is input to a string name is automatically handled as a string. Now, enter

```
12.345
HELLO
123ABC
12,345
HE SAID, "PHOOEY"
```

(handwritten annotation: can not enter commas unless string enclosed in " marks.)

The program will accept letters and numbers in any arrangement. It will accept numbers with decimal points, but still balks at commas. You can force it to accept commas by typing quotation marks around the string like this:

```
"12,345"
"NOW, NOW"
```

In effect, enclosing a string in quotation marks tells the computer that you really do want to use commas in the string, and it must accept them.

When you use INPUT to keystroke characters into a string variable such as X$, leading and trailing spaces are ignored. Spaces between characters or between words are accepted. If leading or trailing spaces are important, you must put the entire expression inside quotation marks, including the leading and trailing spaces. Try it.

You can't force it to accept quotation marks by putting them in standard quotation marks. Enter

```
"HE SAID, "PHOOEY""
```

But you can use single quotation marks:

```
"HE SAID, 'PHOOEY'"
```

Now input ZZ to get out of the loop.

You may be wondering how you will remember all of these details. Don't try. You've planted a seed in your brain. The first time you write a program that doesn't work because of commas, spaces or quotation marks, you will remember some of the details. You may solve the problem by messing around until something works, or you can return to this interesting chapter and read all about it. Eventually, harsh experience will make you remember.

Considering all of those problems with commas, INPUT statements are hardly worth fooling with. They have only one advantage—to force the keyboard operator to input a number when the program expects a number.

I've seen programs with instructions printed on the screen saying *DON'T USE ANY COMMAS*. That's not the way to write a program, friends. Later, I'll show you some ways to solve the comma problem.

LINE INPUT

This statement accepts *anything* you type until ENTER is pressed—with one important exception—*it omits trailing spaces!* Spaces placed between the last character and ENTER are ignored and disappear.

The LINE INPUT statement always treats the keyboard input as a string. You don't have to enclose anything in quotation marks. If you do, the quotation marks become part of the string. LINE INPUT does not use a question mark as a prompt and displays only the cursor.

Please list the program in memory. Then change line 30 to read:

```
30 LINE INPUT X$: REM enter a string and put into memory
```

List it, check it, run it and enter

```
NOW, IS: THE "TIME" FOR 12,345.000 GOOD MEN
```

LINE INPUT doesn't require the keyboard operator to observe any unusual rules. It gobbles up anything that anybody wants to type. If commas or missing spaces at the end cause problems, the problems are the programmer's responsibility—where they belong!

Run the program for a while, entering anything you wish until the joy subsides. Then get out of the loop.

MATCHING TYPES

You must always match types. The type designation of a variable name—numeric or string—must agree with the type of data you input and store under that name. A numeric variable name, such as X, must receive numeric inputs. A string variable name, such as X$, must receive string inputs.

The computer is glad to LINE INPUT X$. From the command mode, ask it to

```
LINE INPUT X
```

and it will scold you because *LINE INPUT works only with strings.* Try it and see.

INCLUDING A PROMPT

A program should always tell the user what to do when user input is required, as line 20 does in this program. You can put a program line just ahead of an INPUT or LINE INPUT statement to say *Type name, rank and serial number* or whatever you wish. It prompts the user to do it.

INPUT and LINE INPUT statements allow you to include a prompt as part of the statement. Please delete line 20 and enter a new line 30 to look like this:

```
30 LINE INPUT "Please enter something now:"; X$
```

Notice the form. The prompt is in quotation marks, followed by a semicolon. If you do it some other way, it won't work. Run it and see how you improved it. Change line 60 so the program will work. Then admire it.

The cursor is too close to the colon. Put one space between the colon and the ending quotation marks. Run it again and enter a few things.

If you want a question mark as part of the prompt with LINE INPUT, you must put it just before the space preceding the ending quotation marks, instead of the colon. Try it, if you wish. I prefer to use a colon.

Change line 30 by deleting LINE so it looks like this:

```
30 INPUT "Please enter something now: "; X$
```

That combines a prompt with an INPUT statement. It will work fine, but it has the same limitations as any other INPUT statement. Run it and notice the display.

It has both the prompt and a question mark. Probably one or the other is enough. You can suppress the question mark by using a comma instead of the semicolon after the ending quotation marks, like this:

```
30 INPUT "Please enter something now: ", X$
```

Run it and notice that the question mark has been suppressed.

Suppose that you want to use an INPUT statement without a prompt and also without a question mark. You have to trick BASIC into thinking that you are using a prompt followed by a comma, like this:

```
30 INPUT "", X$
```

The prompt is there, but nothing is in it. Run it and enter something.

WHERE DOES THE DATA GO?

You can input data to ordinary variable names such as X or X$. Or, you can input data to subscripted variable names such as X( ) or X$( ), which puts the data in the specified locations in an array. You don't have any other choices.

When the designated variable name receives data, the data is labeled with that name and automatically placed in computer memory until it is needed for something.

Getting it from memory is automatic. When you ask for a variable name in a program line, the computer finds the data item with that name and uses it as instructed by the program line.

Getting a data item from memory *does not remove it* from memory. It is still there with the same value until you change it by giving it a new value, or until you null or zero it, or until you clear memory. As long as you don't change its value, you can use the same variable repeatedly and its value will be the same.

CONSTANTS

These are data items that never change, such as the speed of light, the distance to Cincinnati, the number of pints in a gallon, your middle name or your income last year.

Constants are often needed by a program to do its work. If so, they must be in memory when needed, with a name attached so the computer can find them.

Suppose you write a program to figure out how much it will cost to ship a package to Cincinnati. The program needs two kinds of data as inputs. It needs the weight of the package. That changes, depending on what's in the package, so the user must type it in each time.

It also needs the distance to Cincinnati, which is a *constant* from any fixed location. If the user has to enter the same distance each time he runs the program, he will eventually become tired of doing that.

He will make errors when typing it, and people will say that your program broke because the overnight express would never charge $99,999.87 to deliver a parcel to Cincinnati. You can troubleshoot forever and never find the problem in the program, because the problem is the user, not the program.

READ DATA

Constants can be typed into the program itself in a DATA list. Enter this:

```
NEW
20 DATA 1
```

Line 20 is a DATA list, identified by the word *DATA* at the beginning. It has only a single data item on the list—the number 1.

A READ statement tells the computer to find the DATA list in the program and put the data into memory so the computer can use it. Enter

```
10 READ D
30 PRINT D
```

List it, check it and run it a few times. Line 10 asks for one data item to be read and assigned to the name *D*. Line 20 supplies it. Line 30 gets it from memory and prints it, proving that computer science is real.

More Than One Data Item—Usually there is more than one constant to be put in a data list and read into memory. In that case, line 10 should ask for more than one item, line 20 should supply more than one item and line 30 should print more than one item. Try it this way:

```
10 READ X: READ Y: READ Z
20 DATA 1,2,3
30 PRINT X, Y, Z
```

In line 20, the data items are separated by commas used as *delimiters*. They tell the computer where one data item ends and the next one begins. The computer knows that a comma is "de limit of de data." This is why it has difficulty with commas in INPUT statements.

The READ statement causes the computer to read a data item in a DATA list and remember that it read it. It remembers by moving a "pointer" along the list, inside the computer. The pointer always points to the *next data item* to be read. The next READ statement finds the pointer and then reads the next data item. In this way, data items are not omitted or read twice.

When the first data item is read, it goes into memory as X because the READ statement provided that name for the first data item. The second item is read as Y, and so forth. Each READ into a DATA list gets a *new item* and therefore *requires* a new name.

List it and check your typing. Run it. The computer reads each data item, stores it in memory under the specified name and prints it so you can see what it stored.

Reading Data Items with a Loop—For long data lists, you would use a loop to read the data items. Change line 10 to use a loop:

```
10 FOR I = 1 TO 3: READ D(I): NEXT I
```

As you know, the only way a loop can change variable names is to use the form $D(I)$, in which I is the loop counter. It changes value at each pass and thereby supplies a new variable name. These are subscripted variables and are plugged into an array. Line 10 builds a simple array with three data items by reading the data on line 20.

When the array is filled, the program can use the data any way you wish. Let's just print it out. You could use another loop, or just call for the items as you need them and in whatever order you prefer. Write a new line 30 like this:

```
30 PRINT D(3), D(2), D(1)
```

This will display the items in reverse order. Run it and see.

RULES FOR READ DATA STATEMEMTS

1) The READ statement must be executed before the program needs the data from memory. A DATA list can be anywhere in the program, but I usually put it near the READ statement because this makes the program simpler to write and understand.

2) A DATA list can occupy more than one program line. When all of the first line has been read, the program then reads the next line, taking each item in order. If you use more than one program line, each line must begin with the word DATA.

3) The number of READ requests should match the number of data items supplied. If there are more READ requests than data items, the error message *Out of DATA* results. If there are more data items than READ requests, the excess data items are not read.

4) If data items are not used up by one READ statement, and there is a second READ statement later in the program, it will begin reading the data list where the first one stopped.

5) READ DATA statements can be used with either numeric or string data items, provided the variable name types match the data types.

6) If your program needs to read a DATA list more than once, the list must end with a colon and the word *RESTORE*. Or, you can put RESTORE on the next line. RESTORE resets the pointer so it designates the first data item on the list again.

BUILDING A LOOK-UP TABLE

A READ DATA routine is the best way to put look-up tables in your programs and read them into memory. A two-column table uses a two-dimensional array and two nested loops to fill it with data items.

If all data is numeric, the array can have a numeric name, such as Y(R,C). If one column is string data and the other numeric, treat them all as strings and put them in a string array. You can change the numbers back to numeric data later, using VAL( ).

Let's make a simplified employee list with names and department numbers. The first column is names and the second column is department numbers. The array name is EMPL$( ). Please enter this program:

```
NEW
10 CLS
20 FOR R = 1 TO 5
30 FOR C = 1 TO 2
40 READ EMPL$(R,C)
50 NEXT C
60 NEXT R
100 DATA Abe, 11, Bill, 22, Clancy, 33, Don, 44, Ev, 55
```

After the R loop sets a Row number, the C loop reads two data items. Visualize what happens in line 40. When R is 1, the first pass of the C loop creates the variable name EMPL$(1,1), reads the first data item and puts it into memory.

Then the C loop creates the variable name EMPL$(1,2), reads the second data item and puts it into memory. The first data item is the employee name, Abe, and the second data item is a department number, 11.

Then the R loop sets the next row number, 2. Two more variable names are created by the C loop. These receive data items 3 and 4 on the data list, and so forth.

List, check and run the program. To see if it worked, look into memory from the command mode. Enter

```
PRINT EMPL$(1,1)
PRINT EMPL$(1,2)
PRINT EMPL$(5,1)
PRINT EMPL$(5,2)
```

Keep looking until you are satisfied. Now enter

```
PRINT EMPL$(4,3)
```

The computer made the correct response. There is no column 3 in that array. Change line 20 to read

```
20 FOR R = 1 TO 6
```

and run the program. You get an error message. The R loop ran 6 times but there was only enough data for 5 passes.

Change line 20 back so it counts to 5. Then add lines 45 and 55 to display the array.

```
45 PRINT EMPL$(R,C),
55 PRINT
```

List it and then run it. If you don't remember what the PRINT statement on line 55 does, delete the line and run the program again. Then put line 55 back again. Run it with TRON operating.

What About Column Heads?—Every data table printed out should have column heads. They should be printed before the loop operation, so they print just once. Add

```
15 PRINT "EMPL.", "DEPT.": PRINT
```

Run it that way with TRON on and off. Change the program to move the prompt down so it doesn't look like *Ok* is an employee.

USES OF LOOK-UP TABLES

When you've read a look-up table into an array in memory, you can use it for several things. The primary use, of course, is to supply data to the program. When the program needs to know how many days there are in October, the distance to Cincinnati, or whatever, it merely looks in the array.

Always protect the keyboard operator from problems due to typing errors. A program containing employee information would ask the user to type the name of an employee to get data for that person. If the user types it incorrectly, the program doesn't do what the user expected, even though nothing is wrong with the program.

You can prevent that by using the table as a spelling check. After a name is entered, check it against the employee list in the array EMPL$( ). Scan down the first column and compare each name in the array to the name that was entered. If no match is found, the name was entered incorrectly or there is no employee with that name.

The program should tell the user what happened and ask for a correct name.

Data items to be stored permanently, such as employee files, are normally put on disk. After the spelling-check function has been performed, the program can then get the correct personnel file from the disk.

If the big boss suddenly wants to know how many employees are in department 27, you can write a routine to scan down column 2 of EMPL$( ) and count the number of times that 27 is found. It may be necessary to report that there is no department 27—as politely as possible.

If an employee leaves the company, you might copy the data into another file labeled *Former Employees*. Then you should remove the name and data from the file of current employees. To do that, scan across the array at the correct row, and null or zero each location on that row. From the command mode, try zapping Clancy out of the array. Then hire a lady named Cindy to take his place.

Surprises—They happen. *Serendipity* is an overworked word that means finding something good that you weren't looking for. If you organize data in your programs thoughtfully, you will find it easy to do things that may not have been part of the original plan. Everybody will say it is serendipitous, but you and I will know it is luck.

INKEY$

You have already used INKEY$ to input data from the keyboard. As a quick review, the form is:

```
50 KB$ = INKEY$: IF KB$ = "" THEN GOTO 50
```

When that line is executed, it waits for a keystroke and assigns the character produced by that keystroke to the string variable name KB$. The main advantage of INKEY$ is that you don't have to press ENTER after the keystroke.

Each time line 50 executes, it can accept only a single keystroke. A routine that allows you to input more than one keystroke using INKEY$ is in the next chapter.

MEMORY CHECK

A list of BASIC words used in this chapter follows. Please look up each one in the IBM book *BASIC*.

Practice—Please look over the programs in this chapter. Be sure you understand each line. Write some similar programs. For example, write a program that allows you to input a 5x5 array from the keyboard. My version is below.

```
10 'program to fill a 5x5 array. filename "5X5 ARAY"
20 CLS
30 DIM ARAY$(5,5): REM creates array
40 FOR R = 1 TO 5: REM sets Row number
50 FOR C = 1 TO 5: REM sets Column number
60 PRINT "Please enter item for Row "R", Column "C": ";
70 LINE INPUT M$
80 ARAY$(R,C) = M$: REM fills array
90 NEXT C
100 NEXT R
110 CLS: PRINT: PRINT: PRINT;' display array
120 FOR R = 1 TO 5
130 FOR C = 1 TO 5
140 PRINT ARAY$(R,C),
150 NEXT C
160 PRINT: PRINT
170 NEXT R
180 PRINT: PRINT: PRINT
```

7 Strings And Things

This chapter demonstrates methods of string management, an important part of programming. Some people think that computers merely compute numerical answers to mathematical problems. Computers do that of course, but they can also handle words and phrases that are often necessary to make the numbers understandable.

You already know that strings are made up of both letters and numbers that convey literal information, such as *July 1989.* The last symbol of a string name must be a $, such as G$.

CONCATENATION

This is not a BASIC word. In computer lingo, it means connecting *string expressions* together, like freight cars in a train. It's done with the symbol +. When used with strings, + *does not* mean addition. It means *concatenation.* Enter

```
A$ = "HELLO"
B$ = "THERE"
PRINT A$ + B$
```

Do it again and put a space after *HELLO,* inside the quotation marks.

There are two meanings for the symbol +. With numbers, it means add them together. With strings, it means concatenate them. The word *catenate* means to connect or form into a chain. The prefix *con* is redundant, but we all use it.

LEN( )

This BASIC word means LENgth. When you put the name of a string in the parentheses, LEN will tell you how long the string is—the number of spaces that it occupies.

You have just put two strings into memory as A$ and B$. To see them again and find out how many keystrokes are in each string, enter

```
PRINT A$
PRINT B$
PRINT A$ + B$
PRINT LEN(A$)
PRINT LEN(B$)
PRINT LEN(A$ + B$)
```

Why does A$ have one more character than B$? It's the space you put at the end of HELLO.

ALLOWABLE LENGTH OF A STRING

Strings can hold a maximum of 255 characters. One way to get in trouble is to concatenate two long strings so that the combination exceeds 255 characters. If this happens, the error message says *String too long.*

SUMMARY OF WAYS TO MAKE A STRING

X$ = "12ABC34"	Typed *directly* in program line. Defined by quotation marks.
Y$ = "12ABC34": X$ = Y$	The variable X$ is defined *indirectly* by setting it equal to Y$. Y$ is typed directly in program line, defined by quotation marks.
Y = 12345: X$ = STR$(Y)	X$ is obtained by *converting* a numeric, Y, to a string using STR$( ).
INPUT X$	X$ is formed by *inputting* characters to a string variable name. Will not accept commas, leading or trailing spaces.
INPUT X$ Enter *"data"*	Quotation marks surrounding typed input from keyboard. Will accept commas, leading and trailing spaces. Example of keyboard input: "12,345"

RELATIONAL OPERATORS

You can compare strings by using relational operators. The relational operators used with strings are the same as those listed earlier for numerics. They are:

```
=    Equals
<    Less than
<=   Less than or equal to
>    Greater than
>=   Greater than or equal to
<>   Not equal to
```

When relational operators are used to compare strings, the ASCII code number of the first character of one string is compared to the ASCII code of the first character of the other string. Then the second characters of the two strings are compared, and so on. If all characters are identical, the strings are declared equal.

When the computer encounters the first different pair of characters, it makes a decision based on which code is larger. As shown in the list of codes in Appendix G of the IBM *BASIC* book, ASCII codes for letters become larger toward the end of the alphabet. If the strings being compared contain only letters—all upper case or all lower case—then the one with the *larger* ASCII code number belongs nearer the *end* of the alphabet.

ASCII codes for numbers also become larger as the numbers become larger. Strings can contain both numbers and letters. If they do contain both, they will be ranked by the same method, but the ranking may not have any relevance to alphabetical order. Try these:

```
IF "AGE" > "ACE" THEN PRINT "YES" ELSE PRINT "NO"
IF "ACE" > "ACES" THEN PRINT "YES" ELSE PRINT "NO"
IF "ACE 1" > "ACE 2" THEN PRINT "YES" ELSE PRINT "NO"
```

Try all of the relational operators listed earlier to compare a variety of strings, so you know how they work.

USING STRINGS

Strings normally originate at the keyboard. They are then used by your computer program. Please enter this program:

```
NEW
10 CLS: PRINT: PRINT
20 LINE INPUT "Enter your first name: "; N1$
30 LINE INPUT "Enter your middle initial: "; N2$
40 LINE INPUT "Enter your last name: "; N3$
50 PRINT: PRINT "Hello, " N1$ N3$
60 PRINT "What does the "N2$" stand for? ";
70 LINE INPUT N2$: PRINT
80 PRINT N1$ N2$ N3$ " SOUNDS DISTINGUISHED!"
90 PRINT: PRINT
```

List it and check it. Lines 20, 30 and 40 receive three strings from the keyboard and name them N1$, N2$ and N3$. Line 50 greets you.

Line 60 asks for your full middle name. The semicolon at the end of line 60 keeps the cursor on the same screen line. Line 70 receives your middle name as N2$. This string name was used earlier, in line 30, to receive your initial. At line 70, N2$ is changed. It becomes your full middle name, rather than just your initial.

Line 80 then prints all three names and makes a thoughtful observation about them. Run it and supply the keyboard inputs as requested.

Where are the Spaces?—When the program ran, there were no spaces between the words of your name. In lines 50 and 80, a space is typed between the string names. The computer ignored those spaces as it will any space that is not enclosed in quotation marks or typed into a string variable.

Run the program again and press the space bar after each name, before pressing ENTER.

That doesn't work because LINE INPUT ignores trailing spaces. Every version of BASIC that I'm acquainted with has some peculiarities that make me wonder about the logic behind them. This is one such peculiarity.

There are several ways to fix the program. You can change the PRINT statements to print spaces between the strings. Enter

```
50 PRINT: PRINT "Hello, " N1$ " " N3$
80 PRINT N1$ " " N2$ " " N3$ " SOUNDS DISTINGUISHED!"
```

The spaces are enclosed in quotation marks so they are accepted as strings consisting of one space. List the program, check your typing carefully and run it. The space between N3$ and SOUNDS is inside the quotation marks before SOUNDS.

Another way to solve the problem is to use the ASCII code for "space," which is CHR$(32). Try using CHR$(32) instead of " " in lines 50 and 80.

The spaces are not part of the strings as they are stored in memory. They are added in the print statements, when the strings are displayed. If you use the strings again later in the program, you must remember to print spaces between them.

Maybe the best solution is to attach a space to the back of each string when you enter it and store the string in memory with the space attached. This can be done in the program itself.

Do it by concatenating. Put line 50 back the way it was originally. Change line 80 to delete the space ahead of SOUNDS. Add lines 45 and 75.

```
50 PRINT: PRINT "Hello, " N1$ N3$
80 PRINT N1$ N2$ N3$ "SOUNDS DISTINGUISHED!"
45 N1$ = N1$ + " ": N3$ = N3$ + " "
75 N2$ = N2$ + CHR$(32)
```

List it and check it. Line 45 adds a space to the end of N1$ and N3$ after they are entered from the keyboard. Line 75 is needed because N2$ is changed in line 70. The space is a permanent part of those strings. I made a space one way in line 45 and another way in line 75 to remind you that there is more than one way to do it. Now run it. Please list it again.

Notice that a prompt was included in the LINE INPUT statements in lines 20, 30 and 40. The prompt for line 70 was entered separately at line 60 instead of being included with the LINE INPUT statement on line 70. That's because the prompt at line 60 is too complex to be included with a LINE INPUT statement. Line 60 prints *three* separate strings, two of them in quotation marks. INPUT and LINE INPUT can use only *one* string as a prompt.

Mid-Term Exam—If you understand this program, you are doing fine. You may be thinking that you couldn't write it from scratch. That's OK. The important thing now is to understand the structure and flow of programs and be able to make small changes in them. If you can write similar programs, that's even better, but it's not essential right now.

Later, when you want to write a real-world program to do something that interests you, you'll know how to start. Once you have started, programming teaches programming.

As a self-check, improve this program by using a subroutine to clear the screen after each question and its response. Print a period after line 50. You'll use several techniques that were demonstrated earlier. You may need TRON to find out where the program went.

Don't skip doing this. It may take several attempts to get it right. That's normal. If you can't do it, go back and review the preceding chapters. Don't move ahead until you can write that subroutine and solve the related problems. My version is at the end of the chapter, page 110.

LEFT$( )

On magazine address labels, you may have noticed a line printed by a computer that seems to have parts of your name and parts of your address. This is to produce a unique code that nobody else has, probably.

If your name were Joe Smith and the magazine used that name as a way of filing subscription information, all of the Joe Smiths in this great land would rise up in confusion.

The LEFT$( ) instruction makes a new string using characters from the left side of an original string. The original string is not altered. The statement has this form:

```
S1$ = LEFT$(N1$,2)
```

S1$, or any string variable name, is the name of the new string. LEFT$( ) says *take characters from the left side of the original string.* N1$ in this example is the name of the original string. The number 2 says how many characters to take.

You should still have three strings in memory, N1$, N2$ and N3$, holding your first, middle and last names. If not, enter them again with trailing spaces attached. Then try this from the command mode:

```
S1$ = LEFT$(N1$,2)
PRINT S1$
```

The first statement takes the first two letters of your first name and assigns them to S1$. Now, take LEFT$( ) pieces of your other two names:

```
S2$ = LEFT$(N2$,2)
S3$ = LEFT$(N3$,2)
```

Concatenate them and print your own personal Secret Code:

```
SC$ = S1$ + S2$ + S3$
PRINT SC$
PRINT LEN(SC$)
```

Obviously, you could also add on a piece of your address, the color of your eyes and your political persuasion, if you wish.

RIGHT$( )

This is similar to LEFT$( ), except that it takes characters from the other end. Try this:

```
PRINT RIGHT$(N3$,2)
```

The right two characters of N3$ should be displayed. The last character of N3$ doesn't show up as anything because you put a space there. Try printing the last three characters.

MID$( )

You guessed it. MID$( ) takes a chunk out of the middle. The form is M$ = MID$(X$,Y,Z). M$ is the name given to the chunk. X$ is the name of the string. Y is the number of the first character that is included in the chunk, counting from the left. Z is how many characters are removed. X$ is not changed by this. Try it:

```
PRINT N3$
Z$ = MID$(N3$,2,2)
PRINT Z$
```

If your last name has three letters or more, two letters are displayed.

REMOVING AN UNWANTED CHARACTER

Sometimes a string has one or more unwanted characters. Suppose you have another use for

N1$ that doesn't require a built-in space at the end. This trick will remove it. Enter the following statements from the command mode.

```
PRINT N1$
PRINT LEN(N1$)
X = LEN(N1$)
PRINT X
N1$ = LEFT$(N1$,X-1)
PRINT N1$
PRINT LEN(N1$)
PRINT N1$ N2$
```

The fifth statement in the series says that *the new N1$ is the old N1$ without the last character on the right.* X is the length of the old N1$. The new N1$ is X−1 characters taken from the left side. That omits the last character.

The series of statements you just entered does everything slowly, one step at a time. Look at the series again and review what each statement accomplishes. Big-time programmers do the same with one elegant line. Enter

```
N1$ = LEFT$(N1$,LEN(N1$)-1)
```

The statement uses LEN(N1$) directly instead of setting X equal to LEN(N1$) and then using X. Now enter

```
PRINT N1$
```

What happened? The *series* of statements removed the space at the end of N1$. Then the *all-in-one* statement lopped off one more character, which was the last letter of your name. In case that's too painful, let's use another name. Enter these statements:

```
T$ = "NAPOLEON"
PRINT LEFT$(T$,3)
PRINT RIGHT$(T$,4)
PRINT MID$(T$,5,3)
PRINT LEFT$(T$,1) MID$(T$,4,1) RIGHT$(T$,2)
```

Continue entering strings and doing surgery on them with these statements until there are no surprises left.

VAL( )

As you know, the VAL( ) statement tells you the numerical value of a string. LINE INPUT allows you to type commas. Try this:

```
NEW
10 LINE INPUT "Enter a number: ";X$
20 PRINT VAL(X$)
```

Run it and enter 12,345.67 for X$. The comma acts as a delimiter. What we need is a comma eater.

HOW TO BUILD A COMMA EATER

Before you take the VALue of a number that was entered as a string, you should remove any commas. This can be done with a routine using MID$( ). The idea is to look through the entire string, starting with the first character. If any character is a comma, remove it. To see how it works, enter this program:

```
NEW
10 CLS
20 LINE INPUT "Enter a number with commas: "; T$
30 FG = 0: REM initialize flag
40 PRINT "OLD T$: " T$
50 X = LEN(T$): REM number of characters to check
60 FOR I = 1 TO X
70 IF MID$(T$,I,1) = "," THEN FG = I: REM FG locates comma
80 NEXT I
90 IF FG = 0 THEN GOTO 140
100 T$ = LEFT$(T$,FG-1) + RIGHT$(T$,X-FG): REM remove it
110 PRINT "NEW T$: " T$
120 PRINT "TO CONTINUE, PRESS F5";: PRINT: PRINT: STOP
130 GOTO 30
140 CLS: PRINT "FINAL T$ IS: " T$: PRINT
```

List it and check your typing. Leave it listed on the screen so you can look at the program while reading the following discussion.

Lines 10 to 50 should be self-explanatory. Line 60 sets up a loop that will operate as many times as there are characters in T$. The loop will examine each character in sequence to see if it is a comma.

On the first pass, when I is 1, line 70 looks at MID$(T$,I,1). That means it starts at position 1 in T$ and looks at one character—in other words, the first character in T$.

On the second pass, it looks at MID$(T$,2,1), which is one character starting at position 2. It continues moving along in T$, checking each character in sequence.

If it finds a comma, flag FG is set to equal I. The value of the flag is then the location of the comma, counting from the left. Then, line 80 loops back and line 70 examines the next character in T$.

When the loop operation is complete, line 90 tests the flag. If it is still zero, meaning no commas were found, it jumps to line 140 and ends the program. If FG is not zero, line 90 does not execute.

Line 100 is the tricky part. The number held by FG is used to separate T$ into two parts. The LEFT$( ) is FG−1 characters long. That includes characters up to the comma but does not include the comma. The RIGHT$( ) is all of T$ to the right of the comma, not including the comma. The comma is not included in either part, but everything else is. The two parts are concatenated to form a new value of T$.

Line 100 says: *The new value of T$ is equal to the left portion of the old T$, without the comma, plus the right portion, without the comma.* If you don't see that immediately, use pencil and paper. Write down a number with a comma in it and then do exactly what the program says.

Line 110 displays the result. The last comma, if there is more than one, will be missing because the comma eater got it. Line 120 merely slows down the program so you can watch it. Line 130 jumps back to line 30, where the flag is reset to zero, and the operation repeats.

This routine is fun to watch. Run it. Enter a number with two or three commas. Notice that the avid comma eater gets them in reverse order. It may seem that it should gobble up the first comma it finds. If so, list the program and think about it. I'll discuss it in the next paragraph.

The I loop runs to a normal termination each time it operates. The flag is set each time a comma is found, but nothing happens to a comma until the program leaves the loop and gets down to line 90. When the program leaves the loop, the flag has the last value received during the loop operation, so the comma eater snacks on the last comma in T$.

Eating Nearly Everything—To provide more protection against keyboard errors when entering numbers, the comma eater should eat everything that isn't a number or a decimal point.

Line 100 will actually remove *any character* that is designated by the flag. It doesn't ask if the character is a comma. Instead it simply says *tell me where it is and I'll nibble it into history.* If the routine comes out of the loop with the flag set to any number, such as 14, line 100 will remove the character at that location in the string, no matter what it is.

Let's change the routine to set the flag for any character that is not a number or a decimal point. This can be done by checking ASCII code numbers.

Look in the Table of ASCII Code Numbers in Appendix G of the IBM *BASIC* book. Numbers 0 to 9 have codes 48 to 57. Any character with a code number in this range is OK. A period or decimal point has code 46, so that is a good number, too. All codes from 46 to 57 are OK, *except code 47.*

Remember that the expression MID$(T$,I,1) represents one character in T$. When I is 1, it is the first character, and so forth. Suppose the *character* is the number 8. The statement ASC("8") will produce the ASCII code for the number 8, which is 56.

If the character is the number 8, then the expression ASC(MID$(T$,I,1)) is the same as ASC("8"). It will produce the code number 56.

Though the idea is simple, it's the notation that strains the brain. When you see MID$(T$,I,1) think of it as a single character selected from T$.

Please change line 70 as shown. Use Ctrl-ENTER to break the program line into three physical lines. Then enter a new line 75.

```
70 IF ASC(MID$(T$,I,1)) < 46
   OR ASC(MID$(T$,I,1)) > 57
   THEN FG = I
75 IF ASC(MID$(T$,I,1)) = 47 THEN FG = I
```

List it, check it, and leave it on the screen. Line 70 says, *if the ASCII code of the character being examined is less than 46 or more than 57, IT IS NOT OK.*

Line 70 has three parts, on three screen lines. The first part says *IF the code number is less than 46.* The second part says *OR the code number is greater than 57.* The third part says *THEN set the flag equal to I.*

The problem with line 70 is that it will identify code 47 as a good guy, which it is not. Line 75 fixes that by setting the flag to I if the code is 47—which makes 47 a bad guy. Line 80 loops back to examine the next character in T$.

If *any* character other than a number or a decimal point is entered, it will be removed. Check this by running the program. Enter anything on the keyboard.

MANAGING PARENTHESES

Every statement must have the same number of left parentheses as it has right parentheses. Sometimes, to get them even, you must stick a few someplace in the statement. In the preceding program you used this expression:

```
75 IF ASC(MID$(T$,I,1)) = 47 THEN FG = I
```

The MID$( ) instruction operates on an expression in parentheses. The ASC( ) instruction also requires its operand in parentheses. The result is nested parentheses with two together at the end.

When you write a statement with nested parentheses, it's a good idea to count all of the left ones and then all of the right ones. If the number is not the same, the program won't run and you'll get an error message. If you ever learned algebra, you will probably handle parentheses correctly because the rules are the same. If not, you may have to struggle with them occasionally.

SEARCHING FOR A KEYWORD

Programs that store data items on disk and then help you find them are called *database* programs. Word-processor programs store words and allow you to change or edit them. These and similar programs can search through a file looking for a keyword. You can do this with a MID$( ) technique.

Groups of characters in a target string are examined in sequence and compared to the keyword. The groups are the same length as the keyword. The following program will show you the general idea. Enter

```
NEW
10 CLS:FG=0:' finds keyword JKL
20 TS$ = "ABCDEFGHIJKLMNOPQRSTUVWXYZ": REM target string
30 PRINT TS$
40 KW$ = "JKL": REM keyword
50 FOR I = 1 TO 24
60 IF MID$(TS$,I,3) = KW$, THEN FG = I: BEEP
70 NEXT I
80 PRINT: PRINT "Keyword "KW$" found at " FG: PRINT
```

List it, check it and run it. It tells you that the keyword matched three characters in the target string beginning at location 10. To see the program work, enter

```
65 PRINT I "  Is  "MID$(TS$,I,3)"  same as  "KW$ "?"
```

Of course it scrolls, but you can see the pattern. Notice that the counter in line 50 goes only to 24. When you are comparing three characters as a group, in a target string of 26 characters, you can stop with the group beginning at 24. The last three are 24, 25 and 26.

Some Practice Variations—Try these to check your understanding:

1) Slow down the scroll at line 65, so you can see each operation of the loop, or else break it up into screen loads. Put column heads on the display produced by line 65.

2) Change line 40 so you can enter a three-character keyword from the keyboard. Try different keywords, including some that can't be found in the existing target string.

3) Change the program so you can enter both the target string and a keyword. If the keyword is not three characters, change the MID$( ) statement in line 60 so it selects groups of the correct length. Do this automatically, using a LEN( ) statement, if you wish. The form is MID$(TS$,I,LEN(KW$)).

4) If the keyword is to be found only once, all loop operations after that are wasted time. How would you jump out of the loop as soon as the keyword is found?

5) Word-processing programs let you search and find a keyword repeatedly until you arrive at the desired place in the text. How would you do that in this program?

A program that does all of these things is at the end of this chapter, page 111.

USING A MENU

Many programs offer the user a choice of activities through a screen display called a *menu*. Such programs are said to be *menu-driven*.

If the items on the menu are numbered, the user makes a selection by typing the appropriate number. The user can also type a letter corresponding to the initial letter of his choice: Q for Quit, C for Change, or whatever the program requires.

ON N GOTO

From a programming standpoint, menus using numbers are simplest because of the ON N GOTO statement. In this statement, N can be any numeric variable name.

If the menu offers fewer than 10 choices, an INKEY$ routine is a good way to input numbers of one digit. The digit must then be converted to a number using VAL( ). If the menu has choices with numbers greater than 9, get the input using an INPUT statement. The number is assigned to a numeric variable name, such as N.

Here is a routine that will branch according to numbers selected at the keyboard. Please enter

```
NEW
10 CLS: PRINT: PRINT
20 PRINT "PLEASE CHOOSE BY PRESSING NUMBER:": PRINT
30 PRINT "1 - INVENTORY": PRINT "2 - SALES":
   PRINT "3 - BUDGET": PRINT "4 - EXPENSE"
40 N$ = INKEY$: IF N$ = "" THEN GOTO 40
50 N = VAL(N$)
60 ON N GOTO 100, 200, 300, 400
100 CLS: PRINT"INVENTORY": STOP
200 CLS: PRINT"SALES": STOP
300 CLS: PRINT"BUDGET": STOP
400 CLS: PRINT"EXPENSE": STOP
```

List and check the program. Line 40 waits for the user to press a key from 1 to 4. Line 50 converts N$ to the numeric value N.

At line 60, the statement ON N GOTO prepares the computer to act on the selection of a number. The variable name doesn't have to be N. But it must agree with the name of the number selected by the user If the number is X, the statement will be ON X GOTO. In this example, the number is N.

In this routine, if N is 1, the program branches to the first line number on the list. This can be any line number. It is 100 in this example. If N is 2, the program branches to the second number, and so forth. Line 60 can act on values of N from 1 to 4 because four line numbers are listed.

When a number has been selected, line 60 branches to the designated line. At lines 100, 200, 300 and 400, the title of a routine is printed and the program stops. These lines are sometimes called program *stubs*. They are written in this form to allow the programmer to test the program and see that it branches properly. Later, the programmer writes the complete routines beginning at those lines.

Please run the program several times. Input the numbers 1 to 5. It works as advertised until you input the number 5. List it again to see why.

If a number or character outside the expected range of 1 to 4 is not delivered to line 60, it does not execute. The program moves past line 60 and executes line 100, no matter what is typed. To protect against user error, enter

```
55 IF N < 1 OR N > 4 THEN GOTO 40
```

This is an unsophisticated *error trap*. It merely ignores invalid entries. You may prefer to tell the user that the entry was invalid and ask for another selection.

ON N GOSUB

This works the same way as ON N GOTO except that the program branches to a subroutine.

USING LETTERS TO MAKE A CHOICE

A menu routine is a little more complicated if the choices are made by letter, but I prefer letters anyway. Use the initial letter of the function being selected—for example, B for Budget.

Suppose the choices are A through C. The choice is made by an INKEY$ routine, assigning the name V$ to the chosen letter. A branching routine can look like this:

```
80 V$ = INKEY$: IF V$ = "" THEN GOTO 80
90 IF V$ = "A" THEN GOTO 500
100 IF V$ = "B" THEN GOTO 1000
110 IF V$ = "C" THEN GOTO 2000
120 GOTO 80
```

Line 120 protects against keyboard error. If the keystroke is not A, B or C, the program jumps back to 80. This line can display a message to the user, inviting him to try again.

Lines 90—110 compare the letter typed at the keyboard, held in V$, to the upper-case letters A, B and C. If the user intends to select the letter *A,* but types lower-case *a* instead, this routine will not work properly.

The result may be that the user presses a valid key, but the computer fails to recognize it and keeps asking for a repeat input. A practical solution is to use lines like this:

```
100 IF V$ = "B" OR V$ = "b" THEN GOTO 1000
```

Then, no matter which way the letter is typed, the computer will recognize that a valid choice has been made.

KEY

Several statements in BASIC begin with the word KEY. They relate to the 10 function keys and to the display on the bottom line of the screen. Pressing one of these keys will automatically type characters on the screen, and in some cases automatically enter those characters. To display what each of these keys prints, enter

```
KEY LIST
```

The small arrow symbol, such as after RUN, represents ENTER. It means that RUN is both typed and entered when you press F2. Now, clear the screen and press F9 followed by F1. Then press ENTER.

These are called *soft keys* because what they do can be changed. When you turn the computer on, they are automatically set to print standard strings. You can set any key to print any string of up to 15 characters by entering the key number, followed by the desired string. Enter

```
KEY 6, "GOSUB 1000"
```

Now press F6. Notice that the number 6 display at the bottom of the screen has changed. This display does not show the complete string. List the soft-key strings again to see all of it.

Using Function Keys for Menu Selection—You can use program lines to set the function keys to print whatever you wish, up to 15 keystrokes. You can use function keys in a menu, as a way for the user to make selections. If you do, pay careful attention to error trapping. Pressing some of the keys, when they're set to print the standard characters, can cause an error message and a return to command level.

Setting a function key to print a null disables it, which may be the best thing to do with keys that aren't used for the menu.

Fun with F2—Look at the bottom of the screen to verify that F2 types and enters the word RUN. Then disable F2 by entering

```
KEY 2, ""
```

Notice that the display at the bottom of the screen changes to show that pressing F2 types nothing. List the key strings to verify that. Press F2 and you'll see that it is disabled.

Now, restore its previous function. Set it to type RUN followed by ENTER. If you did what I did the first time, it didn't work. Look at the display for key 2. Do you see the little arrow? List the key strings again. Is the arrow there? You should have a program in memory. Does pressing F2 run it as it should? Try pressing F2 followed by ENTER.

When I intended to restore the function of F2, I typed RUN and then pressed ENTER, hopefully. The computer understood the ENTER keystroke to mean enter the expression, which it did. What it entered was just RUN, not RUN followed by the keystroke ENTER.

Then I remembered that if you package a keystroke as a CHR$( ), the computer will treat it as a string. To get the little arrow and the ENTER function back again, we must do some concatenating. Enter

```
KEY 2, "RUN" + CHR$(13)
```

As you know, CHR$(13) represents the keystroke called ENTER.

INKEY$

You have used the INKEY$ method of inputting data from the keyboard. It's often used in menus and to get quick replies to questions that can be answered by a single keystroke. For example, *Do you want to print this report? Y/N.*

The user types *Y* or *N,* which is used to control a branch point in the program. The user does not have to press the ENTER key after typing the response. The keystroke must correspond to a string variable name in your program. Therefore, everything input by an INKEY$ routine is a string.

When using this method to input data, you can combine single keystrokes to make a word or sentence. Here is a routine to do that. Enter

```
NEW
10 CLS
20 LETTER$ = "": REM null
30 SENTENCE$ = ""
40 PRINT "Please type a sentence:": PRINT
50 LETTER$ = INKEY$: IF LETTER$ = "" THEN GOTO 50
60 PRINT "LETTER$ IS: " LETTER$
70 SENTENCE$ = SENTENCE$ + LETTER$
```

(Program continued on next page.)

```
80 PRINT "SENTENCE$ IS: " SENTENCE$
90 PRINT
100 IF LETTER$ = CHR$(13) THEN GOTO 120
110 GOTO 50
120 PRINT: PRINT
```

List it and check your typing. Lines 20 and 30 initialize the two string variables to nulls. Line 40 is an instruction to the user. Line 50 accepts one character at a time from the keyboard and names it LETTER$. Line 60 announces that it is going to display LETTER$ and then does it, so you can see what you typed.

Line 70 builds SENTENCE$, one character at a time. It concatenates the LETTER$ characters, one at a time, calling the result SENTENCE$. The string variable, SENTENCE$, starts with nothing in it because of line 30. On each pass through the loop, a new character is typed and added to the end of SENTENCE$. Line 80 displays the sentence string, so you can see it grow one character at a time.

In line 100, if the LETTER$ that was most recently typed is ENTER, the program leaves the loop and goes to line 120. If the user does not press ENTER, line 100 does not execute. Line 110 loops back to line 50, and the INKEY$ routine accepts another character from the keyboard. This adds another character to the end of SENTENCE$.

Now, run the program and type a short sentence. If you make a typing error, don't try to fix it. Keep typing. At the end of the sentence, press ENTER.

Fixing Typos—This routine isn't practical because it fails when the user makes a typo and wants to fix it. There are ways to solve that problem. Here's the general idea:

Put in a line that recognizes BACKSPACE, which is CHR$(8), when that key is pressed. Lop off the last character of SENTENCE$, using a LEFT$ statement. Display the result. Get the next keystroke. If it is another backspace, do it again. You must clear the location on the screen where SENTENCE$ prints. Each new SENTENCE$ is shorter, but the display won't show that unless you clear the previous SENTENCE$ first. This is an oversimplified demonstration:

```
5 'Improved INKEY$ routine inputs sentence, allows backspace
10 CLS
20 SENTENCE$ = ""
30 PRINT "Please type a sentence:": PRINT
40 PRINT SENTENCE$: PRINT
50 PRINT "TO CORRECT, USE BACKSPACE KEY."
60 LETTER$ = INKEY$: IF LETTER$ = "" THEN GOTO 60
70 IF LETTER$ = CHR$(8) THEN
    SENTENCE$ = LEFT$(SENTENCE$,LEN(SENTENCE$)-1): GOTO 100
80 SENTENCE$ = SENTENCE$ + LETTER$
90 IF LETTER$ = CHR$(13) THEN GOTO 110
100 CLS: GOTO 30
110 PRINT: PRINT
```

This is only a partial fix because the user may want to use the cursor-control keys instead of BACKSPACE. You can do that also, if you wish. It's fun and keeps you occupied until about 2:00 AM.

REVIEW

It's probably a good idea to look over the programs in this chapter again. When you understand them, congratulate yourself because you probably won't have any difficulty with the rest of this book.

Following is a list of BASIC words used in this chapter. Please look them up in the IBM book *BASIC*.

BASIC WORDS USED IN THIS CHAPTER

ASC( )	LINE INPUT
CHR$ ( )	MID$( )
CLS	ON N GOTO
INKEY$	ON N GOSUB
KEY	RIGHT$( )
LEFT$( )	VAL( )
LEN( )	

This is the answer to the programming exercise from page 99:

```
5 ' improved "NAMES" program uses subroutine
    to clear screen after each response
10 CLS: PRINT: PRINT
20 LINE INPUT "Enter your first name: "; N1$
25 GOSUB 500
30 LINE INPUT "Enter your middle initial: "; N2$
35 GOSUB 500
40 LINE INPUT "Enter your last name: "; N3$
42 GOSUB 500
45 N1$ = N1$ + " "
50 PRINT: PRINT "Hello, " N1$ N3$"."
55 N3$ = N3$ + " "
60 PRINT "What does the "N2$" stand for? ";
70 LINE INPUT N2$: PRINT
72 GOSUB 500
75 N2$ = N2$ + CHR$(32)
80 PRINT N1$ N2$ N3$ "SOUNDS DISTINGUISHED!"
90 PRINT: PRINT
100 END
500 CLS: PRINT: PRINT: RETURN
```

Here's the answer program for the exercise on page 105:

```
10 'improved KEYWORD program. Input target$, KW$, find KW$
20 CLS:FG=O:REM FG is flag for found keyword
30 INPUT "ENTER TARGET STRING: "; TS$
40 INPUT "ENTER KEYWORD: "; KW$
50 FOR I = 1 TO LEN(TS$) - LEN(KW$) + 1
60 IF MID$(TS$,I,LEN(KW$)) = KW$, THEN FG = I
70 CLS: PRINT: PRINT: PRINT: PRINT
80 PRINT " I", "MID$(TS$,I,LEN(KW$))", "KW$": PRINT
90 PRINT I, MID$(TS$,I,LEN(KW$)),, KW$: PRINT
100 FOR DL = 1 TO 800: NEXT:' delay loop
110 IF FG < I THEN GOTO 160
120 PRINT "FIND IT AGAIN? Y/N?": BEEP
130 AGAIN$=INKEY$: IF AGAIN$ = "" THEN GOTO 130
140 IF AGAIN$ = "N" THEN I = LEN(TS$) - LEN(KW$) + 1:' stop
150 IF AGAIN$ = "n" THEN I = LEN(TS$) - LEN(KW$) + 1
160 NEXT I
170 PRINT
180 IF FG <> O THEN PRINT "KEYWORD "KW$" FOUND AT " FG
190 IF FG = O THEN PRINT "KEYWORD NOT FOUND"
200 PRINT: PRINT: PRINT
```

8 Mathematical Operations

Your computer can do as much math as you can tell it to. It has symbols for everything we do in arithmetic—multiply, divide and so forth. It also has the symbols and the capability needed for virtually everything we do in algebra, including nested parentheses.

It understands logarithms and trigonometry. In higher fields of mathematics, such as calculus, it can provide answers by *number crunching*—repeated operations with numbers.

The difficulty in discussing these operations is that some will be appreciated only by people who understand the relevant math. If I say that the computer can take the natural logarithm of a number, that's good news to log fans but no news at all to people who think that logs grow on trees.

The easy way out is merely to describe and demonstrate some of the more common mathematical operations. Without hesitation, I will take the easy way.

ARITHMETIC OPERATORS

The first thing is to learn the symbols and the keystrokes used to produce them. You know most of them already:

```
=     Equals
+     Add
-     Subtract
*     Multiply
/     Divide
\     Divide with an integer result
^     Exponentiation (Raising a number to a power.)
MOD   Divide until the remainder is smaller than the
         divisor. Keep remainder. Discard everything else.
()    Evaluate the expression inside the parentheses.
         Brackets and braces are not used.
```

Examples—Here are some examples showing various uses of mathematical operators. Please enter them individually and observe the results.

```
X = 2: PRINT X
X = 2 + 3: PRINT X
X = 5 - 3: PRINT X
X = 5*3: PRINT X
X = 15/4: PRINT X          (Ordinary division)
X = 15\4: PRINT X          (Integer division)
X = 5^2: PRINT X           (This means five squared.)
```

(Program continued on next page.)

```
X = 12 MOD 10: PRINT X      (Divide until remainder is
                             smaller than divisor.
                             Keep remainder.)
X = 2*(2+2): PRINT X        (Answer is 8, not 6.)
```

With a minus sign you can do *negation,* which means to change the sign of a number. In the expression $Y = 2 * (-X)$, negation is performed inside the parentheses.

There's an order of precedence for mathematical operations. For example, if you tell the computer to add and multiply, it will multiply and then add unless you bend it to your will by using parentheses.

ORDER OF PRECEDENCE

```
()          Evaluation of parenthetical expressions
^           Exponentiation
-           Negation
* or /      Multiplication or Division
\           Integer division
MOD         Modulo division
+ or -      Addition or Subtraction
```

I don't think anybody actually memorizes this order. If you remember a little algebra, you will probably write equations correctly.

When you write a mathematical routine, always test it in several ways. Test within the normal range of numbers you expect it to handle. Test very carefully at the limits of that range. Then test exceptions. What if a number is negative when you expect it to be positive? What if it is zero? Sometimes an apparently rock-solid math routine fails when there is a special case or an unfortunate combination of events.

The computer will divide by zero. The result is a very large number. This is discussed in Chapter 11.

Suppose a mathematical routine doesn't give the correct answer, and you can't see any reason why: Carefully check your typing and what is input to the routine. Then check the mathematical logic itself and the order of operations.

ARITHMETIC FUNCTIONS

These are BASIC words followed by an expression in parentheses, which is shown as *(exp).* The result is that the expression is altered in a specific way, or converted from one form to another.

To explain, I will show a function, describe it briefly and then show simple examples that you can run.

ABS(exp)

This takes the ABSolute value of the expression in parentheses. The idea is to make the number positive even if it is negative. Try these:

```
PRINT ABS(8)
PRINT ABS(-8)
X = 2*(-4)
PRINT X, ABS(X)
```

INT(exp)

This produces the INTeger value of the expression in parentheses. If Y is the integer of X, then Y is the largest whole number that is *not larger* than X. Enter

```
PRINT INT(8.1)
PRINT INT(8.999)
PRINT INT(7.999)
PRINT INT(0)
PRINT INT(-4.1)
PRINT INT(-3.9)
```

The last two examples are significant. Observe that -4 is the largest whole number that is not larger than -3.9. In other words, -4 is the integer value of -3.9.

AN ALGORITHM TO CONVERT UNITS OF MEASURE

The word *algorithm* means a *method* or *formula*. If you are writing a program that deals with ounces and pounds, you will probably do all of the arithmetic in ounces. At the end, convert to pounds and ounces because that's what people expect. Enter

```
NEW
10 CLS: REM converts ounces to pounds and ounces
20 INPUT "Please enter the number of ounces. "; OZ
30 LB = INT(OZ/16): REM get number of full pounds
40 OZ = OZ MOD 16: REM get remaining ounces
50 PRINT: PRINT "That is "LB" pounds and "OZ" ounces."
60 PRINT: PRINT: PRINT: GOTO 20
```

Here's how the program works. Suppose you input 35 ounces at line 20. Line 30 divides 35 by 16, which is 2.1875. Then it takes the integer value, which is 2. There are two full pounds in 35 ounces, plus some ounces left over.

Line 40 divides the total number of ounces by 16 until the remainder is smaller than 16: $35/16 = 2$ with a remainder of 3. It keeps the 3 and discards the rest. The remaining number of ounces not used to make full pounds is 3.

Test this algorithm by inputting several values of ounces, including 0. To save time and typing in these demonstration routines, I am not putting in a way to get out of the loop. Do it by pressing Ctrl-Break until the computer notices it.

FIX(exp)

FIX chops off the decimal part of any number and discards it. It truncates the number at the decimal point, yielding an integer. Enter

```
A = 12.5
PRINT FIX(A)
Y = A - FIX(A)
PRINT Y
A = -12.5
PRINT FIX(A)
```

```
Y = A - FIX(A)
PRINT Y
```

The difference between FIX and INT is in the treatment of negative numbers.

```
A = -12.5
PRINT FIX(A)
PRINT INT(A)
```

SQR(exp)

This takes the square root of the expression. It does not work for negative values of (exp).

```
PRINT SQR(16)
```

EXPONENTIATION

This is raising a number to a power. The power is called an *exponent*. The symbol is ^.

```
PRINT 4^2
```

means to print the value of 4 raised to the second power, which is 4 squared. The exponent does not have to be a positive integer. It can be a fraction or a negative number.

LOG(exp)

This takes the *natural* logarithm of the expression.

```
PRINT LOG(25)
```

EXP(exp)

The base number used in natural logarithms has the symbol e. Its value is approximately 2.71828. Using e as the base, this function raises e to the number in parentheses. EXP(3) means e to the 3rd power.

```
PRINT EXP(3)
PRINT EXP(1)
```

SGN(exp)

This gives an indication of the sign of (exp). Sometimes you will want a program branch to be decided by the sign of a number—whether it is positive, zero or negative—without regard to the actual value of the number. Balancing your checkbook is an example.

```
A = 4: B = 0: C = -27
PRINT SGN(A), SGN(B), SGN(C)
```

If (exp) is positive, SGN(exp) is 1. If (exp) is 0, SGN(exp) is 0. If (exp) is negative, SGN(exp) is −1. To branch based on the value of SGN(exp), you can use the ON N GOTO statement. However, that statement cannot accept values of N that are zero or negative. This form will work:

```
ON SGN(exp) + 2 GOTO 1000, 3000, 5000
```

Adding the number 2 to SGN(exp) changes the range of numbers it can produce. Insead of −1 to +1, the range becomes 1 to 3.

RND(x)

This produces random numbers between 0 and 1. You can use RND(x) to simulate a roll of dice, the luck of the draw, or events in nature.

Your computer has a built-in random-number generator. It generates a long list of random numbers that you can use. RND is the name of the *next random number* on the list. Enter

```
PRINT RND
PRINT RND
```

If you see strange-looking numbers such as 2.54690E-02, accept them as numbers between 0 and 1. I'll explain them later in this chapter.

To use a random number in a program, you may wish to assign it to a variable name, such as Y:

```
Y = RND
PRINT Y
```

Do that several times and notice that you get a different value of Y each time.

If you add parentheses with a number in them, represented by the form RND(x), the number affects operation of the random-number generator. If the x in RND(x) is any positive number except zero, operation is the same as you have already seen—it produces the next number on the list. In the command mode, enter

```
FOR I = 1 TO 5: PRINT RND(I): NEXT I
```

and you get the next five random numbers. Try this:

```
FOR I = 1 TO 5: Z(I) = RND: PRINT Z(I): NEXT I
```

That calls up the next five random numbers, assigns them to five array names and prints them. The numbers went into an array in memory as you can see by entering

```
PRINT Z(1)
```

Are They Really Random?—Electronic random-number generators begin operation with a quantity called a *seed*. They derive the series of random numbers from that seed. Every time you turn on your computer, clear memory, or enter RUN, the random-number generator starts with the same seed and produces the same series of numbers. Try this, noticing the number produced each time:

```
CLEAR: PRINT RND
CLEAR: PRINT RND
CLEAR: PRINT RND
```

Because the series repeats, some people will argue that the numbers are not really random because anything that repeats can be predicted. Anything predictable is not random. The numbers are *pseudo-random.* If you write a program that uses random numbers, you may not want to feed it the same series of numbers each time.

Reseeding the Generator—You can change the seed to produce a different series of random numbers. If you put a negative number in the parentheses, such as RND(−3), a different series of numbers is produced, but it will be the same each time you seed the generator with −3.

To use this method, you must reseed the generator only once for each series of numbers that you use. Try this:

```
PRINT RND(-3)
PRINT RND(-3)
```

You get the same number both times because each statement reseeds the generator—it starts over with the first number of that series. The trick is to reseed it once and then change to another method of calling for random numbers. Try this:

```
PRINT RND(-3)
PRINT RND
PRINT RND
```

You are seeing the series of numbers produced by the seed −3. Try other seeds, if you wish, or try −3 again.

If the value in parentheses is zero, the last random number is repeated. Enter

```
PRINT RND(0)
```

to see this work.

The form RND(x) looks like a subscripted variable because of the number in parentheses. It isn't. When a number is used to change the way a statement works, the number is sometimes referred to as a *switch*. This means that it switches from one type of operation to another. The x in RND(x) is a switch.

SHOOTING CRAPS

Here's a routine that uses random numbers to simulate throwing dice. It also demonstrates a very useful technique to put a pause in a program. Please enter

```
NEW
10 CLS: REM filename "CRAPS"
20 D1 = INT(RND*10)
30 IF D1 <1 OR D1 >6 THEN GOTO 20
40 D2 = INT(RND*10)
50 IF D2 <1 OR D2 >6 THEN GOTO 40
60 PRINT D1, D2, "=", D1 + D2, "PRESS SPACE BAR"
70 PAUSE$ = INKEY$: IF PAUSE$ = "" THEN GOTO 70
80 GOTO 20
```

List it and check your typing. The RND function generates decimal numbers between 0 and 1. Line 20 multiplies RND by 10 to make the numbers in the range of 0 to 10. Then it takes the integer value so D1 is a whole number. D1 represents the first die of the pair of dice.

Line 30 checks to see if the number is in the range of 1 to 6. If not, it jumps back to line 20 and gets another random number.

Lines 40 and 50 do the same thing to produce a value for D2, which represents the second die. Line 60 prints the number on each die and the total. It also displays an instruction that will roll the dice again.

Line 70 contains a very useful technique. It uses an INKEY$ routine to wait until a keystroke is made, which is received as PAUSE$. Nothing is done with PAUSE$. The purpose of line 70 is merely to stop the program until a key is pressed. Even though the instruction on the screen says to press the space bar, almost any key will do. I prefer to give specific instructions.

Line 80 loops back to do it all again. Run it, but don't gamble. I don't know if these results are statistically valid or not. If you think the screen display is horrifying, I agree. Chapter 10 shows how to do it better.

When you've lost interest, press Ctrl-Break. You may have to do it more than once to get the machine's attention. If you run the program again, it will repeat the sequence of numbers unless you reseed the generator.

RANDOMIZE

If you are running an honest crap game, you will reseed the random-number generator every time you run the program. The easiest way to do that is to put a RANDOMIZE statement on a line at the beginning of the program. When that line executes, it asks for a new seed number to be entered from the keyboard.

List the program in memory and add

```
15 RANDOMIZE
```

Run it. When the program asks, type and enter a seed number in the indicated range. If you repeat the seed number when running the program again, the series of numbers repeats. Save this program as CRAPS.

TRIGONOMETRIC FUNCTIONS

These operations include sine, cosine, tangent functions and combinations of them. They allow you to solve problems relating to angles and right triangles. In each case, the *(exp)* must be in radians. Change degrees into radians by multiplying degrees by $(2\pi/360)$.

SIN(exp)

Takes the sine of (exp).

```
X = SIN(1)
PRINT X
```

COS(exp)

Takes the cosine of (exp).

```
X = COS(1)
PRINT X
```

TAN(exp)

Takes the tangent of (exp).

```
X = TAN(1)
PRINT X
```

ATN(exp)

This is an inverse trig function that you may know as arctan(exp). It means *the angle in radians whose tangent is (exp)*.

```
X = ATN(1)
PRINT X
```

DERIVED FUNCTIONS

With SIN, COS and TAN, you can derive other trig functions. Formulas are in Appendix E of the IBM book *BASIC*.

FLOATING-POINT NOTATION

You may have learned this in school as *powers of ten*. It's also called *scientific notation*. Pocket calculators use this method to display large numbers. When floating-point notation is used to display a number, the display will have three parts and look like this:

```
1.234568E+09
```

The number to the left of the decimal is always in the range of 1 to 9. The numbers between the decimal point and the letter E are the decimal portion of the number being displayed.

The number following the letter *E* is called an *exponent*. It tells *how many places* to move the decimal point to show the number as you and I would write it in ordinary notation.

If the exponent is a positive number, move the decimal point to the right that number of places, filling in zeros where needed. If it is negative, move the decimal point to the left that number of places, filling in zeros where needed.

The number 1.234568E+09, in ordinary notation, is 1234560000. You get it by moving the decimal point nine places to the right and filling in zeros where necessary.

The computer will use floating-point notation only when it has to. Enter this program to demonstrate that:

```
NEW
10 INPUT X
20 PRINT X
30 GOTO 10
```

Run it and enter a series of numbers, each one digit longer. Enter 1, then 12, then 123, then 1234 and so forth until you force the computer to use floating-point notation.

It happens when you enter a number with eight digits. Notice that only seven digits are displayed, plus an exponent to tell you where the decimal point would be in ordinary notation.

Now enter 123456789. Again, seven digits are displayed, plus an exponent. In both of these examples, the numbers are rounded off to seven digits and displayed along with an exponent. Press Ctrl-Break to get out of the loop.

Degree of Precision—The number of digits used to display a number indicates the degree of precision. The numbers just printed have a precision of 7 digits.

Accuracy in Floating Point—Because of the automatic round-off to seven places, a number in floating-point notation may not be identical to the original number entered.

When you entered 12345678, the computer printed 1.234568E+07. Moving the decimal point seven places to the right yields 12345680, which is the number actually in memory.

In a bookkeeping program, that would produce an error of two dollars—not good enough. Bookkeepers expect accuracy to the nearest penny. You can ask the computer to use *more digits* of precision by using a type declaration.

OVERFLOW

If the computer is running a program and the result of a calculation is too large for the computer to store in memory, it will display an error message: *Overflow*.

What happens depends on what caused the overflow. I will discuss overflow at appropriate places in the remainder of this chapter.

TYPE DECLARATIONS

Type declarations are symbols used as the last character of a variable name. They tell the computer how it should deal with that variable. You already know that $ identifies a literal string.

Numeric variables also have type declarations. They control the degree of precision and the amount of memory space needed to store a number. The important consideration here is degree of precision. There are three type declarations for numeric variables:

```
X% is an integer.
X! is a single-precision number.
X# is a double-precision number.
```

If you omit the type declaration with a numeric variable, the computer assumes that it is single precision. So far in this book, you have omitted the type declaration by using variables such as X and Y to represent numbers. You've been using single precision.

When you declare the type of a numeric variable, the computer will round off accordingly, when necessary. You will understand this easily if you watch it happen by entering the following examples.
Integers—Floating-point notation is never used for integers because integers are whole numbers. The limits for an integer are $+32767$ to -32768. Try this:

```
X% = 12345.6789
PRINT X%
```

The number is rounded off and then stored in memory as an integer. Now enter

```
X% = 55555.55
X% = -55555.55
```

The error message *Overflow* means that these numbers are outside the range of integers.

If an overflow occurs because an integer number is out of range, the program stops running and displays the overflow error message and the line number at which the overflow occurred.
Single Precision—When a single-precision number is stored in memory, it is limited to seven digits plus an exponent if needed. This doesn't mean that you can enter only seven-digit numbers. You can enter huge numbers, but there's a limit.

If necessary, the computer uses floating-point notation and rounds off to seven digits. The seventh digit may be different from the one you entered because of a round-off. The default declaration for numeric variables is single precision. X and X! are treated the same way. List the program in memory. The variables are single precision. Run it and enter

```
1234567
12345678
```

Floating-point notation was necessary. The number was rounded off. Press Ctrl-Break. Save this as PROGRAM.

If an overflow occurs because a single-precision number is out of range, the overflow message is displayed, but the program continues to run. To see this happen, enter

```
NEW
10 X = 1E+20
20 X = X*X
30 PRINT X
```

Enable TRON and run the program. The number printed by line 30 is the largest number that the computer can store in single precision.
Double Precision—This declaration stores 17 digits and displays 16 digits. The 17th digit is rounded off, but the 16th isn't—except in one special case, explained below. When necessary, double precision uses floating-point notation. If a double-precision number is displayed using floating-point notation, the exponent letter E is changed to D to indicate double precision.

Load the program saved as PROGRAM. Change X to X# wherever it is used. Now the program is set to use double-precision numbers. Run it and enter

```
1234567890123456
12345678901234567
```

The special case in both single and double precision is a number made of a bunch of nines. Try it. There isn't any place to stop rounding off. Run the program for a while and then press Ctrl-Break to get out of the loop.

If an overflow occurs because a double-precision number is out of range, the overflow message is displayed, but the program continues to run.

HOW DO YOU DECIDE WHICH TO USE?

Your choice of integer, single precision or double precision, depends on how large the numbers are going to be and what they mean.

A program that reports the population of East Bottlecap to be 123.7 people looks ridiculous. Things that occur naturally as integers should be reported as integers.

In many fields, large numbers are rounded off even when known to greater precision. For example, if the average weekly traffic on a toll road is 127,254 cars, most people will be happy to accept 127,000 as the number.

In most branches of engineering, rounding off and using floating-point notation are customary. Yet I want my bank statement accurate to the penny. There are no fixed rules, but you should use the degree of precision appropriate to the task. Usually, this is the *lowest* degree of the precision of the numbers involved. Remember this truism: A chain is only as strong as its weakest link.

WHAT TO DO ABOUT OVERFLOW ERRORS

When you write a program that uses mathematics, you should consider the possibility of an overflow condition. If a keyboard input or a calculation can produce an overflow error, you should probably write the program to prevent the error. You can do that by limiting the range of numeric variables, using relational operators. Then you should test the routine to be sure that an overflow can't happen.

ENTERING LARGE NUMBERS FROM THE KEYBOARD

If you enter large numbers from the keyboard, in response to an input statement from a program, the result will be the same as described earlier. If the number is an integer, the program will stop. If the number is single precision or double precision, the program will continue running. Either way, it displays the overflow message.

If you enter a single-precision or double-precision number from the keyboard in the command mode, and that number causes an overflow, the result is unpredictable. The computer may display an overflow message and continue to operate.

Or, it may lock up. If it locks up, the cursor will disappear and the computer will be unresponsive to all keyboard commands. To resume operation, you must turn the computer off and then turn it back on again. You will lose everything in memory. No harm is done to the computer.

THE RULE FOR ROUNDING OFF NUMBERS

Numbers are automatically rounded off for two reasons: to suit the type declaration and when displayed in floating-point notation.

The round-off rule is: If the digit being dropped is 5 or more, the digit to its left is increased by one. If the digit being dropped is 4 or less, the digit to its left is not changed. This is called the *5/4 round-off rule.*

A ROUND-OFF ALGORITHM

You may want to do a 5/4 round-off in a program. Do it by adding 0.5 to the number and taking its integer value.

Suppose the number is 8.5 or larger, but smaller than 9. By the 5/4 rule, that number should round off to 9. Adding 0.5 will make the number 9 or larger. Taking the integer will result in the number 9.

Suppose the number is 8 or larger, but smaller than 8.5. That should round off to 8. Adding 0.5 will make it 8.5 or larger, but smaller than 9. Taking the integer will result in the number 8. Try this by entering

```
NEW
10 CLS
20 INPUT "Please enter a number: "; X
30 X = INT(X + .5)
40 PRINT "Integer = "X
50 PRINT: PRINT: GOTO 20
```

Run it a few times and enter positive numbers. Notice that the algorithm makes the entered number larger, then uses INT( ) to round off to the first number to the left of the decimal place. In other words, it produces rounded-off whole numbers.

Now enter −2.4, −2.5 and −2.6. Notice that the round-off of negative numbers does not follow the 5/4 rule.

ROUNDING OFF TO TWO OR MORE DECIMAL PLACES

When dealing with money, it's customary to round off to the nearest penny, which is the second decimal place.

The same general method will work, but you must first multiply the number being rounded off by 100. Then you have a number of pennies with a decimal fraction, instead of a number of dollars with a decimal fraction.

The result of the round-off is still a whole number, but the last digit actually represents a penny. Divide the result by 100 to put the decimal place back where it belongs. Change line 30 to read

```
30 X = INT((X*100) + .5)/100
```

Notice that you multiply by 100 first, then add 0.5 to the result. Line 30 now rounds off to the second decimal place. Run it a few times with various numbers to round off. If you don't see how it works, do it with pencil and paper.

If you use 1000 as the factor instead of 100, it will round off to the third decimal place, and so forth.

TINY ERRORS

Computers make tiny errors for obscure technical reasons. I am reluctant to suggest that your computer makes errors similar to mine, but it may. For example, if I ask mine to

```
PRINT 12.3 - 12
```

it displays

```
.3000002
```

The answer should be .3 without that tiny error. The displayed number is too large by 0.0000002, which is insignificant but looks bad. It could erode public confidence in computing.

The error would be invisible if the computer were not using single precision. Using integers to display the number won't work because the entire number would disappear.

When your program is about to display a number, and there may be a tiny error in the far-out decimal places, clean it up by a round-off routine. Then show it to the world. You should still be running the round-off routine. Enter

```
.3000002
```

Run the routine as long as it interests you and then get out of it.

THE GOLDEN DREAM

Periodically, we read about some enterprising person who claims to own England or Mesopotamia because his ancestor deposited a pence in the bank there and never took it out. It earned compound interest for many years, and the sum is now a zillion dollars.

Computers are ideal for doing complicated financial calculations. This program can help you figure out which country you own. The formula for compound interest is

```
SUM = PRINCIPAL * (1+RATE)^N
```

SUM is the value of an interest-bearing account after N years or months, or whatever the accounting period is. If the bank says that your money is compounded daily or monthly, the accounting period is one day or one month.

PRINCIPAL is the original deposit or investment. RATE is the interest rate as a decimal number, not a percent. ^ means exponentiation, or raising to the power of N.

To solve an equation like that in a program, first write program lines to establish values for all of the necessary variables, such as PRINCIPAL, RATE and N. Then enter the equation on a program line and let the computer calculate SUM for you. Enter

```
NEW
10 CLS: PRINT: PRINT
20 INPUT "Enter original investment $",PRINCIPAL#
30 INPUT "Enter interest rate as percent %",RATE
40 RATE = RATE/100: REM convert to decimal
50 INPUT "Enter number of accounting periods: ",N%
60 SUM# = PRINCIPAL# * (1 + RATE)^N%
70 PRINT: PRINT "The sum is $"SUM#: PRINT
```

Notice that I used some type declarations. These declarations are tedious, but essential. This program uses commas instead of semicolons in the INPUT statements. A comma suppresses the question mark.

If you insist on entering commas at line 20, put in your comma-eater subroutine. Test the program by investing $100 for one accounting period at 10%. The sum should be $110.00.

My computer made a tiny error! Perhaps yours did also. It may do that when you force it to print a small number with single or double precision. The error will disappear if you round off to two decimal places. Enter

```
65 SUM# = INT((SUM#*100) + .5)/100
```

Now you have the advantage of double precision when you need it without the penalty of double precision when you don't need it. Run it again. Invest $100 for 1 year at 10%.

Example Problems—Try these for fun and maybe profit, too.

1) You may have wondered if daily compounded interest really gets you richer quicker. If the annual rate of interest is 10%, the daily rate is 10%/365, which is about 0.028%. Try investing $100 for 365 periods at an interest rate of 0.028%. Some banks use 360 days in these calculations.

2) Suppose your grandpappy invested a dollar at the Big Bank of the Kentuky in 1850 at 3% per year and forgot to take it out. Do you own the Kentuky?

3) What if he had invested $1000?

4) What if the interest rate had been 8% or 20%? Compound interest over a long period is powerful, but it is much more powerful at higher interest rates.

Financial wizards have equations to calculate the present value of future money, the future value of present money, mortgage payments, how much you should invest annually to have a big pile someday, and many other miracles.

To take charge of your financial destiny, get a book on personal finance. Program the equations and figure out how to provide for your retirement in luxury somewhere.

When you make it, there in golden sunshine, you will probably show your neighbor the actual computer program that made it all possible. Then he will show you his.

MIXING TYPES

As you know, you cannot mix numeric and string variables because it causes an error message saying *Type mismatch*. But you can mix numeric variables that have different type declarations. There are several rules that govern the result. The most important one is illustrated by this statement:

```
X! = 2 * Z#
```

This produces a result with single precision because X! is declared to be single precision. It doesn't matter that Z# is double precision. If the statement were

```
X# = 2 * Z#
```

then X# would be double precision. What do you think the following statement will do?

```
X# = 2 * Z!
```

It will display X# to double precision, but you can't believe all of the digits because it was derived from a single-precision number, Z!. The result can't be more precise than Z!.

CONVERTING TYPES

There are three commands to convert numeric types to other numeric types: CINT( ), CSNG( ) and CDBL( ).

CINT(exp)

Converts the expression in parentheses to an integer.

```
X = 12.34
PRINT CINT(X)
```

CSNG(exp)

Converts the expression to single precision.

```
PRINT CSNG(123456789012345.123)
```

CDBL(exp)

Converts the expression to double precision. This doesn't add any precision to a number that was an integer or single precision. It can force the result to more digits, so you can see what they are. The added digits in the result may not be valid.

```
PRINT 2/3
PRINT CDBL(2)/CDBL(3)
```

STR$( )

It's often necessary or convenient to convert a number to a string. You can do string operations on the number, such as RIGHT$( ). However, if the number of digits forces floating-point notation, that will greatly confuse string operations.

One form is X$ = STR$(number). The number must be in parentheses. Here are some examples:

```
X$ = STR$(1234567890)
PRINT X$
PRINT RIGHT$(X$,3)
X$ = STR$(12345678901234567890.123)
PRINT X$
PRINT RIGHT$(X$,3)
```

When you use STR$(number), the computer expects the number to be a valid expression with some value. Try this:

```
X$ = STR$(123.ABC)
```

The command STR$(number) is used only to convert valid numbers into a string. Using the following notation, you can declare almost anything to be a string.

```
X$ = "123.ABC"
PRINT X$
```

WATCH FOR SPACES

When a number is displayed, a space is provided at the front for a sign. If the number is negative, a minus sign will print. If the number is positive, the first space will be blank. This can confuse string operations if you don't know that the blank space is there. Try these:

```
X$ = STR$(-123.456)
PRINT X$
PRINT LEN(X$)
```

```
X$ = STR$(123.456)
PRINT X$
PRINT LEN(X$)
```

If you look at the screen carefully, you can see the leading blank space. If you attach X$ to the back of another string by concatenation, expect a blank in the middle if you didn't remove it first.

CONVERTING A STRING TO A NUMBER

The command VAL( ) produces the numerical value of a string that is placed inside the parentheses. If the string has no numerical value, the result is 0. Try these examples:

```
Y$ = "ABC"
PRINT Y$
PRINT VAL(Y$)


Y$ = "123ABC"
PRINT Y$
PRINT VAL(Y$)


Y$ = "ABC123"
PRINT Y$
PRINT VAL(Y$)


Y$ = STR$(123.456)
PRINT Y$
PRINT VAL(Y$)
```

Notice that VAL( ) will evaluate numbers at the beginning of a string, even if letters follow. It will not evaluate a string that begins with a letter.

DEFINING VARIABLE TYPES IN GROUPS

You can put a statement near the beginning of a program that defines a group of variable types. It may say that all variable names beginning with the letters A, B and C are integers. Then you can type names in this range without type-declaration characters at the end of each variable name.

This saves some space in memory, but I think it makes programs harder to read. I prefer to be reminded of variable types each time I use them. Notice that in the following examples, parentheses are not needed around the specified letter range.

DEFINT (letter range)

All variable names beginning with a letter in the specified range are integers.

DEFSNG (letter range)

All variable names beginning with a letter in the specified range are single precision.

DEFDBL (letter range)

All variable names beginning with a letter in the specified range are double precision.

DEFSTR (letter range)

All variable names beginning with a letter in the specified range are strings. Here are some examples:

```
DEFSTR A-D: DEFINT I-K
A = "HOWDY"
PRINT A
J = 123.456
PRINT J
```

You can make an exception to a DEF( ) statement, later in the program, by a type declaration for a specific variable name.

```
DEFSTR A-D
A! = 123.456
A = "HOWDY"
PRINT A!
PRINT A
```

USING INTEGERS AS LOOP COUNTERS

Integers are stored in a smaller amount of memory and can be handled faster by the computer than single- or double-precision numbers. Therefore, using integers as loop counters makes loops run faster. FOR I% = 1 to 1000 will run faster than FOR I = 1 to 1000. With nested loops and long complicated programs, this can make a noticeable difference.

It's good practice to use integers as loop counters. If you have some standard letters that you normally use, such as I, J and K, defining them as integers at the beginning of the program takes care of it. Then you can type I, rather than I%.

TIME$

Whether you entered the correct time or not when you turned on the computer, a clock is running in there. You can see what time it is by entering

```
PRINT TIME$
```

What you are seeing is hours: minutes: seconds. You can set the clock and display the time by entering

```
TIME$ = "12:12:12"
T$ = TIME$
PRINT T$
PRINT TIME$
```

Time marches on.

ARE INTEGER LOOP COUNTERS WORTH THE TROUBLE?

Probably. Please enter and run this demonstration:

```
NEW
10 CLS: PRINT: PRINT
20 PRINT "START AT 00:00:00"
30 TIME$ = "00:00:00": REM set clock
40 PRINT: PRINT "COMPUTER IS COUNTING TO 10,000"
50 FOR I = 1 TO 10000: NEXT I
60 PRINT: PRINT "STOP AT " TIME$: PRINT
```

Change I to I% in both places where it is used in line 50. Run it again. When you are ready, save this program as TIME.

DATE$

This statement works like TIME$. If you time execution of a really long program, you may also have to invoke DATE$.

CHAPTER MARCHES ON

As usual, I suggest that you review this chapter. Following is a list of BASIC words. Please look them up in the IBM book *BASIC*. You'll find some things I didn't tell you.

In the same book, read from the beginning of Chapter 3 to the section entitled *Input and Output*. In my copy of that book, this is the first 32 pages. Study Appendix E, if you're that sort of person. In Appendix I, read the section entitled *Tips and Techniques*.

BASIC WORDS USED IN THIS CHAPTER

ABS	DEFINT	RANDOMIZE
ATN	DEFSNG	RND
CDBL	DEFSTR	SIN
CINT	EXP	SGN
CLEAR	FIX	SQR
COS	INPUT	STR$
CSNG	INT	TAN
DATE$	LOG	TIME$
DEFDBL	MOD	VAL

9 Disk Operations

Essential disk operations include putting information on disk and getting it back off again. Information stored on disk is called a file and has a *filename*. Disk files include the operating system and BASIC, plus the following kinds of files.

Application programs do something useful, such as figure your income tax or calculate the dimensions of roof beams. These programs are often written in BASIC, but they can also be written in other programming languages.

Data files are created by an application program. If you have a program that keeps track of your income, it will create a file with a filename such as INCOME. This file will be kept on disk. When you run the program, it brings the file from disk into memory, helps you bring it up to date and then puts it back on disk.

Utility programs allow you to change the names of files, move files from one disk to another and perform similar operations.

FILENAMES
Filenames are labels used to identify files. They can use up to eight characters and can begin with a number or a letter. Spaces are allowed.

FILENAME EXTENSIONS
It is customary to add a file-type indicator, which is a period and three letters following the filename. This is sometimes called a filename *extension*. List the files on disk A by entering

FILES

and you will see filenames with several different extensions.
.BAS—The extension .BAS means that the file is a program written in BASIC. When you save programs written in BASIC, the computer automatically adds the extension .BAS to the filename, so you don't have to type it.

To load or run a program written in BASIC, it is necessary to use only the first part of the filename—the extension is not required.
.COM—The extension .COM means that the file is a program written in assembly language. It can be run from the operating system by entering the first part of the filename. The extension is not required. BASIC is a .COM file.

Names for data files don't have an extension unless you add one. I often use an extension indicating the name of the program that created the data file. For example, a FINANCE program could create a data file named INCOME.FIN or something similar.

SAVING PROGRAMS ON DISK
To be saved, a program must be in in computer memory. While it is still in RAM, decide two things: a filename for that program and the device, such as a disk drive, that you wish to send it to. The form of the command is

```
SAVE Device:"FILENAME"
```

The closing quotation marks are optional. The device and filename taken together are called the file specification or *filespec*. Device names for the disk drives are *A:* and *B:*. The colon is part of the device name. If the device name is omitted, drive A is used.

With two disk drives, three SAVE commands are possible:

```
SAVE "FILENAME"
SAVE "A:FILENAME"
SAVE "B:FILENAME"
```

The first two are equivalent. If a file with the same filename already exists on the disk, it will be replaced by the file being saved from memory.

LOADING PROGRAMS FROM DISK

Similarly, with two disk drives, there are three possible commands to load a program from disk into computer memory:

```
LOAD "FILENAME"
LOAD "A:FILENAME"
LOAD "B:FILENAME"
```

The LOAD command loads the program but does not run it.

LOAD AND RUN WITH ONE COMMAND

To load and run a program in one command, enter one of these commands

```
RUN "FILENAME"
RUN "A:FILENAME"
RUN "B:FILENAME"
```

DATA FILES

As a program operates, it is usually fed data from the keyboard. This data can be manipulated by the program, assigned a filename by the program and put onto a disk by the program. The program can also get files from a disk and use them.

Files that are created and managed by a program are called *data files*.

KINDS OF DATA FILES

Individual data items are placed in *records*. There are two ways to place records in a file on disk and retrieve them. Therefore, we say there are two kinds of data files.

SEQUENTIAL DATA FILES

Records can be filed in sequence, one behind the other. Between the records is a character called a *delimiter,* which indicates where one record ends and the next begins. To read any individual record, the computer scans the file in sequential order, starting with the first record in the file, until the desired record is found.

RANDOM DATA FILES

These files hold individual records, each with an identification number called the *record number*. To put a record on disk, you can specify a record number, such as 37, and the record will be placed in location 37 of the file—following location 36. To read a record, you retrieve it from the file by asking for its record number. Then it can be returned and another record brought into computer memory. Records can be put on disk and retrieved at random.

BUFFERS

A buffer is a *temporary parking place* for data. It's a designated area of the computer memory, with a limited capacity to hold characters. If a buffer holds 128 characters, we say that it is 128 characters long. It could hold a sentence that was entered using 128 keystrokes.

The operating system puts information on disk and plays it back when asked to. When a program has a record to put on disk, it delivers the data to a buffer and asks the operating system to file it.

The operating system takes the data from the buffer and puts it on disk. When the program asks the operating system to give the data back, it is returned to the buffer. The program then picks it up from the buffer and uses the information.

The program must designate a buffer for each filename. If the program says *use buffer #1 for the file named INCOME,* then both the program and the operating system will route all data for that file through buffer #1.

Three data buffers are automatically available to each program. They can be active at the same time. If more are needed, there is a way to request a larger number.

OPENING A DATA FILE

Before a data file can be used by the program, it must be opened. An OPEN statement does several things. In this statement,

```
OPEN "INCOME" FOR OUTPUT AS #1
```

the word *OPEN* means to open a file. The filename is INCOME. The device name is omitted, so drive A will be used. The words FOR OUTPUT mean that data will flow *from the computer* to the disk, through a buffer. AS #1 means that buffer #1 will be used.

The OPEN statement ties the buffer number and the filename together. This association between buffer number and filename is valid until the file is closed.

FOUR WAYS TO OPEN DATA FILES

The OPEN statement determines how a file can be used. There are four ways:

```
OPEN "FILENAME" FOR OUTPUT AS #1        Seq
```

opens a sequential file using buffer #1. The computer can output—meaning send—data to the disk. When a sequential file is opened for output, data cannot flow from disk to computer.

```
OPEN "FILENAME" FOR INPUT AS #2         Seq
```

opens a sequential file using buffer #2. The computer can receive data from the disk, but cannot send data to the disk.

```
OPEN "B:FILENAME" FOR APPEND AS #3      Seq
```

is used when a *sequential* file already exists on disk and the program wishes to add, or *append,* a data record to the end of the sequential file. In this statement, drive B and buffer #3 will be used.

```
OPEN "FILENAME" AS #1                    Ran
```

opens a *random* file for *both input and output,* using buffer #1.

The way to know how a file has been opened, and therefore how you can use it, is to observe the form of the OPEN statement. Notice that the three ways of opening a sequential file all have conditions: FOR OUTPUT, FOR INPUT, FOR APPEND. If there is no condition, the file is opened for random access.

CLOSING DATA FILES

The word *CLOSE,* used in a program, closes *all* data files by canceling all buffer assignments.

When you do this, the computer won't know where to put data for a particular filename. If you ask it to, it displays an error message.

If you don't want all files closed, you can close files selectively.

```
CLOSE #1
```

closes the file that was using buffer #1. It disassociates buffer #1 from a filename and makes it available for another assignment. The commands END, NEW, RUN and CLEAR close all files automatically. STOP doesn't close any files.

USING A SEQUENTIAL FILE

Here is a program that will open a sequential file, send some data to a disk, get it back and print it. The name I have chosen for the program is SEQDEMO, meaning *sequential demonstration*. When it runs, the program itself creates a data file on disk A, which it names TESTFILE. Please enter

```
NEW
10 CLS: REM filename "SEQDEMO"
20 OPEN "TESTFILE" FOR OUTPUT AS #1
30 PRINT #1, "Data Item 1"
40 PRINT #1, "Data Item 2"
50 CLOSE #1
60 OPEN "TESTFILE" FOR INPUT AS #1
70 INPUT #1, X1$: PRINT X1$
80 INPUT #1, X2$: PRINT X2$
90 CLOSE #1
```

List it, check it and run the program. Then list it again. Line 20 opens a sequential data file for output through buffer #1 and gives it the name TESTFILE.

Line 30 sends one data record to the disk. The statement PRINT #1, means *I am sending something to buffer #1. Put it on disk, using the filename that is associated with buffer #1.*

This is still another use of the PRINT command. When used with a buffer number, it means to put a record onto a disk. What is to be placed on the disk is typed directly after the statement. It can be the name of a variable, either string or numeric, in which case the computer finds that variable in memory and puts it on the disk. Or, it can be data typed on the program line itself.

In line 30, what is to be placed on the disk is typed into the program line itself. It is the string "Data Item 1".

Line 40 executes another PRINT #1, statement and supplies "Data Item 2" as the data. It goes onto the disk in sequence, following item 1.

When the program executes, drive A runs and two data records are put on the disk under the name TESTFILE. The file is closed by line 50. You must close a file before you can open it again in a different mode.

To get the data back into the buffer and then into memory, line 60 opens the file again using the same buffer number and filename. The difference is that the file is opened FOR INPUT, which means that data will flow *from the disk to the computer.*

The statement INPUT #1, in line 70 brings the first record back. Line 70 does several things. It brings a record from the disk. It puts it in buffer #1. It gives it a name, X1$. It places the data in memory under that name. The variable X1$ receives the data and trots over to memory with it. Then, a separate statement on line 70 prints X1$ so you can see what it is. Line 70 has then finished with the data in the buffer, so it's OK to put the next record in the buffer.

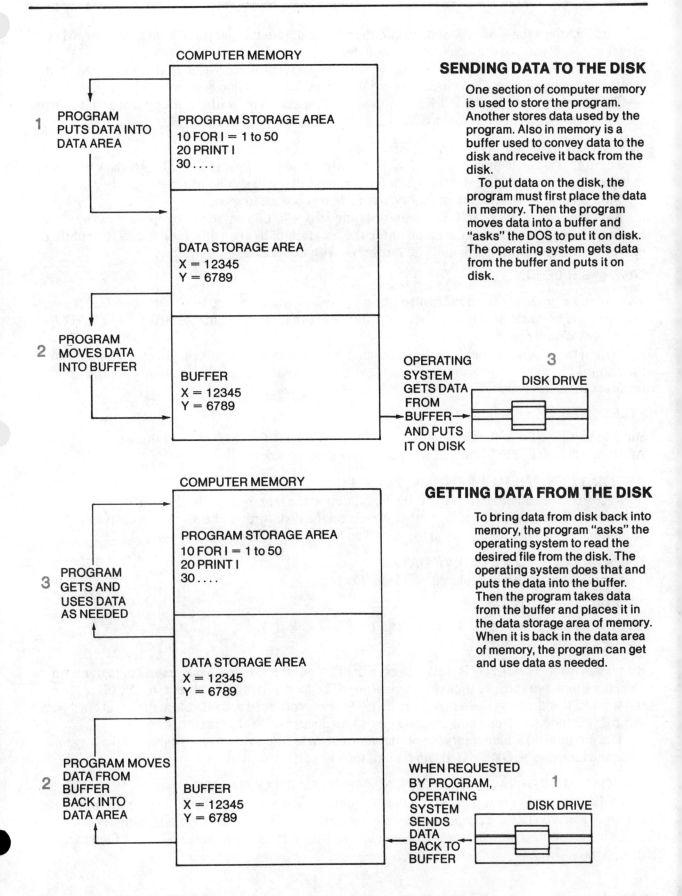

SENDING DATA TO THE DISK

One section of computer memory is used to store the program. Another stores data used by the program. Also in memory is a buffer used to convey data to the disk and receive it back from the disk.

To put data on the disk, the program must first place the data in memory. Then the program moves data into a buffer and "asks" the DOS to put it on disk. The operating system gets data from the buffer and puts it on disk.

GETTING DATA FROM THE DISK

To bring data from disk back into memory, the program "asks" the operating system to read the desired file from the disk. The operating system does that and puts the data into the buffer. Then the program takes data from the buffer and places it in the data storage area of memory. When it is back in the data area of memory, the program can get and use data as needed.

Figure labels (top diagram):

COMPUTER MEMORY

1 PROGRAM PUTS DATA INTO DATA AREA

PROGRAM STORAGE AREA
10 FOR I = 1 to 50
20 PRINT I
30 . . . .

DATA STORAGE AREA
X = 12345
Y = 6789

2 PROGRAM MOVES DATA INTO BUFFER

BUFFER
X = 12345
Y = 6789

OPERATING SYSTEM GETS DATA FROM BUFFER AND PUTS IT ON DISK

3 DISK DRIVE

Figure labels (bottom diagram):

COMPUTER MEMORY

PROGRAM STORAGE AREA
10 FOR I = 1 to 50
20 PRINT I
30 . . . .

3 PROGRAM GETS AND USES DATA AS NEEDED

DATA STORAGE AREA
X = 12345
Y = 6789

2 PROGRAM MOVES DATA FROM BUFFER BACK INTO DATA AREA

BUFFER
X = 12345
Y = 6789

WHEN REQUESTED BY PROGRAM, OPERATING SYSTEM SENDS DATA BACK TO BUFFER

1 DISK DRIVE

Line 80 brings the *next* record back into the specified buffer, names it X2$ and displays it. The new record replaces the previous record in the buffer.

You must assign a *different name to each record,* as the records are placed in the buffer and then moved to memory. Line 70 inputs to the variable name X1$, and line 80 inputs to X2$.

This is another use for the INPUT command. When associated with a buffer number, it prepares the computer to accept data from a disk.

PROGRAM FILES AND DATA FILES

There are two filenames associated with the program in memory. In line 10 a REMark indicates that the filename is SEQDEMO. This is *only a reminder* that you should use that name to put the program on disk and load it into memory again when you want to use it.

A program never files itself. The remark at line 10 doesn't do anything except serve as a reminder so you don't forget the name or file the program under two different names. To put that program onto disk with that name, you must do it with a SAVE statement. Enter

```
SAVE "SEQDEMO"
```

This creates a *program file* on the disk, containing that program. Notice that there is no buffer involved and no question about sequential or random order. The commands SAVE and LOAD are used *only with program files.*

Within the program, lines 20 and 70 contain two program statements that open a data file with the name TESTFILE. A program opens and closes its own data files, puts them on disk and retrieves them as needed. Enter

```
FILES
```

and you will see a list of files on disk A. One will be SEQDEMO, which was put there by you. Another will be TESTFILE, which was put there by the program.

RECORD LENGTH IN A SEQUENTIAL FILE

Records in a sequential file can be any length, up to the length of the buffer, which is 255 characters. The records follow each other closely on the disk, with no blank space in between. Short sequential records use less space on the disk than long sequential records.

USING A LOOP TO RETRIEVE DATA

Lines 70 and 80 can be replaced by a loop. Enter

```
70 FOR I = 1 TO 2
75 INPUT #1, X$(I): PRINT X$(I)
80 NEXT I
```

Run it and list it. The display is the same as in the first program. If you have several data items on disk, it's simpler to retrieve them by using a loop. The loop will provide repetitive INPUT #1, statements. It will also assign a new name to each newly retrieved record automatically at each pass through the loop. This loop puts the data items into an array X$( ) in memory.

The program now in memory is not the same as it was when you saved it earlier. Save it again, using the filename SEQDEMO. It will replace the old version on disk.

CHOOSING ORDINARY VARIABLE NAMES OR ARRAY NAMES

In the first version of this program, data from the disk was received by X1$ and X2$. These are not array names. They are simply two different string names to identify strings in memory.

In the second version, data was received by the array names X$(1) and X$(2) and filed in a string array, X$( ).

If there are a lot of data items, using a loop and an array to hold the data is preferable. If there are only a few data items, use the method that works best for the program you're writing.

THE SEQUENTIAL-FILE POINTER

The operating system operates the disk drives. For sequential files, it uses an electronic *pointer* that works like a bookmark in a book. When a sequential file is being read from the disk, the pointer moves along the file from beginning to end so that no record is omitted or read twice. The pointer normally remains at the end of the file. When a new record is appended, the pointer says *Put it here at the end, friend.*

HOW TO LOSE THE CONTENTS OF A SEQUENTIAL FILE

Every time a sequential file is opened for *output,* the pointer is positioned at the *beginning* of the file, ready to accept a *completely new* file from the computer. When a sequential file is first opened, that's OK because the file is empty anyway.

But if you put data in it, close it and then open it for output again, the pointer moves to the beginning of the file again, *ready to make a new file.* All data in the file is lost.

HOW NOT TO LOSE THE DATA

There are two ways to prevent losing data already in a sequential file when you need to add more data to the file. You can open it for input and read the entire file from the disk into memory, using the INPUT # statement. Then add new data to the file in memory, or change it as you wish. Then put the whole thing back on disk, entirely replacing what was there before. The other way is to open it for *append.*

OPEN FOR APPEND

If you have a lot of work to do in a sequential file, you may as well bring it into memory and work on it. If you merely want to add something to an existing file, the append method is better. Please list the program in memory. Change the following lines as shown:

```
20 OPEN "TESTFILE" FOR APPEND AS #1
30 PRINT #1, "Data Item 3"
40 PRINT #1, "Data Item 4"
70 FOR I = 1 TO 4
```

List and check it. Line 20 opens the sequential file in the APPEND mode. This leaves the pointer at the end of the file so no records are lost. Lines 30 and 40 will append two new data items to the file, one behind the other. The lines beginning at 60 will open the file for input and display all four data items. Run it. List it again. Don't bother saving it.

What would happen if you ran it again? It would append two more data items. The file would have data items 1,2,3,4,3,4 because 3 and 4 were appended twice. Line 70 would retrieve and display only the first four items. Change line 70 to count to 6 and then run the program again. Don't save it.

KILLING DATA FILES

When you are testing a program that creates data files, the files will get mixed up if the program makes mistakes or if you run an append program several times. Sometimes it's best to kill the data file and start over, particularly if you have made a program change. Begin by listing the files, so you can be sure of what you are killing. If the filename has an extension, you must use it. Enter

```
FILES
```

Look for TESTFILE. It's there, with no extension. Enter

```
KILL "TESTFILE"
```

List the files again. It's gone.

DELIMITERS

For this demonstration, use the version of SEQDEMO that you have on disk, not the altered version in memory. Enter

```
LOAD "SEQDEMO"
```

The program from disk will replace the one in memory. List it. It should be the preceding version. If not, fix it. Then change lines 30 and 70. Notice the commas added to line 30.

```
30 PRINT #1, "Data, Item, 1"
70 FOR I = 1 TO 4
```

You killed the data file TESTFILE, so the program will make a new one. List it, check it and run it. List it again.

Line 70 gave you a clue. Commas act as delimiters when the data is taken back off the disk by an INPUT # statement. There are now four data items in memory—three from line 30 and one from line 40. To read them all, it is necessary to run the loop four times, which line 70 did.

COPING WITH DELIMITERS

Using commas for delimiters in sequential files allows you to put several related items of data on disk as one record, using just one PRINT # statement.

Other Delimiters—With sequential files, other characters may serve as delimiters. It depends on the form of the data item being placed in the file.

If it is numeric data, delimiters are spaces, carriage returns, line feeds or commas. This is discussed in a minute.

If it is an ordinary string, as illustrated by line 30, delimiters are carriage returns, line feeds and commas, but *not spaces*. In this string, the quotation marks at each end are used to *define* the string. They are not part of the string.

You may need to handle a data item with commas in it as a single item—which means that you don't want the commas to act as delimiters. To do this, you must create a special kind of string, called a *quoted* string. Quotation marks are part of the string. When this is done, the only delimiter is the second set of quotation marks—or 255 keystrokes, whichever comes first.

This means that you must use quotation marks to define a string that *includes* quotation marks, perhaps ""''abcdef''". That won't work, but if it did, the resulting string would be "abcdef" because the outside set of quotation marks define the string to include the inside set.

The reason it won't work is that the second pair of quotation marks in a quoted string acts as a delimiter. In other words, the first pair of quotation marks starts it; the closing set of quotation marks stops it. Nothing would go on disk.

You can make a quoted string with ASCII "trickery." For the outside quotation marks, use ASCII code CHR$(34)—the code for quotation marks. Change line 30 to read

```
30 PRINT #1, CHR$(34)"Data,Item,1"CHR$(34)
```

The string is *defined* by the two CHR$(34) characters. The string itself now *includes quotation marks* at the beginning and the end. Run the program.

When the data is brought back from the disk, there are now only two data items, but line 70 still wants four items. You get an error message: *Input past end in 75.*

Change line 70 to ask for two data items. Run it again. It works, and there are only two data items. Making a quoted string by using CHR$(34) to define the string to include quotation marks is not often needed. The LINE INPUT # statement discussed in the next section is normally used for that purpose. Don't save the program in memory.

Delimiters may seem unduly complicated. If so, just remember that sequential files are affected by delimiters. When you are writing a program that uses sequential files, look up the information again and use it. The discussion of INPUT # in the IBM book *BASIC* will remind you about delimiters.

LINE INPUT

If you put a data string on disk and the string includes delimiters, you may want it back in one piece. LINE INPUT # does that. It brings back the complete string and puts it in memory as a single data item. Remove the CHR$(34) from both places in line 30. Change line 75 to read

```
75 LINE INPUT #1, X$(I): PRINT X$(I)
```

and run the program again.

You see two lines on the screen again.

SEQUENTIAL DATA FILES WITH NUMERIC DATA

So far, you've been using strings as input and output. You can also store numeric data. When you do this, every delimiter works as a delimiter. Change lines 30, 40, 70 and 75 like this:

```
30 PRINT #1, 1,2,3,4,5
40 PRINT #1, 6,7,8,9,10
70 FOR I = 1 TO 10
75 INPUT #1, N(I): PRINT N(I)
```

List and check it. Lines 30 and 40 provide 10 data items separated by commas. The last item on each line doesn't need a comma because ENTER is a delimiter. Run it.

Using a loop to put data items into a sequential file will insert delimiters automatically. Change lines 30 and 40, and add line 45.

```
30 FOR I = 1 TO 10
40 PRINT #1, I
45 NEXT I
```

Run it. The data items are separated by carriage returns produced automatically by each PRINT statement. Don't save this version.

This method works very well for reading data items from an array in memory and putting them on disk. Notice that it is practically automatic. You don't have to worry about delimiters either when putting the data on disk or when getting it back.

EOF( )

This means *End Of File*. The computer automatically marks the end of a sequential file by placing CHR$(26) at the end. When reading the file, it knows when it has reached the end because it finds that character. EOF tells you that it has reached the end.

This provides a good way to be sure that a loop runs the correct number of times to input all of the data from the disk. It also prevents *Input past end* errors.

Use a loop without a counter and depend on EOF( ) to jump out of it. To see this work, enter

```
70 I = 1
72 IF EOF(1) THEN GOTO 90
80 I = I + 1: GOTO 72
```

List and check it. EOF(1) means the end of the file that is reached through buffer #1. EOF(2) would query the file associated with buffer #2.

Run it. Save it in this form. Then reduce the number of data items in line 30 and run it again. The program adjusts automatically to the reduced number of records.

Remember that N( ) is an array. If you increase the number of data items without a DIM statement, you will get an error message.

**What is CHR$(26)?**—If you inadvertently put CHR$(26) in the middle of a sequential file by including it in a data item, the computer will stop right there and think that it has reached EOF. If you forget what CHR$(26) is, enter

```
PRINT CHR$(26)
```

It's printable, but there isn't any way you can enter one by a single keystroke. Instead, you enter one by typing CHR$(26). Put one at the end of line 40 and run the program. Don't save this version and don't let anybody see it.

SOURCES OF DATA FOR A SEQUENTIAL FILE

For simplicity, this program supplies data by including it in the program. In a real-world program, you probably won't do that. The data that you want to put on disk will normally be in memory. If it is identified with ordinary variable names, such as X or B$, put the variable names after a PRINT # statement like this:

```
30 PRINT #1, B$
```

Whatever is held in memory as B$ will go onto the disk. If you have data in an array, use a loop to read it out. For example

```
30 FOR K = 1 TO 50: PRINT #1, A(K): NEXT K
```

will read 50 items from the array A( ) and put them in a sequential file on disk.

You can also enter data at the keyboard, process it in the program and then file it on disk.

THE NEW-PROGRAM DILEMMA

If a program opens a sequential data file for *output,* and the file does not already exist on disk, the program will create the file. The computer doesn't care if you put any data into the file or not. The file exists on the disk even if empty.

If a program opens a sequential file for *input,* and the file does not exist, the program stops running, returns to the command mode and prints an error message: *File not found.* The computer assumes that your program needs data from that file, or it wouldn't have asked for it. If it can't find the file, it becomes confused and shuts down the operation.

Many programs begin by taking data from the disk, doing something to the data and then sending it back to the disk. Therefore, the first use of a sequential file in the program is to open it for *input* to the computer.

For example, if you have a program that keeps track of your income, and you actually get some, you would joyfully run that program. The first thing it does is bring the INCOME file from disk, so you can add something to it.

If the program is new and has *never run before,* it will arrive at a statement that opens the file for input, which is OK if the file exists on the disk. But if it has never run before, the file does not exist, so the program stops.

An essential part of programming is to prevent program failures for any reason. Some programming problems can be solved two ways—by brute force or by a more elegant method. Here's the brute-force solution:

```
150 OPEN "SOMETHIN" FOR OUTPUT AS #1: CLOSE #1
160 OPEN "SOMETHIN" FOR INPUT AS #1
```

The first time the program is run, line 150 creates the data file that will be needed and then does nothing except close it again. It's empty, but it exists. Line 160 can then open the file for input without causing an error because the file exists. If there is no data in the file, the program should be written to cope with that. Then the program can enter data as needed and proceed.

After that one-time use, line 150 is unnecessary. It runs the disk drive briefly and slows down execution a little bit. But that line—or a more elegant method—is essential or the user will *never* get the program started. The elegant method of opening files for input is discussed in Chapter 11.

RANDOM DATA FILES

This implies *random access*. You put data on the disk or read it from the disk with just one OPEN statement. You can work with records one at a time, without affecting the other records in the file. Each record has its own record number. You call for records by that number. When you put a record onto the disk, you specify its record number.

For that convenience, there are some disadvantages. Random files accept *only strings*. The record length is fixed. If you don't fill the allocated space for each record, you waste some space on the disk. Programming is a little more complicated.

There are four steps required to open a random file and put data in it: OPEN, FIELD, LSET or RSET, and PUT. Please enter

```
NEW
10 CLS: REM filename "RANDEMO"
20 OPEN "RANDFILE" AS #1
30 FIELD #1, 10 AS B1$, 20 AS B2$, 40 AS B3$
40 M1$ = "Dear":
   M2$ = "Mr. Smith":
   M3$ = "You may already have won $1,000,000.00!"
50 LSET B1$ = M1$: LSET B2$ = M2$: LSET B3$ = M3$
60 PUT #1, 3
```

The OPEN statement in line 20 is for random access using buffer #1. It creates a data file with the filename RANDFILE.

The FIELD statement in line 30 *prepares the buffer* to receive data. It assigns segments or *fields* in the buffer and gives each field a string name. This statement assigns 10 spaces for B1$, 20 for B2$ and 40 for B3$, arranged from left to right in the buffer. The total buffer space used by these three fields is 70 spaces.

Line 40 provides three strings that will be used in a form letter. You can change the salutation, the name and the amount already won by changing the messages, M1$, M2$ and M3$.

To get these three strings onto a disk, they must first go into the buffer. Line 50 places the three strings in the buffer in an orderly way. Field B1$ receives M1$. B1$ has 10 spaces allocated by the FIELD statement. It receives M1$, which is the word *Dear*. That word uses only four spaces, so there is plenty of room in that field. B2$ receives M2$. B3$ receives M3$.

B1$, B2$ and B3$ are names for buffer fields. Don't use them for anything else in the program.

In line 50, LSET means that the string is placed all the way to the *left* in its field. If there are unused spaces, they will be at the right and will be filled with blanks. If you use RSET, the string is placed at the *right* end of the field and filled with leading blanks as needed.

If the string you put in a buffer field is too long for the space provided by the FIELD statement, it will be cut off to fit the available space. LSET preserves the left end of the string, and the right end is truncated if necessary. RSET does it the opposite way.

Now the buffer has the three strings in the designated fields. Line 60 PUTs it all on disk. The number following the word PUT is the buffer number. The number following the comma is the record number. This line puts the contents of buffer #1 onto the disk as record 3 in a random data file named RANDFILE.

You can use any record number. If you skip some, they remain empty. They can be filled later, if you wish. If you send data using a record number that already exists, the new data will replace the old data on disk. Now the data items are on the disk. Please enter

```
70 GET #1, 3
80 M1$ = B1$: M2$ = B2$: M3$ = B3$
90 PRINT M1$ M2$ M3$
100 CLOSE
```

Check your typing. Run the program and then list it. In line 70, the GET statement brings record number 3 back into buffer #1. The computer already has FIELD instructions for buffer #1. The record will be divided up into three parts and placed in three buffer fields, exactly as they were when the record was PUT onto the disk. To get them out of the buffer, for use, you must use the buffer-field names—B1$, and so forth.

Line 80 assigns the contents of each buffer field to a string variable. When that line executes, the contents of each field are automatically placed in memory with the name you assigned to them. The contents of buffer field B1$ go into memory as M1$, and so forth.

You can use any string names to receive data items back from the buffer. You can put data on the disk from one string name and retrieve it into another string name, if you wish. Line 90 finds the three strings in memory and prints them. Line 100 closes the file.

Run the program. You have some repairs to do. In the FIELD statement, 10 spaces were allocated to B1$, 20 and 40 spaces to the other two field names. When you get them back into memory, that's the length of each string, even if some characters are blanks. In the screen display, you are seeing the length of each string as it was fielded in the FIELD statement. That's why there is space between *Dear* and *Mr. Smith.* Enter

```
PRINT LEN(M1$)
PRINT LEN(M2$)
PRINT LEN(M3$)
```

Shorten the first field so there is only one space after *Dear.* This means that the field needs only five spaces instead of ten. Put a comma after *Smith.* Print M3$ on the next line with five spaces for a paragraph indent. Changing these lines as indicated should do those things:

```
30 FIELD #1, 5 AS B1$, 20 AS B2$, 40 AS B3$
40 M1$ = "Dear":
   M2$ = "Mr. Smith,":
   M3$ = "     You may already have won $1,000,000.00!"
90 PRINT M1$ M2$: PRINT M3$
```

List it and check your typing. Run it to see the improvement. Notice that not all of the characters in M3$ print. It is cut off at the right end. Count the characters in M3$ in the program, including the five spaces you added at the front. There are more than 40, but the buffer was fielded for 40 characters. Some were cut off. Change the FIELD statement to allow 45 characters for B3$. Run it again. Save this program on disk as RANDEMO.

PUT # AND GET

PUT # and GET # are used only with random files. The statement

```
PUT #2, 7
```

will put record number 7 onto the disk in the designated disk drive, into the designated filename. These designations are done by the OPEN statement, using buffer #2. The statement

```
GET #3, 9
```

brings record 9 back from the designated file in the designated disk drive and puts it in buffer #3, fielded as it was originally.

RECORD LENGTH IN A RANDOM FILE

BASIC allows you to set the record length of a random file as part of the OPEN statement. The number of spaces in the buffer is the same as the record length. Once set, it remains at that value. Here is the form:

```
20 OPEN "RANDFILE" AS #1 LEN = 80
```

The statement at the end sets record LENgth to 80 characters. To conserve space on the disk, use a record length that is no longer than necessary. But, be sure the buffer fields have enough room to hold everything that the program will put into them. A field that is comfortable for Mr. Smith may do violence to Mr. Higginbotham.

If you don't specify record length, the default value of 128 is used. The maximum record length that you can specify is 32,767 characters.

RANDOM FILES REQUIRE STRINGS

Random files accept only strings. If you have numbers to store, convert them to strings first. Change them back to numbers when they return from the disk.

There are special functions for making numbers into strings to put into a random file and then converting them back into numbers after you get them back. These are MKI$, MKS$, MKD$, CVI, CVS and CVD. These are not discussed in this book. You can read about them in the IBM book *BASIC*.

You've seen the simple way of turning numbers into strings for random-file use: Z$ = STR$(Z) works just fine, along with Z = VAL(Z$) to get the number back again.

EOF( ), LOF( ), LOC( )

EOF( ) is not used with random files. There are two similar functions that work with random data files, but they are not very useful.

LOF means *Length Of File*. It is the number of characters assigned to a file on the disk, even if some are blanks. In computer language, a character is called a *byte*. LOF(1) returns the number of bytes assigned to the file that is reached through buffer #1. This works only when the file is still open. Enter

```
PRINT LOF(1)
```

and you see the problem. The file is closed. List the program in memory and delete line 100. Run it and it will leave the file open. Enter

```
PRINT LOF(1)
```

384 bytes are assigned to RANDFILE. Enter

```
PRINT 384/128
PRINT LOF(1)/128
```

The file has enough space for three records, each with 128 bytes.

This program put only one record on the disk, but it was record number 3. The computer allocated space for records 1 and 2 even though they are empty.

You can use LOF( ) to find the number of the last record in a random file, *provided the record length is 128.* It won't work with any other record length. Usually, you want to know the number of the last record so you know where to put a new record without overwriting something that is already on the disk. This statement will do that:

```
300 PUT #1, (LOF(1)/128) + 1
```
next record.

If the last record is number 3, this will put the next record in slot 4 of the file—*but only when record length is 128 bytes.*

PRINT LOC(1) produces the record number of the last random record that was accessed. *Accessed* means put a record on the disk or read from the disk.

WRITE TO A RANDOM RECORD BEFORE READING IT

BASIC will allow you to call up a random record that has never been written to in that program. It will put the record in the designated buffer, field it and put it in memory in the normal way. This can be troublesome if the record is empty because you will have variable names in memory representing blanks.

Often, an unused random record *will not be empty.* The computer maintains a directory, on each disk, of files on that disk and their locations. When you kill a file, the name and location are deleted *from the directory* so the computer no longer knows where to find that file. But, the file itself is not changed.

The computer has only one way to erase data in a disk file—by writing new data on top of it. If you create a random data file and put data in records 1 to 3 and 5 to 8, record 4 has not been used so far in your program.

If that space on the disk has ever been used for anything, the old data will still be there. If your program calls it up, the result can be confusing—both to your program and to you. When that happens, what you get from the disk is called *garbage.*

Avoid the problem by not reading a record number until the program has written that record number on the disk. Another way is to test one field of each record as it is read, using relational operators. Test for a key word or number that makes sense to your program. If old data is found, it should not pass the test. And, that record should not be used in the program.

MORE THAN ONE RANDOM RECORD

The program RANDEMO shows how to put a random record on disk and get it back. It handles only one record, number 3, so it doesn't really demonstrate random access. The next version will allow you to input names from the keyboard and assign any record number to file the data.

These changes will be tedious to enter, but perhaps worth the effort. Please list the program. Using the edit keys, change line 40 to look like this, or else just retype it.

```
40 M1$ = "Dear":
   M3$ = "      You may already have won $1,000,000.00!"
```

Then enter these lines:

```
42 LINE INPUT "Enter last name: "; M2$
44 M2$ = M2$ + ","
```

```
46 INPUT "Enter record number: ", RN
60 PUT #1, RN
70 CLS
75 FOR I = 1 TO LOF(1)/128: GET #1, I
78 PRINT: PRINT "PRINTING RECORD NUMBER " I
92 STOP
95 NEXT I
97 PRINT "END OF FILE"
```

List it and check your typing. Entering those lines and getting them right was a lot of work. Protect it by saving the program as RANDEMO again. The line numbers are a mess. Renumber it by entering

```
RENUM
```

List it. Add line 180 to make the program look exactly like this. When it does, protect against a power failure by saving it again.

```
10 CLS: REM filename "RANDEMO"
20 OPEN "RANDFILE" AS #1
30 FIELD #1, 5 AS B1$, 20 AS B2$, 45 AS B3$
40 M1$ = "Dear":
   M3$ = "       You may already have won $1,000,000.00!"
50 LINE INPUT "Enter last name: "; M2$
60 M2$ = M2$ + ","
70 INPUT "Enter record number: ", RN
80 LSET B1$ = M1$: LSET B2$ = M2$: LSET B3$ = M3$
90 PUT #1, RN
100 CLS
110 FOR I = 1 TO LOF(1)/128: GET #1, I
120 PRINT: PRINT "PRINTING RECORD NUMBER " I
130 M1$ = B1$: M2$ = B2$: M3$ = B3$
140 PRINT M1$ M2$: PRINT M3$
150 STOP
160 NEXT I
170 PRINT "END OF FILE"
180 CLOSE
```

Line 40 now provides M1$ and M3$, but not M2$. Line 50 asks you to enter M2$. When you run it, enter names like *Mr. Jones* or *Mrs. Williams*. Line 60 adds a comma.

Line 70 asks you for a record number. Use whatever you like, but keep them under 20 so the program doesn't take a long time to run. Skip record numbers so some are not used by this program. Line 90 puts the record on disk, using the record number you supplied.

Line 110 sets up a loop that will print all records in the file. Line 120 tells you which record number is being printed. Line 150 stops the program to slow it down. Use F5 to start it again. When all records have been displayed, line 170 executes.

Run the program a few times, entering different names and record numbers. You may pick up some garbage when printing records that have not been written to by this program. If so, the result is unpredictable. The garbage may clear the screen or beep the beeper.

You will see that you can put random records anywhere in a random file. This does not demonstrate retrieving them at random. The simplest way to see that is to change line 110 to get any record number that you want to see, such as

```
110 GET #1, 13
```

and delete lines 120 and 160. Run it.

The fancy way to demonstrate random retrieval is to write a routine that asks you to input the desired record number from the keyboard and then gets and displays that record. Do that. My version is called RANDEMO 1. It's at the end of this chapter, page 148.

MANAGING RECORD NUMBERS IN A RANDOM FILE

Random record numbers should be managed very carefully by the program—specifically, by the programmer. If record numbers are significant to the program, such as employee numbers or part numbers in an inventory, then record number 100 must be record number 100, and the program should put it there. When you want that information, get record number 100. Simplicity is the advantage of that method.

But doing it the simple way may waste a lot of space on the disk. If your program uses record number 10 and then number 100, all of the intervening spaces are allocated on the disk even though they are empty. If the intervening spaces are filled later, that's OK. If they are never used, disk space is wasted.

Sometimes, it's better to use random record numbers only as addresses for data on the disk. Fill each record space in order, leaving no gaps. When you add a new record to the file, put it at the end. In each record, put a number or keyword that will identify that record.

For example, in the FIELD statement for a random file, the first field spaces could be a part number. FIELD #1, 3 as PN$ could allocate three spaces to the Part Number. Then the record number is incidental, not important to the data stored in that file.

If you file random records like this, there are several ways to get a desired data record back into memory so you can use it. One is to look at all of the records in the random file until you find the one with the identification number or keyword that you need. Don't enter this, just look at it:

```
500 OPEN "DATAFILE" AS #1
510 FIELD #1, 3 AS PN$, 20 AS A$, 30 AS B$ (and so forth)
520 I = 1
530 GET #1, I
540 IF VAL(PN$) = (desired number) THEN GOTO 700
550 (test for end of file. if end, GOTO 600)
560 I = I + 1: GOTO 530 (loop back to examine next record)
600 (desired record not found)
700 (record found, do something with it)
```

If VAL(PN$) matches the desired part number, the routine jumps to line 700. If no match is found in the entire file, the program jumps to line 600.

Another way to get a data record back into memory is to read the entire file, or chunks of it, into memory. While reading it, use the information in each record to organize the data in memory in an array. Then you can get individual data items by addressing them in memory, which is independent of record numbers on the disk. When you're through, put the data back on disk.

Another method of locating a desired random record is to have a separate index file. One column is a list of identifiers, such as numbers or keywords. The second column is the record numbers. Look it up in the index file and then call for the indicated record number.

DELETING A RECORD IN A RANDOM FILE

When using random files, you may want to delete one. For example, if a part number becomes obsolete, you could call up that record, set all of the field names equal to "" and put it back on disk.

The record would still exist on the disk, filled with blanks. Record numbers, once used, can never be deleted except by KILLing the entire file.

The meaning of a blank record may be ambiguous because it could be confused with an unused empty record.

A better way is to put the letters KIL or KL in the first field. This tells the program to disregard that record, with no ambiguity. This has another advantage. When you need to put a new record in the file, scan it to find the first one with KIL at the beginning of the record. Use that record number for the new record. This keeps the file as short as possible.

MOVING THE ENTIRE FILE INTO MEMORY

Moving records one at a time between disk and memory is practical if a program does it infrequently. If the program does it repeatedly, it will be slow and the disk drive will run a lot.

A faster method is to read the entire file into an array in memory. Then you can use the data in the file as much as you wish. The disk drive does not run as often. When you are through with the file, put it all back on disk.

SAVING A PROGRAM IN ASCII

Normally, when a program written in BASIC is saved to disk, the BASIC words are replaced by special abbreviated codes to save space on the disk.

A program can be saved in ASCII codes, which are direct translations of each letter in each BASIC word. This takes more space on the disk. To save a program in ASCII, add ,A at the end of the SAVE command. For example,

```
SAVE "RANDEMO",A
```

Notice that ,A is outside of the quotation marks. The reason you might want to save a program in ASCII is so you can merge it with another program.

MERGE

You may want to combine two programs—one in memory and the other on disk—or add some lines from a program on disk to a program in memory. This is done from the BASIC command mode by the command

```
MERGE (filename)
```

The filename is the program *on disk* that is to be merged with the program in memory. If the program on disk has any line numbers that are the same as the program in memory, they will replace the lines in memory.

Here are some things you should do before entering a MERGE command: Examine both programs and write down a plan for the entire merge operation. You can put the merged program lines below, above or in the middle of the line numbers of the program in memory. Decide what you are going to do and arrange line numbers as necessary.

Let's consider Program M as the main program. It will receive lines from another program. Program D is on disk and will be merged with Program M.

After you have made a plan and made room in Program M for Program D, save Program M to disk and load Program D.

Prepare Program D to be merged. You may want to delete or change some lines. You may wish to renumber the remaining lines. If so, do it. When you have it ready to be merged, return it to disk in ASCII format by typing *,A* after the filename.

If you return the altered Program D to disk with its original filename, the original version will be lost. If you don't want that to happen, return the program to disk with a different name. I usually use MERGE,A.

Then load Program M back into memory. Now you are ready to perform the merge. If you used MERGE as the name of the program on disk, enter

```
MERGE "MERGE"
```

Don't use *,A* at the end. Otherwise, an error message results. List the program and check the merged lines. When you are satisfied that the merge worked, you can KILL the program MERGE on disk, if you wish.

Often, merging programs causes problems that you didn't anticipate. For example, GOTO and GOSUB statements may address the wrong line numbers, or the same variable name may be used twice. Run the new program and troubleshoot it if necessary. If you don't plan carefully, merging programs can be very troublesome.

You have a program named RANDEMO on disk. The last line number in RANDEMO is 180. This procedure writes another program with only one line, line 190, and saves it as "MERGE",A. Then it merges the one-line program with RANDEMO. Enter

```
NEW
190 END
SAVE "MERGE",A
LOAD "RANDEMO"
MERGE "MERGE"
LIST
KILL "MERGE.BAS"
```

The merge operation happens in memory. Only the version of RANDEMO in memory has a line 190. If you want your permanent copy of the program to have that line, you must save the version in memory.

CHANGING A FILENAME

You may want to change the name of a file after it is already on disk. With BASIC, this can be done either from the operating system or from the command mode. In BASIC, the command is NAME. The form is

```
NAME oldname AS newname
```

If you want an extension with *newname,* include it. You have a file on disk named TESTFILE that was created by the program SEQDEMO. Because TESTFILE uses sequential file procedures, a better name might be SEQFILE. Enter this:

```
NAME "TESTFILE" AS "SEQFILE"
```

List the files and the name should be changed.

RUNNING ONE PROGRAM FROM ANOTHER

BASIC will recognize the command RUN "FILENAME" either in the command mode or as a program line. If the desired program is not already in memory, BASIC will load it from disk and run it. You can use one program to call and run another. This is a good way to organize a menu of programs.

If you have several related programs on a disk, you can write a menu program in BASIC. When executed, it displays the available programs and asks the user to choose one.

When the choice is made, the selected program is run by a line in the menu program. The selected program is moved into memory, replacing the menu program. The last line of the selected program calls the menu program again, so the user can make another choice.

There must be a way to terminate operation, or else there will be an endless loop among programs. The first calls the second and the second calls the first. This routine demonstrates one program running another. Enter this one-line program:

```
NEW
10 RUN "SEQDEMO"
```

List it. Then run it. After you run it, list the program in memory.

CLEANUP

Delete a file from the command mode by using the KILL command. You have some files on disk that were created in this chapter. Please list the files by entering

```
FILES
```

If you ran SEQDEMO a moment ago, then you created five files in this chapter: RANDEMO, RANDFILE, SEQDEMO, SEQFILE, and TESTFILE.

You changed the name of a file *on disk* from TESTFILE to SEQFILE, but you didn't change the program itself. When SEQDEMO ran again, it created a new TESTFILE. Now you have one of each. The next time something like that happens, you'll spend less time figuring out why.

You don't need to keep any of the data files. Kill them with these commands:

```
KILL "TESTFILE"
KILL "SEQFILE"
KILL "RANDFILE"
```

List the files to see how you're doing.

REVIEW

As with other languages, the BASIC programming language has grammar, punctuation and standard usage. BASIC is rigid and unforgiving about the rules of use. You won't become fluent in BASIC until its grammar and standard usage are so familiar to you that you can use them correctly almost without thinking about it.

A good thing about languages, including BASIC, is that you *can* use them intelligently without knowing every word and every rule. So far, I have been asking you to look up BASIC words in the IBM book *BASIC*. You are finding things there that you probably don't understand. It's impossible to understand everything in one gulp. The thing to do is nibble at it and use what you know correctly.

Please look through this chapter again. Glance down each of the program listings to review what each line does. If you are unsure about any part, read that part again and repeat the programming exercises.

The accompanying box lists BASIC words used in this chapter. Please look them up in the IBM book *BASIC*. In chapter 3 of the same book, read the section called *Files*. In that section, the expression *File Number* is used to mean what I have called the *buffer number*. Then read Appendix B.

BASIC WORDS USED IN THIS CHAPTER

CLOSE	KILL	MKS$
CVD	LINE INPUT #	NAME
CVI	LSET	OPEN
CVS	LOAD	PUT #
EOF( )	LOC( )	RENUM
FIELD	LOF( )	RSET
FILES	MERGE	RUN
GET #	MKD$	SAVE
INPUT #	MKI$	

Here's the program described on page 144:

```
10 CLS: 'Random-access demo modified to allow getting
        or putting to specified record numbers.
           filename "RANDEMO1"
20 OPEN "RANDFILE" AS #1
30 FIELD #1, 5 AS B1$, 20 AS B2$, 45 AS B3$
40 PRINT: PRINT
50 PRINT "Do you wish to GET or PUT records,";
60 PRINT " or QUIT and end program?"
70 PRINT: PRINT "==> Press G or P or Q."
80 CHOICE$ = INKEY$: IF CHOICE$ = "" THEN GOTO 80
90 IF CHOICE$ = "G" OR CHOICE$ = "g" THEN CLS: GOTO 220
100 IF CHOICE$ = "Q" OR CHOICE$ = "q" THEN CLS: GOTO 280
110 IF CHOICE$ <> "P" AND CHOICE$ <> "p" THEN GOTO 40
120 M1$ = "Dear";
    M3$ = "      You may already have won $1,000,000.00!"
130 CLS: PRINT: PRINT: PRINT
140 LINE INPUT "Enter last name: "; M2$
150 M2$ = M2$ + ","
160 PRINT: PRINT: PRINT
170 INPUT "ENTER RECORD NUMBER: ", RN
180 LSET B1$ = M1$: LSET B2$ = M2$: LSET B3$ = M3$
```

(Program continued on next page.)

```
190 PUT #1, RN
200 CLS: PRINT: PRINT: PRINT M2$ " FILED IN RECORD "RN
210 PRINT: PRINT: GOTO 50
220 CLS: PRINT: PRINT: INPUT"ENTER RECORD NUMBER: ", RN
230 CLS: GET #1, RN
240 PRINT: PRINT: PRINT "PRINTING RECORD NUMBER " RN
250 M1$ = B1$: M2$ = B2$: M3$ = B3$
260 PRINT: PRINT M1$ M2$: PRINT M3$
270 PRINT: PRINT: PRINT: GOTO 50
280 PRINT: PRINT "END OF PROGRAM"
290 PRINT: PRINT: PRINT: END
```

10 Managing The Display And The Printer

The first part of this chapter applies to the standard monochrome display for the IBM Personal Computer. Monochrome means *one color*—green—against a dark background. Color displays, with more than one color, are available for this computer but are not discussed in this book.

The last part of this chapter discusses the dot-matrix IBM PC Printer. Dot-matrix printers form characters by printing patterns of dots on paper, rather than by forming solid characters.

THE GOAL

If you let the computer manage the display on the screen, it will be a mess. You've already seen some excellent examples. You can do a lot better if *you* manage the display.

The screen display, and pages from a printer if you have one, are what the outside world sees of your programs. If the display is confusing and disorganized, users will think your program is the same way, even if it is a model of logic and clear thinking.

The presentation on the screen or page must be clear and easy to understand. Every program and every section of a program should begin with a clean screen showing only a title, a question to the user or an indication of what the computer is doing.

Questions and prompts to the user should be erased as soon as they are answered unless the user will need to refer to them. If there will be a lengthy pause while the computer processes data, the screen should tell the user what is happening. Data must have labels and column heads to explain it. For long lists displayed on the screen, scrolling must be controlled.

Screen and page organization are like remarks in a program. It takes a little thought and some time to do it right, but it pays off for the life of the program.

MANAGING THE SCREEN DISPLAY

To do this, you should know how to clear the screen, clear part of the screen, control *where* characters print, control *how* characters print and use screen graphics to draw lines and boxes. You already know one of these things.

The screen has 25 lines, each with 80 spaces. It can be set to print only 40 spaces wide using the WIDTH statement. All routines in this book use 80-space screen lines.

PRINT CHR$( )

To use this command, put an ASCII code number or a *control code* number in the parentheses. ASCII numbers are standard and mean the same thing to all computers. Some control codes are standard, some are not. In Chapter 3, you ran a routine that displayed the codes and what they do.

PRINT CHR$( ) has two possible meanings. If the number in parentheses is the ASCII code for a printable character, such as *A,* then that character will be displayed on the screen.

If the code does not represent a printable character, it has another purpose, such as moving the cursor up or down, clearing the screen, performing carriage returns and similar actions. These numbers are *control codes.*

Please refer to Appendix G of the IBM book *BASIC* for a list of codes and what they print. Some code numbers have different effects when delivered to different devices. A code that does one thing on the screen may do a different thing at the printer.

HOW NUMBERS PRINT

Faced with these challenging uncertainties, the programmer's secret weapon is to write it, run it and observe the result. Enter

```
PRINT 12345
```

You know that the space at the left is for the sign. You don't know what happens at the right end of that number because the computer moves the cursor down one line and all the way to the left. Then, it displays the BASIC prompt. Enter

```
PRINT 12345"X"
```

Either the number carries a space behind it or the string "X" carries a space ahead of it. To find out which, enter

```
PRINT "12345""X"
```

Numbers carry both a *leading space* for the sign and a *trailing space* to separate them from whatever prints next. Strings don't.

CURSOR CONTROL

The way to control where something prints is to control the location of the cursor. Enter

```
PRINT "12345" CHR$(29)
```

After the string of numbers has printed, CHR$(29) causes the cursor to move one space to the left. You don't see it happen because nothing is printed with the cursor at that location. Then the prompt symbol appears. Enter

```
PRINT "12345" CHR$(29) "X"
PRINT "12345" CHR$(29) " "
PRINT "12345" CHR$(29) CHR$(29) " "
PRINT "12345" CHR$(29) CHR$(65)
```

The location of a character on the screen is determined by the location of the cursor when it prints. If one character is printed over another, the old character disappears and the new character remains. In these examples, CHR$(29) was used to backspace and then print something.

Other control codes are used in a similar way. For a closer look at how they work, enter

```
NEW
10 FOR I = 1 TO 32
20 CLS: PRINT: PRINT: PRINT "CODE", "EFFECT": PRINT
30 PRINT I, "(" CHR$(I) ")"
40 PRINT: PRINT: PRINT
50 PRINT "PRESS F5 TO CONTINUE": PRINT: PRINT: STOP
60 NEXT I
```

List it, check it and run it. You see the effect of code 1, printed inside parentheses. Whatever the code does happens after the first parenthesis and before the second.

To continue, press F5. Notice that codes 11 and 13 do the same thing. You know that code 26 is used as an EOF indicator in sequential data files. Avoid that one when programming. Codes 28 through 32 are useful for controlling screen displays.

CONTROL CODES THAT AFFECT THE DISPLAY

CODE	EFFECT ON SCREEN DISPLAY
7	Beep
9	Tab
10	Line feed
11	Cursor home
12	Clear screen and home cursor
13	Carriage return
28	Cursor right
29	Cursor left
30	Cursor up
31	Cursor down
32	Space

DON'T TRY TO MEMORIZE ALL OF THESE CODES

This chapter is filled with codes and procedures that will seem complicated because there are so many. If you try to memorize them, you may become bogged down. All you need to remember is that these things can be done, along with a general idea of how to do them.

When you want to program some of these tricks, look them up. Put paper clips on pages with lists of codes, so you can find them easily. Or, give the code program that is now in memory a filename and save it to disk.

If you use certain codes frequently, you will gradually remember them. If you use some infrequently, it's better to look them up anyway to be sure you get them right.

CARRIAGE RETURNS

A carriage return moves the cursor down one line and fully to the left on the screen. You can produce carriage returns in several ways.

When a PRINT statement is executed, it is followed *automatically* by a carriage return—unless the last character in the PRINT statement is a semicolon. There is one exception that I will discuss soon.

When one line on the screen is filled with characters, a carriage return is produced automatically, so printing can continue on the next line. The trigger for this carriage return is something printed in the last space of the line.

The statement PRINT CHR$(13) produces a carriage return.

STRING$( )

This is a BASIC statement you can use to print a character a specified number of times. The form is STRING$(x,y) in which y is a code number and x is how many times you want it printed or executed. It's used as part of a PRINT statement. Enter

```
PRINT STRING$(80,219)
PRINT STRING$(38,42) " XX " STRING$(38,42)
```

What is the difference between STRING$( ) and STR$( )? If you are not sure, look them up in the IBM book *BASIC*.

SPC( )

This produces spaces only. If you put a number inside the parentheses, the command will print that number of spaces, starting from the cursor location when the statement is executed. It is used in a PRINT statement. Try this:

```
PRINT "X" "X"
PRINT "X" SPC(20) "X"
```

If the number in parentheses is greater than 80, what it actually prints is MOD 80. Enter

```
PRINT "X" SPC(100) "X"
```

The result is the same as if SPC(20) had been used because 100 MOD 80 = 20. Enter

```
PRINT "X" SPC(80) "X"
```

No spaces are printed because 80 MOD 80 = 0. If SPC( ) is the last item on a print list, such as

```
PRINT "X" "Y" SPC(30)
```

the line executes as though a semicolon were at the end, but you don't have to type one. This is the exception mentioned earlier.

The best use of SPC( ) is to tab from the current cursor position. Enter

```
PRINT "HELLO" SPC(5) "THERE" SPC(5) "BUDDY"
```

LOCATE

This statement is used to locate the cursor on the screen. Try this:

```
LOCATE 12,40: PRINT "A"
```

In that statement, the first number is the number of screen lines from the top. The second number is the number of spaces from the left—80 is the maximum number of spaces on a screen line.

HOW THE CURSOR PRINTS

The LOCATE statement can be followed by as many as five numbers separated by commas. Here's the form:

```
LOCATE row, column, cursor, start, stop
```

You have seen how row and column work. If 0 is typed for *cursor,* the cursor is turned off and is invisible. The number 1 for *cursor* turns it on. This does not affect the cursor at the command level or when statements such as INPUT are executed.

The last two numbers control the appearance of the cursor. Characters on the screen are printed by dots. Each character is in a "box" that is 14 dots tall and 9 dots wide. Characters are formed by glowing dots that produce the desired pattern.

The cursor is normally formed by two rows of dots at the bottom of the box. You can use more than that, if you wish. The *start* number selects the first row used, counting from the top. The *stop* number selects the last row used. The rows are numbered from 0 to 13. If numbers are omitted from a LOCATE statement, they retain their former values. Enter

```
LOCATE,,,0,13
```

The cursor retains that appearance until changed or until you turn the computer off and back on again. Enter

```
LOCATE,,,12,13
```

and the cursor is normal again. Try different specifications to see what they do.

KEY OFF

The screen has 25 lines, starting with line 1 at the top. The 25th line does not scroll and is normally occupied by the list of soft-key numbers and their functions. This list is of more interest to programmers than to those who run programs. You can turn it off when it is not needed. Enter

```
KEY OFF
```

You can now print something there that you don't want to scroll, such as an instruction to the user. Use LOCATE to place the cursor at that line.

You should have a program on disk A with the name CRAPS. It needs improvement. Please load and list the program. Change it to look like this:

```
10 CLS: REM filename "CRAPS"
11 KEY OFF
12 LOCATE 5,15
13 PRINT "TO START CRAP GAME, PLEASE RANDOMIZE"
14 LOCATE 10,15
15 RANDOMIZE
16 CLS
17 LOCATE 25,10
18 PRINT "FOR NEXT ROLL, PRESS SPACE BAR.     TO QUIT, PRESS Q"
20 D1 = INT(RND*10)
30 IF D1 <1 OR D1 >6 THEN GOTO 20
40 D2 = INT(RND*10)
50 IF D2 <1 OR D2 >6 THEN GOTO 40
55 LOCATE 10,1: PRINT STRING$(50,32)
60 LOCATE 10,1: PRINT D1, D2, "=", D1 + D2;
70 PAUSE$ = INKEY$: IF PAUSE$ = "" THEN GOTO 70
80 IF PAUSE$ = "Q" THEN KEY ON: CLS: END
90 GOTO 20
```

List the program and check your typing on the new lines. Then run it for a while. List it again. What the new lines do should be obvious, except for line 55. It goes to row 10 on the screen and prints a string of 50 blanks to erase anything on that row. Then line 60 prints the numbers from the last roll of the dice. Renumber the program and save it again, if you wish.

The screen is going to get pretty messy during the next few demonstrations. Clear it as often as you wish by pressing Ctrl-Home.

CSRLIN

This means *cursor line*. Its value is the screen line number where the cursor is, counting from the top. Enter

```
LOCATE 15,50: PRINT CSRLIN
```

The cursor's screen line number is printed at location 15,50, which means row 15, column 50.

POS(C)

This gets the column number of the cursor location. It doesn't matter what you put in the parentheses. Put in a *C* to remind you that its value is the POSition of the cursor. Enter

```
LOCATE 12,66: PRINT POS(C)
```

and the number 66 is displayed at that location. The cursor was at row 12, column 66 on the screen when it printed POS(C).

ERASE TO END OF LINE

Sometimes you want to print something on a screen line that has been used to print something else. If the new item has fewer characters than the old item, some of the old stuff will remain visible. One way to remove it is to print a string of blanks on that screen line before printing the new item. You saw that work in the crap game. Here's another way. Enter

```
LOCATE 12,1: PRINT "NOW IS THE TIME FOR ALL GOOD MEN"
LOCATE 12,1: PRINT "DEARLY BELOVED"
```

It would be better to erase the rest of the line after printing the new item. The cursor is in the first space past BELOVED and POS(C) knows exactly what space number that is. You know that the screen has 80 columns. Printing a number of blank spaces equal to 80 − POS(C) should do it. Enter

```
LOCATE 12,1: PRINT "DEARLY BELOVED" STRING$(80-POS(C),32)
```

That seems to work, but I have been wrong before. Suppose a new item occupies 40 spaces. When it prints, the cursor stops in space 41, so its position will be 41. Now, 80 − 41 is 39. That method stops one space short. If there were a character in space 80, it would not be erased. Do some experimental programming. Enter

```
10 LOCATE 12,1: PRINT STRING$(80,65)
20 LOCATE 12,1: PRINT STRING$(40,66) STRING$(80-POS(C),32);
```

Run that. Yes, the string of blanks needs one more character. Change line 20 to read

```
20 LOCATE 12,1: PRINT STRING$(40,66) STRING$(81-POS(C),32);
```

Use this practical algorithm to clear to the end of a screen line:

```
PRINT STRING$(81-POS(C),32);
```

ERASE TO END OF SCREEN

Another handy routine erases from the cursor position through screen line 24. Line 25 is not included in this routine, but it can be cleared separately if you wish.

The first step is to erase to the end of the current screen line using the algorithm just discussed. When that is done, the cursor is at the beginning of the next line on the screen.

CSRLIN knows which screen line the cursor is on. The number of complete screen lines that should be erased is from CSRLIN through 24. This requires a loop. Enter

```
15 LOCATE 18,1: PRINT STRING$(80,67);
   REM print something near bottom of screen
30 FOR ERASEND = CSRLIN TO 24: LOCATE ERASEND,1:
   PRINT STRING$(80,32);: NEXT
40 GOTO 40
```

List it. Line 15 prints something near the bottom of the screen so you can see if it is erased. Line 20 erases to the end of the current screen line. Line 30 should finish the job.

Line 40 is to prevent the program from returning to command level and printing the BASIC prompt at the bottom of the screen—which would confuse the display by causing a scroll. It creates an endless loop at line 40. Clear the screen by pressing Ctrl-Home and then run it.

It works, but the string of B's that should remain on the screen is bumped up one screen line, which is intolerable.

The reason is that space 80 of screen line 24 was filled with a CHR$(32), which caused an automatic wrap-around. This forced a one-line scroll because screen line 25 is protected. An item printed on screen line 24 cannot wrap around into screen line 25. The semicolon at the end of the PRINT statement *will not* solve this problem because the wrap-around happens before the program *sees* the semicolon. Press Ctrl-Break to get out of the endless loop. Change line 30 like this:

```
30 FOR ERASEND = CSRLIN TO 23: LOCATE ERASEND,1:
   PRINT STRING$(80,32);: NEXT: PRINT STRING$(79,32);
```

The loop erases through screen line 23. Then the PRINT statement erases 79 characters of screen line 24.

It doesn't matter that the last character is not erased because it's impossible to put a character in space 80 of screen line 24. If you do, it scrolls up one line and becomes the last character of screen line 23. Try it.

Run the routine. Then get out of the endless loop.

Finally—Now you have a routine to clear to the end of the current screen line and then to the end of the screen, except screen line 25 and the last character of screen line 24, without scrolling:

```
PRINT STRING$(81-POS(C),32);:
FOR ERASEND = CSRLIN TO 23: LOCATE ERASEND,1:
PRINT STRING$(80,32);: NEXT: PRINT STRING$(79,32);
```

This will all fit on a single program line. If you use this whopper very much, make it a subroutine.

It may seem that I spend a lot of your time on trivial problems—character returns, one-line scrolls and such. In my experience, the real time-wasters in a program are not big things that go wrong. They are obscure little things such as unnoticed typing errors, not realizing that $80 - 41 = 39$ and unexpected scrolls.

Some versions of BASIC used with other brands of computers have control codes to clear the current screen line and to the end of the screen. This book is written for IBM PC BASIC versions 1.10 and earlier, which don't have such codes. The documentation for the computer suggests keystrokes for both functions, to be used in programs written in assembly language.

SPACE$( )

This is another way to print blank spaces. If you think you have seen too many already, I agree. Ordinarily, I wouldn't mention this one, but you're bound to find it anyway. It may have a built-in surprise.

If you put a number in the parentheses, SPACE$( ) will print that number of spaces. The number must be in the range of 0 to 255. Enter

```
NEW
10 FOR I = 1 TO (24*80-1): PRINT "X";: NEXT
```

(Program continued on next page.)

```
20 LOCATE 10,1: PRINT "*" SPACE$(70) "*"
30 LOCATE 15,1: PRINT "*" SPACE$(90) "*"
40 GOTO 40
```

Line 10 fills the screen with Xs, except at location 24,80 and line 25. Line 20 prints an asterisk at location 10,1 followed by 70 spaces and another asterisk. Line 30 should print an asterisk at location 15,1 followed by 90 spaces and another asterisk. Line 40 loops to prevent displaying the prompt. Run it.

On my computer, line 20 works as expected. Line 30 doesn't. Computer manufacturers sometimes make small changes to software without announcing it. Your computer may run line 30 as expected. If not, you have plenty of other ways to make spaces. You can get out of the loop now by pressing Ctrl-Break.

CLEARING PART OF THE SCREEN

This will be easy if we avoid screen line 24. Assume X is the first line to be cleared and Y is the last. The form is

```
FOR I = X TO Y: LOCATE I,1: PRINT STRING$(80,32);: NEXT
```

You already know what to do about screen line 25. Clear it with the KEY OFF command.

CLEARING THE ENTIRE SCREEN

You already know how to use CLS.

PRINT TAB( )

This instruction spaces to the right, counting from *the beginning of the screen line*. PRINT TAB (15) will tab over 15 spaces and then print something. Try this:

```
NEW
10 CLS: LOCATE 10,1
20 PRINT "12345678901234567890"
30 PRINT TAB(5) "FIVE" TAB(20) "TWENTY"
40 LOCATE 20,1
```

Notice where the words print.

COLOR AND GRAPHICS MODES

When you look up BASIC words used in this chapter, you will find references to COLOR, the SCREEN statement, and text and graphics modes.

Graphics modes and the SCREEN statement are used with a color display and a Color/Graphics Monitor Adapter plugged into your computer.

With a monochrome display, the computer is always in the text mode. When looking up BASIC words, use this book as a guide to what you should now understand and use.

COLOR STATEMENT (TEXT)

Some COLOR statements are used with the monochrome display. The form is COLOR *foreground, background*. Foreground means the character displayed. Background means the surrounding dots. By using numbers in the statement, you control how an item prints on the screen. With a monochrome display, your choices are white—actually green—and black, plus some tricks.

The logic of it is that adding 8 to the base number causes high-intensity white characters. Adding 16 causes blinking. Adding 8 + 16 causes both. There is no high-intensity black.

"COLOR" CODES FOR MONOCHROME DISPLAY

FOREGROUND NUMBER	RESULT
0	Black character
1	White character, underlined
7	White character
1 + 8 (9)	High-intensity white character, underlined
7 + 8 (15)	High-intensity white character
0 + 16 (16)	Blinking black character
1 + 16 (17)	Blinking white character, underlined
7 + 16 (23)	Blinking white character
1 + 8 + 16 (25)	Blinking high-intensity white character, underlined
7 + 8 + 16 (31)	Blinking high-intensity white character

BACKGROUND NUMBER	RESULT
0	Black background
7	White background

With a computer, you could probably figure out how many combinations of these numbers are possible. It's a dazzling array of dazzles. The normal condition is COLOR 7,0. You can omit either of the numbers and the existing value is used. Enter

```
COLOR 7,0
LIST
```

Listing is just to print something so you can see what happens. Enter

```
COLOR 0,7
LIST
```

TV engineers call that *reversed video*. Enter   *Reverse video   0,7*

```
COLOR 16,7
LIST
COLOR 25,7
LIST
```

Had enough? Let's do one more. Enter

```
COLOR 7,0
```

Clear the screen. Enter

```
NEW
10 CLS: REM filename "VIDEO"
20 LOCATE 5,1: PRINT "Where did you hide the money?"
30 LOCATE 10,1: COLOR 0,0: LINE INPUT H$: CLS
40 LOCATE 5,1: COLOR 15,7: PRINT "AHA!"
50 LOCATE 7,1: COLOR 0,7: PRINT " YOU HID THE MONEY "
60 LOCATE 10,1: COLOR 25,7: PRINT H$
70 LOCATE 20,1: COLOR 7,0: PRINT CHR$(7)
```

Humor me by entering the truth about that money. Save this program under the name VIDEO. Fool around with COLOR statements as long as you wish.

Attributes—The COLOR statements, as you have been using them, change a characteristic of whatever is printed on the screen—its appearance. Characteristics are also sometimes called *attributes.* In computer lingo, you have been setting attributes for the screen display.

When display attributes are set by a COLOR statement, they remain in effect until changed by another COLOR statement or until you turn the computer off and back on again.

GRAPHICS CHARACTERS

In Appendix G of the IBM book *BASIC,* the codes starting at 169 print graphics characters on the screen. Even though a computer with a monochrome display doesn't have a graphics mode, you can print these characters. Others are between codes 0 and 31. With a color display and the graphics mode, you can do fancier things.

DRAWING A HORIZONTAL LINE

Use STRING$( ) to print a string of graphics characters on the same line. Enter

```
NEW
10 CLS: LOCATE 6,1
20 PRINT STRING$(80,219)
30 PRINT "X"
40 LOCATE 20,1
```

Notice the double carriage return when space 80 is filled. Add a semicolon to the end of line 20 and run it again. Use different code numbers in line 20 if you wish.

DRAWING A VERTICAL LINE

Do this with a loop. Enter

```
NEW
10 CLS
20 FOR I = 1 TO 20
30 PRINT TAB(20)CHR$(221)
40 NEXT I
```

This prints a vertical line, tabbed in 20 spaces from the left margin. How would a line made with CHR$(222) differ from this one? Try it with CHR$(176).

MAKING A BOX

A box is just a combination of horizontal and vertical lines. The locations of the lines are controlled by LOCATE, TAB( ) and ingenuity. Boxes call attention to what is in the box. In a game, for example, you can put a box in a corner of the screen and print the players' names and scores inside the box.

Write a routine to draw a box. Notice the great variety of characters available. After you make a box, use LOCATE to print something in it.

While you were making your box, I made one:

```
NEW
10 CLS: REM BOX
20 LOCATE 5,40: PRINT STRING$(20,219)
30 LOCATE 10,40: PRINT STRING$(20,219)
40 FOR I = 5 TO 10: LOCATE I,40: PRINT CHR$(219): NEXT
50 FOR I = 5 TO 10: LOCATE I,60: PRINT CHR$(219): NEXT
60 LOCATE 7,49: PRINT "BOX"
```

CONTROLLING HOW A NUMERIC EXPRESSION PRINTS

To control the way numbers print on the screen, set up a model *format string* using symbols that show the numbers as you want them to look. Give the model string a name, such as FORMAT$, or F$ to reduce typing.

Later in the program, instead of PRINT, use PRINT USING and reference the format string. Here's an example. Please enter and run it.

```
NEW
10 CLS
20 F$ = "$#####,.##": REM Format string
30 N1 = 1234.56
40 N2 = 22.338
50 N3 = 7.89
60 PRINT N1: PRINT N2: PRINT N3
70 PRINT
80 PRINT USING F$; N1: PRINT USING F$; N2: PRINT USING F$; N3
```

Line 20 is the Format string. Line 60 prints the three numbers without using the format string as a reference. Line 80 prints the three numbers using the format string.

You can control where PRINT USING will place a number on the screen by LOCATE or TAB( ). The forms are

```
LOCATE r,c: PRINT USING F$; N
PRINT TAB(c) USING F$; N
```

As usual, *r* is row and *c* is column. These statements locate the first space provided by the format string and thereby also position the decimal point. If numbers are printed one above the other and some of them don't fill the format string, the decimal points still line up vertically, making a proper display.

FORMAT-STRING SPECIFIERS
FOR NUMERIC EXPRESSIONS

SYMBOL	WHAT IT DOES
#	Provides a space for a number. If the number doesn't fill the available space, blanks appear at the left.
decimal point	Locates the decimal point in the field of #s
comma	Causes commas to be inserted, separating numbers to the left of the decimal point into groups of three. Place the comma anywhere to the left of the decimal point in the format string. Only one comma is needed.
**	At the beginning of the format string, prints * if there are not enough numbers to fill all locations of the format string. The two asterisks add two more locations in the format string to be filled.
$$	At the beginning of the format string, causes a dollar sign to be printed immediately to the left of the first digit. This is called a *floating* dollar sign.
**$	Fills unused locations in the format string to the left of the decimal point with *, then places a $ at the extreme left. This is a *fixed* dollar sign.
^ ^ ^ ^	At the end of the format string, causes the number to print in scientific notation.
+	At the beginning or end of the format string, causes either a + or − sign to print at the left of the number, according to the sign of the number.
−	At the end of the format string, causes a minus sign to print at the end of negative numbers.
yy	*yy* is one or more characters. If included in a format string along with other symbols, the character or characters represented by *yy* print where shown.

The accompanying table is a list of format-string symbols, or *specifiers,* for numeric expressions and what they mean. Refer to the table, find the specifiers used in F$, and then look at the result of line 80 to see if they did what they are supposed to.

PLACING THE FORMAT STRING IN THE PRINT USING STATEMENT

If you will use the format string only once, you can put it in the PRINT USING statement:

```
80 PRINT USING "$####,.##"; N
```

USING PRINT USING

Here's a routine that will help you learn the great variety of things you can do with PRINT USING statements. Enter it and run it a while. Try all of the specifiers for numeric expressions.

Try inputting too many characters, not enough characters, positive and negative numbers, wrong character types, commas and anything else that you are curious about. Try putting the word EXACTLY at the beginning of the format string and at the end. Try inserting spaces in the format string.

If you enter a number requiring more spaces than provided in the format string, a % symbol appears in front of the number when printed. If necessary, the computer will round off the number to fit the format.

```
NEW
10 CLS: KEY OFF: LOCATE 6,1
20 PRINT "Enter a Format string. Quotation marks not needed."
30 LOCATE 8,1 : LINE INPUT F$
40 LOCATE 10,1: INPUT "Enter a numeric expression: ", N
50 LOCATE 12,1: PRINT "This is the result: ";
60 PRINT USING F$; N
70 LOCATE 25,1: PRINT "PRESS SPACE BAR TO REPEAT. Q TO QUIT.";
80 C$ = INKEY$: IF C$ = "" THEN GOTO 80
90 IF C$ = "Q" OR C$ = "q" THEN CLS: KEY ON: END
100 GOTO 10
```

PRINT USING WITH STRING EXPRESSIONS

A separate and smaller group of string specifiers can be used to control how strings print. They are shown in the table on the next page.

They are used *within* each PRINT USING statement. Here are some examples to try:

```
A$ = "ABCDEFGHIJ"
PRINT USING "!"; A$
PRINT USING "\ \"; A$
PRINT USING "&"; A$
PRINT USING "XYZ!"; A$
```

Write a program to input the name Francis Xavier Smith, and then print it as F. X. Smith.

Here's one way to do it, along with some simple screen management techniques. Enter

```
NEW
10 CLS: ' filename "PRNTNAME
20 LOCATE 10,10: INPUT "Enter First name:   ", F$
30 LOCATE 12,10: INPUT "Enter Middle name: ", M$
40 LOCATE 14,10: INPUT "Enter Last name:    ", L$
50 CLS
60 LOCATE 10,10: PRINT "Full Name is:    "F$" "M$" "L$
70 LOCATE 12,10: PRINT "Salutation is: ";
80 PRINT USING "!."; F$;
90 PRINT USING " !."; M$;
100 PRINT USING " &"; L$
110 LOCATE 20,1
```

**FORMAT-STRING SPECIFIERS
FOR STRING EXPRESSIONS**

SYMBOL	WHAT IT DOES
!	At the beginning of the format string, causes only the first character of the string to print.
\\	If x is the number of spaces between the \\ symbols, x + 2 characters at the left of the string will print. The symbol \\ prints two characters.
&	Specifies that all the characters in the string are to be printed.
xyz	*xyz* represents any characters. When included with the print specifier, the *xyz* characters print where shown in relation to the specifier.

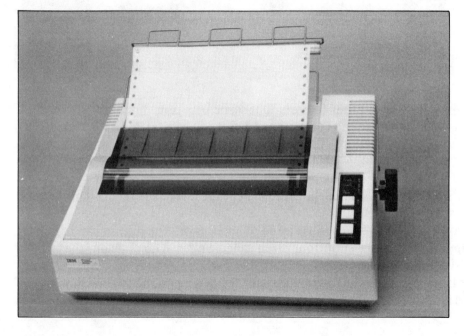

This is the standard dot-matrix printer. It forms characters by imprinting closely spaced dots on the paper.

Notice that the last set of quotation marks in lines 20, 30 and 40 line up. This causes the keyboard inputs to line up on the screen as they are entered. Line 60 prints the three lines as typed.

The semicolons at the ends of lines 70, 80 and 90 keep the cursor on the same line. The PRINT USING statement in line 80 prints the first initial of F$ followed by a period. The PRINT USING statement in line 90 prints a space, followed by the first initial of M$, followed by a period. The PRINT USING statement in line 100 prints a space and then all of L$. Line 110 moves the prompt down and to the left.

Run it and input three names.

MANAGING THE PRINTER

This discussion relates to the dot-matrix IBM Personal Computer Printer. Other printers can be

The dot-matrix printer is controlled by these pushbuttons. The on-off switch is on the right side, near the back.

used. Some of this information will apply to other printers, but some may not.

I assume that your printer is connected to the computer and plugged into an AC outlet, and that you have followed the paper-loading instructions. The gadget that advances the paper is called a *tractor*.

Printers have two kinds of on-off switches. The power switch turns on the AC power to the machine, so it can operate. It's on the right side of the printer, near the back. Turn it on. The indicator light labeled *Power* should glow.

The other on-off switch controls data input to the printer. When it is on, the printer can receive and print data from the computer. This is a pushbutton, often called *Select*. When it is on, the printer is *selected*. On the IBM printer, it is labeled *Online* and has two indicator lights. One is beside the Online button, the other labeled *Ready*. When you first turn the power on, both glow. Press Online and both go off. Press it again. When these indicators glow, the printer can accept data and print it.

TOP OF FORM

The paper for your printer is a continuous strip, with perforations at standard length and width. The perforations at the top of a page identify *Top Of Form*.

Setting Top Of Form—To establish where the printer will print the first line on each page, you must set Top Of Form. Turn the Power switch off. For the rest of this chapter, tip up the printer cover. Rotate the knob at the right to advance paper until a horizontal perforation is visible near the bottom of the tractor. The print head is about an inch below the tractor. It will print the first line at that location on the paper. Turn the power back on.

Now, the printer will advance paper to that location each time it receives a Top Of Form command. You can give it the command by pressing the button on the printer labeled *Form Feed*. It works only when the Ready light is off. Press the Online button to turn it off. Press Form Feed. You just wasted a sheet of paper.

The Line Feed button will advance one line at a time, when the printer is deselected. Try it. Then press Online again to select the printer.

SELF-TEST

You have probably done this already. If not, turn the Power switch off. While holding down the Line Feed button, turn the power switch on again. The printer can make 96 ASCII characters, plus 9 symbols, plus 64 block graphics characters. It normally prints 80 characters on a line. First, it prints characters 0 to 79, then 1 to 80, 2 to 81, and so forth for a long time. You can stop it by turning the power off.

Checking Line Centering—If the margins are not about the same on each side of the page, stop it. Release both ends of the tractor by moving the gray levers toward the front. Move the ends of the tractor to the left or right as needed, and lock them again by moving the gray levers toward the rear.

LPRINT

The LPRINT statement does at the printer what PRINT does at the screen.

WHAT CAN THE PRINTER PRINT?

You saw all of the printable characters when you ran the printer self-test. It's handy to have a list of codes and what they do. Enter

```
NEW
10 CLS: PRINT "LINE PRINTING CODES 0 TO 255"
20 LPRINT "PRINTING CODES 0 TO 255"
30 FOR I = 0 TO 255
40 PRINT I, "(" CHR$(I) ")"
50 LPRINT I, "(" CHR$(I) ")"
60 PRINT: NEXT I
```

You've seen line 40 before. It displays the code number on the screen and then prints the result of that number inside parentheses. Line 50 does the same thing on the printer. The printer and screen do not make the same response to all codes. Be sure the printer is online and at the top of the form. Run the program, and don't be alarmed if it does a form feed.

One of the tedious things about programming is shown by lines 40 and 50. If you want to PRINT and LPRINT identical things, it takes two statements to do it.

Look over the printout and get some clues about what the printer can do. When it printed nothing in the parentheses, the corresponding code didn't print anything. If it is not obvious what somes codes do, refer to Appendix G of the IBM *BASIC* book.

PRINTING WHAT IS ON THE SCREEN

Pressing a shift key with the key labeled *PrtSc,* meaning *Print Screen,* causes the printer to duplicate on paper whatever you have displayed on the screen, if that's possible. An obvious exception is characters on the screen that the printer can't print. Put something on the screen and try it.

Some of the screen attributes cannot be printed. You have a program in memory with the filename VIDEO. Please load it. Maybe you can get someone else to run it. Then print the screen. Notice which attributes LPRINT can print and which it can't.

CONTROL CODES

As you know, control codes do something other than print a character. In the IBM book entitled *Guide To Operations,* find the index for Section 3. Use it to find the *ASCII Control Code Chart*—in my book it is section 3-15. I'm not going to discuss all of those codes.

This chart has three columns. The left column shows code numbers. The next column shows the common name or result of that code number as used in the communications industry. The third column shows what each code does when sent to the printer.

Single Control Codes—The code numbers shown in the chart without asterisks are executed by the statement of this form:

```
LPRINT CHR$(code)
```

in which *code* represents one of the numbers without asterisks.

An asterisk beside a code number between 0 and 24 means that it may not work unless you add 128 to that number, for a technical reason. Code 0 should produce the same result as code 128, code 1 is the same as code 129, and so forth. Code 24 is the same as 152. If one of the lower set of numbers doesn't work as it should, add 128.

All single-control codes are entered like this:

```
LPRINT CHR$(7)
```

Preventing a Line Feed—When a printer-control code is executed, the printer accepts the instruction and then performs a line feed—unless the line feed is suppressed by a semicolon at the end of the statement.

Double-Control Codes—Some control functions use a double code—that is, one code number followed by another. The first number is always 27, which is called the ESCape code. In some computers, the escape code breaks out of a routine.

In this application, 27 tells the printer to give the following code a different meaning than it would if received as a single code. For example,

```
LPRINT CHR$(27) CHR$(69)
```

causes the printer to make bold-face characters. But CHR$(69) used alone prints the letter *E*. When the second number is the ASCII code for a letter, you can use the number or the letter. These two statements have the same result:

```
LPRINT CHR$(27) CHR$(69)
LPRINT CHR$(27) "E"
```

Following is a table of printer-control codes that you should learn to use.

PRINTER-CONTROL CODES

EFFECT	CODE		ALTERNATE CODE	
Line feed	10		138	
Form feed	12		140	
Carriage return	13		141	
Double width	14		142	
Cancel double width	20		148	
Compressed	15		143	
Cancel compressed	18		146	
Emphasized	27	69	27	"E"
Cancel emphasized	27	70	27	"F"
Double strike	27	71	27	"G"
Cancel double strike	27	72	27	"H"

LINEPRINTER CHARACTERS PER LINE

TYPE STYLE	CHARACTERS PER INCH	CHARACTERS PER LINE
Normal	10	80
Double width	5	40
Compressed	16.5	132
Compressed double width	8.25	66

The printer can produce several type styles. To see some of them, enter and run the following program. Print it out and save it.

```
NEW
10 CLS: REM filename "TYPESTYL"
20 LPRINT "This is normal type"
30 LPRINT CHR$(14) "Code 14 produces double width."
40 LPRINT "But only for one line"
50 LPRINT CHR$(20) "Code 20 turns off double width."
60 LPRINT CHR$(15) "Code 15 produces compressed type."
70 LPRINT CHR$(18) "Code 18 turns off compressed type."
80 LPRINT CHR$(27) "E" "Escape E emphasizes type."
90 LPRINT CHR$(27) "F" "Escape F cancels emphasized type."
100 LPRINT CHR$(27) "G" "Escape G causes double strike."
110 LPRINT CHR$(27) "H" "Escape H cancels double strike."
120 LPRINT "This is normal type again"
130 LPRINT CHR$(15) CHR$(14) "Code 15 compresses code 14."
140 LPRINT "But only for one line."
150 LPRINT "Code 15 is in effect until canceled."
160 LPRINT CHR$(18) "Code 18 restores normal type."
```

In the double-strike mode, each character receives two impressions to make it blacker. The printer head makes two passes along the same line, printing it twice. The second impression is offset slightly downward from the first to make the characters appear both larger and darker. This is equivalent to bold face.

In the emphasized mode, each character receives two impressions in the same pass.

Double width remains in effect only to the end of the line. The other attributes remain in effect until canceled by the turn-off code. You can print emphasized compressed type by entering both codes. You can't print normal double-width type. When two conflicting codes are entered, the latter one takes effect. You can use several type styles in one line, but it may take some experimenting to make it work.

Please experiment with printer-control codes until you are satisfied that you can look them up again later and use them.

PRINTING FROM A PROGRAM

In general, a program that prints letters and numbers on the screen can print the same things on the printer. The statements LPRINT and LPRINT USING are equivalent to PRINT and PRINT USING.

Commas, semicolons and tabs work the same on printer and screen. LOCATE statements work on the screen but not the printer. If your program displays characters on the screen that can't be printed by the printer, such as CHR$(150), the printer makes a blank space at that location.

USING THE PRINTER AS A TYPEWRITER

With this short program, you can use your printer as a typewriter—with some advantages that an ordinary typewriter doesn't have. Enter

```
NEW
10 CLS: KEY OFF: REM filename "TYPEWRITER"
20 LOCATE 25,1:COLOR 0,7:
   PRINT TAB(15) "TYPEWRITER MODE.";
30 PRINT SPC(12)"TO QUIT, PRESS F5" SPC(20)
40 LOCATE 1,1: COLOR 7,0
50 LINE INPUT L$
60 IF L$ = "CONT" THEN GOTO 100
70 LPRINT L$
80 GOTO 50
100 CLS: KEY ON
```

List it and check your typing. Line 10 clears the screen, including screen line 25. Lines 20 and 30 put an instruction at the bottom of the screen in reversed video. This causes the screen line to be 79 characters long. With 80 or more characters, screen line 25 does an interesting wrap-around. Observe it by changing SPC(20) to SPC(21) in program line 30.

Line 50 accepts a keyboard input of up to 255 keystrokes. I suggest entering one line at a time so you can control wrap-around. Line 60 is a way of getting out of the loop. Line 70 lineprints the string entered at line 50. Line 80 loops back to get the next line.

The instruction at the bottom of the screen tells the user to press F5 to quit. The F5 key automatically types CONT followed by an ENTER, just as though it had been typed at the keyboard. If the user presses F5, line 60 recognizes CONT and jumps to line 100.

With the printer online and Top Of Form set, run it. Type a letter to somebody. Before entering each line, you can use editing procedures to correct or change it. When each line is correct, press ENTER. When you are through writing the letter, press F5. Then use the Form Feed button on the printer to extract your letter.

The Finished Letter—The sprocket holes on each side of the paper are on a perforated strip so you can tear them off. When the IRS sends out ''Dear Taxpayer'' letters, they leave the sprocket holes on. I find this intimidating. When I reply, I leave the sprocket holes attached also, hoping they will think that I'm one of them. If you write me a letter, please remove the sprocket holes.

Word-Processing—What you're doing with this program is primitive word-processing. It's acceptable for letter writing.

You can improve it by storing strings in memory and printing them when needed. Print a letterhead automatically, using fancy type. Print the date automatically, using DATE$. Print time with TIME$. Put strings in an array in memory and use them to print standard paragraphs in your letters. Add an automatic form feed at line 110 using code 12.

If you save the preceding program with an eight-letter name, you must use TYPRITER or

TYPERITE or some other misspelling that will be hard to remember. In line 10, I recommend saving it as TYPEWRITER. Try it. Then list the files and see what happens. See if you can get it back by loading TYPEWRITER.

THE KEYBOARD BUFFER

It's possible to type something when the computer is not ready for it, or to type faster than a program can accept the data. The keyboard has a buffer that holds 15 keystrokes until they're accepted by the computer. Therefore, keystrokes aren't lost if the typist gets ahead of the computer. If the buffer is full, the computer beeps—which means, "Stop typing!"

PRINTING WITH THE PRINTER OFF

The computer documentation says that you may lose data if you run a program with the printer connected to the computer but not turned on. To avoid this problem, turn the printer on before turning the computer on.

Printing with the Printer Offline—Occasionally, I try to print something with the printer offline. When that happens, the computer locks up temporarily. Whatever you type goes into the keyboard buffer until the buffer is full. More typing makes more beeps. This can be confusing—if you don't know what is happening.

A timer in the computer will bring it back to life in a short time. It will display an error message about the printer and then display characters that were stored in the keyboard buffer.

A program can provide some protection against this user error with a routine like this. Don't enter it, just look at it.

```
550 PRINT "PLEASE PREPARE PRINTER."
560 PRINT "WHEN PRINTER READY, PRESS SPACE BAR."
570 RDY$ = INKEY$: IF RDY$ = "" THEN GOTO 570
580 IF RDY$ <> CHR$(32) THEN GOTO 570
590 LPRINT (data)
```

THE HARDCOPY OPTION

Many programs produce displays on the screen. You may wish to give the user a choice of also printing a display on paper—called *hardcopy*. I use an INKEY$ routine like this. Read through it but don't enter it:

```
490 HC$ = "": REM initialize
500 PRINT "DO YOU WANT HARDCOPY?  Y/N?"
510 HC$ = INKEY$: IF HC$ = "" THEN GOTO 510
520 IF HC$ = "Y" OR HC$ = "y" THEN HC$ = "Y" GOTO 600
530 IF HC$ = "N" OR HC$ = "n" THEN HC$ = "N" GOTO 600
540 PRINT "ERROR. PLEASE CHOOSE AGAIN": GOTO 510
600 IF HC$ = "Y" THEN LPRINT (DATA)
```

Line 500 asks for a keystroke *Y* or *N*. Line 510 accepts the keystroke and names it HC$, for Hard Copy. Lines 520 and 530 allow the user to type either upper or lower case and convert lower to upper case. If the program reaches line 540, something was typed other than *Y* or *N*. It asks you to try again.

I usually ask the hardcopy question only once, and use the answer for the entire program. After it is answered, there is a variable in memory, HC$, that is either Y or N. At line 600, and other lines later in the program, it will lineprint or not, depending on HC$.

CONTROLLING THE NUMBER OF LINES ON A PRINTED PAGE
When printing from a BASIC program, you must control the number of lines per page by a routine in the program. Enter and run this:

```
NEW
10 FOR I = 1 TO 100
20 LPRINT I
30 IF I = 56 THEN GOSUB 200
40 NEXT I
50 LPRINT CHR$(12): END
200 LPRINT CHR$(12): RETURN
```

Line 200 skips over the perforations connecting sheets of paper. A standard page is 8.5x11 inches. The printer is set to print 6 lines per inch, so it could print 66 lines on a page. Because I is limited to 56, some unprinted space remains at the bottom of the page. You can print closer to the bottom of the page by allowing I to reach a larger value. Try it.

LOOP BACK
The amount of information per page in this chapter is probably greater than the others in this book. Logical things are usually easy to remember because the thread of logic ties all of the pieces together. Much of this chapter is seemingly arbitrary facts, such as attributes and format strings. I try to cope with such things by taping charts and lists on the wall. When I want to produce reversed video or an automatic underline, the wall helps me.

Please review this chapter to be sure you can use the information. Remember the big ideas and don't worry about the details. When you want details, look them up.

You have some more BASIC words in your vocabulary. In the IBM *BASIC* book, look up the accompanying list. In Section 3 of the *Guide to Operations,* browse through the section about the Printer again.

BASIC WORDS TO LOOK UP

BEEP	PRINT USING
CHR$( )	SPACE$( )
COLOR STATEMENT (TEXT)	SPC( )
CRSLIN	STR$( )
KEY	STRING$( )
LOCATE	TAB( )
LPRINT	WIDTH
LPRINT USING	WRITE
POS( )	WRITE#
PRINT	

---

11 Programming And Debugging Techniques

This chapter is oriented more toward techniques than toward BASIC words. You will develop techniques of your own when a program you are writing doesn't work. If you are persistent and willing to experiment, you will eventually find a way to solve problems. That's how programming techniques are born.

VERIFYING KEYBOARD INPUTS

Keyboard operators make typing errors—fewer than programmers, of course, but still too many. A program user is frustrated when an error is right there on the screen, but there is no way he can fix it.

Use program statements to ask the user to examine and verify a keyboard input. Provide a way to correct errors. The method depends on the program, the screen organization and the data.

If there are several data-entry points in a program, I use a subroutine to avoid typing the same lines repeatedly. Here is an example. Don't enter it.

```
100 (CLEAR SPACE FOR DATA, position cursor)
110 LINE INPUT "Please enter data: "; DATA$
120 GOSUB 3000: REM verify
130 IF V$ = "Y" THEN GOTO 200: REM data OK
140 GOTO 100: REM not OK
200 (PROGRAM CONTINUES)
```

Lines 100—140 are the mainstream of the program. The key points are to provide a specific location on the screen for the data input request and to display the typed data. This is done by lines 100 and 110.

Line 120 goes to a subroutine that asks if the data is correct. I'll show an example soon.

When the program returns from the subroutine at line 130, a variable V$, for *Verify,* has been given a value by the subroutine. V$ is either *Y* or *N,* meaning *Yes* or *No.* If *Y,* the program jumps to line 200, where the data is used.

If line 130 does not execute, then V$ *must be N* and the user will want to key in the data again. The program jumps back to line 100, where the screen is again prepared to display the data.

When you do this, you can erase the erroneous data and start over. This routine does that by jumping to line 100. Or, you can leave the erroneous data in view while the user types it correctly. That would happen if the routine jumped to line 110 instead of 100. Sometimes one is better than the other, depending on the program and the type of data.

Here is an example of a subroutine that asks for verification. Don't enter it.

```
3000 PRINT "Is data correct?  Y/N?"
3010 V$ = INKEY$: IF V$ = "" THEN GOTO 3010
3020 IF V$ = "Y" OR V$ = "y" THEN V$ = "Y": RETURN
```

(Program continued on next page.)

```
3030 IF V$ = "N" OR V$ = "n" THEN V$ = "N": RETURN
3040 GOTO 3010
```

Lines 3020 or 3030 end the subroutine and return to the main program if a valid choice is made. They allow the user to type either upper or lower case. They send upper case back to the main program.

If an invalid key is pressed, line 3040 jumps back to line 3010. The computer ignores an invalid response. The response doesn't appear on the screen because a keystroke to an INKEY$ statement does not print. Nothing happens. Normally, the user will respond again and do it correctly.

You can make the subroutine more elaborate by telling the user that he made a keyboard error. When you do things to make a program trap errors and appear friendly, the program gets longer and longer. Many program lines sweep the floor and wash the windows instead of doing the main job. But this is what makes a good program, rather than a vague and confusing one.

SORTING

Many programs use lists or tables. Usually it is desirable to put the items in alphabetical or numerical order. This is called *sorting*.

SWAP

This statement is used in sorting routines to interchange the values of two variables. Enter

```
X(1) = 11
X(2) = 22
PRINT X(1), X(2)
SWAP X(1), X(2)
PRINT X(1), X(2)
```

This demonstrates interchanging the values of two array elements, X(1) and X(2). SWAP also works with ordinary variables, such as X and Y. It also works with strings. Try it with X$="Hello" and Y$="there".

THE BUBBLE SORT

For short lists, this method is practical. As the list of items to be sorted becomes longer, this method becomes slower. For long lists, you will prefer a faster procedure.

A bubble sort begins by comparing the top two items on the list, using a sorting rule to make decisions. A typical rule is that the list should end up in numerical order, with the smallest number on top. This discussion is based on that sorting rule.

If Item 1 on the list is smaller than Item 2, nothing is done. If Item 1 is larger than Item 2, then the two items are *interchanged* to put them in order. Here are some examples.

Item 1 = 7
Item 2 = 4

These two items must be interchanged to follow the sorting rule, so they end up like this:

Item 1 = 4
Item 2 = 7

Then Items 2 and 3 on the list are compared and interchanged if necessary.

Item 1 = 4
Item 2 = 7
Item 3 = 6

Items 2 and 3 of this list should be interchanged. Then, Items 3 and 4 are compared. The program works down the list, comparing two items all the way down. As the sorting routine operates, the smaller numbers rise to the top, like bubbles in a glass of champagne.

Items to be sorted must be in an array. This sort is done by a loop. For each pass down the list, an item can move up only one position.

The worst case is to have the smallest item at the bottom when the sort begins. If the list has 20 items, it will take 19 passes to move it from the bottom to the top. That's why this procedure is slow when you need to sort a large list.

BUBBLE-SORT DEMONSTRATION

This program is a graduation exercise. As you enter the program you'll know what the statements do, and most of the logic will be obvious.

The first part of the program uses the random-number generator to fill an array, A( ), with 10 random numbers to be sorted. Enter

```
NEW
10 CLS: RANDOMIZE
20 CLS: PRINT SPC(25) "BUBBLE SORT DEMONSTRATION": PRINT
30 PRINT SPC(23) "(Each column shows one sort.)": PRINT
40 LOCATE 6,1
50 FOR I = 1 TO 10
60 X = RND
70 A(I) = INT(100*X): REM make integers from 10 to 100
80 PRINT A(I): REM display unsorted list
90 NEXT I
```

What Happens—Line 60 produces random numbers, named *X,* between 0 and 1. Line 70 multiplies X by 100 and then takes the integer. This produces random whole numbers from 10 to 100, which are placed in the array A( ) and then displayed. The display begins at screen line 6, as set by program line 40. Test this routine by running it. It should display a column of 10 numbers at the left side of the screen. Then enter

```
100 K = 1: FG = 0
110 FOR C = 1 TO 9: REM make 9 compares
120 IF A(C) > A(C+1) THEN SWAP A(C), A(C+1)
130 NEXT C
```

Line 100 initializes some variables that will be used later. The routine from line 110 to line 130 is a bubble sort. On the first pass through the C loop, when C is 1, A(C) in line 120 is the array element A(1) and A(C+1) is A(2).

Display the Sorted List—When this routine has executed, one sorting pass down the list has been done. To display the sorted list, enter

```
140 GOSUB 1000: REM tab and print sorted list
150 STOP
1000 K = K + 5: REM tab 5 spaces from last column printed
1010 FOR P = 1 TO 10
1020 LOCATE P + 5,K: PRINT A(P)
1030 NEXT P: RETURN
```

Line 140 jumps to line 1000, which is a subroutine to print the sorted list. Line 150 is a temporary

STOP to keep the program from going to the subroutine by an invalid route.

At line 1000, K is incremented by 5. K will be used to space each column of numbers to the right by five spaces. Line 1010 sets up a loop to print 10 numbers.

Line 1020 is inside the loop. The first statement locates the cursor to print each of the ten numbers. The first column on the screen, the unsorted list, began at screen line 6. Line 40 did that. The second column on the display, which is the first sorted list, should also begin at screen line 6.

Line 1020 says LOCATE P + 5, K. When P is 1, that puts the cursor on screen line 6. When P is 2, the cursor will be on screen line 7, and so forth until 10 numbers are printed—one below the other. The second part of the LOCATE statement is K. On this pass, K is 6. During this execution of the print-out loop, the cursor will be placed at 6,6 7,6 8,6 and so forth. To print the next sorted list, K will be incremented by 5, so the next list will print at 6,11 7,11 7,12 and so forth.

Run it. You see the unsorted list and the result of the first sort. Notice that smaller numbers moved up one space. Run the sorting loop again by entering

```
GOTO 110
```

Another sort is performed and displayed, five spaces to the right of the preceding sort. Notice that the cursor returns to the GOTO statement you just typed. To run it again, press ENTER.

Continue running it until the sort is complete. The last list will be the same as the one before, and all numbers will be in correct order—according to the rule used for sorting.

The maximum number of sorts necessary is one less than the number of items to be sorted. With 10 items, this is nine sorts. If your list of random numbers needs nine sorts, do it all again until you get a set of numbers that sorts in less than nine passes. Try several different seeds.

Using a Flag—You can always sort this list by making nine passes. But when the list is sorted, remaining passes are just wasted time. Put a flag in the sorting routine to signal when it has done its job. The flag, FG, is initialized to zero at line 100. Put the cursor at the end of line 120 and add another statement. Then enter lines 150 and 160.

```
120 IF A(C) > A(C+1) THEN SWAP A(C), A(C+1): FG = FG + 1
150 IF FG > 0 THEN FG = 0: GOTO 110
160 PRINT: PRINT "SORT COMPLETE": LOCATE 20,1: END
```

List and check it. At line 120, if a swap occurs, FG is incremented by one. At the end of the loop, FG will be equal to the total number of swaps that were made. If it is still zero, there were no swaps and the sort is complete.

At line 150, the flag is tested. If it is not zero, it is reset to zero and the following statement sends the program back for another pass through the sort loop.

At line 150, if the IF statement does not execute, nothing on that line will be executed. The program moves to line 160 and ends.

Run it a few times with different seed numbers. If there are two identical numbers on the list, the sorting routine will have no problem.

Even though small numbers move up only one line at each pass, large numbers drop like a rock. That's because a large number moves down at each swap and is compared again to the number below it after the swap. It can participate in repeated comparisons and swaps during one pass down the list.

A real-world program would not display all of these columns. It would show and use only the final sorted list. If you put the array on disk after it is sorted, you don't have to sort it again the next time you run the program unless some of the items are changed.

SORTING STRINGS

The bubble sort works for both numeric expressions and strings. When relational operators are used, strings are compared one character at a time, starting at the left. When the first pair of characters is not the same, a decision is made as to which string is larger. This decision is determined by the ASCII codes for the characters.

Rewrite this program so it sorts a list of words. Change the first segment to accept 10 words typed at the keyboard. Delete lines 10, 70 and 80. Enter

```
60 LINE INPUT A$(I)
```

Then change A to A$ throughout the rest of the program. Run it and enter words with five letters or less so they will fit into the column spacing on the screen display. Without using any capital letters, enter these words: *now is the time for all good men to come.* Then, try entering five words twice—with the initial letter capitalized and without.

OTHER SORTING ROUTINES

The bubble sort is a *linear* method because the routine starts at one end of the list and plods through it in one direction.

A category of faster sorting routines is called *binary.* The general idea is to go through the list and sort items into two piles. You put all of the items above some arbitrary value into one pile and all below into another.

Then divide each pile into two smaller piles in a similar way and continue doing that until all piles have only one item and their order is known. Even though binary sorts are more complicated to program, they run faster because there are fewer passes through the entire list.

Some sorting methods have colorful names. One version of a binary sort is called *heapsort.*

CHEAPSORT

Once I was trying to devise a way to put some items in numerical order. I wrote some elaborate routines that wouldn't work. After I made them even more elaborate, they still wouldn't work. Finally, I had an idea that was absurdly simple.

I created an array. Then I put Item 7 into array location 7, Item 12 into location 12, and so forth. When the items were all plugged into the array, they were in order. I won't say how many hours it took to rise to that level of simplicity. I was so pleased with my "invention" that I called it *cheapsort* because it doesn't take much time or effort to do it.

INSERTING AN ITEM INTO A SORTED LIST

If you add an item to a list, the list must become one item longer. The easiest place to make an array longer is at its end. Stick the new item onto the end of the array. Then do comparisons and swaps, working upward from the bottom, until you find where the new item fits. You can do that in one pass.

ERROR MESSAGES

As you have seen, when something goes wrong during execution of a program, an error message is displayed. To see a list of error messages, look in Appendix A of the IBM book *BASIC.* These are only a few of the ways an ardent programmer can get into trouble. That Appendix uses the word *direct* to mean *command mode.*

To see what error messages look like in living video, enter

```
ERROR 1
ERROR 67
ERROR 255
```

The numbers you just typed are called *error codes.* There are 255 possible codes, of which 73 are presently used.

If you type

```
ERROR 256
ERROR 257
```

you get the same error message. This is actually ERROR 5. The computer is trying to tell you that the numbers 256 and 257 are invalid because they are too large. Error messages are sometimes difficult to interpret.

WHAT HAPPENS WHEN AN ERROR OCCURS?

It depends on the error and how it happened. If it is a type mismatch from the keyboard, the computer will ask you to type it again. If the computer can't do what the program asks, it will stop execution and go to the command mode. If there is a syntax error in a program line, it goes to the edit mode, displaying that line number—ready to be fixed. Sometimes the computer tells you that an error has occurred and continues running the program.

ERROR

This BASIC word simulates errors to see results or to test a program. Enter and run

```
NEW
10 GOTO 50
20 STOP
```

The two-line program encountered an error at line 10. The program has no line 50. The computer stopped execution, displayed an error message and returned to the command mode. Enter and run

```
10 ERROR 8
```

The result is the same. ERROR 8 simulates a program line that says GOTO a nonexistent line.

ERROR TRAPPING

Error trapping is the technique of detecting errors and doing something to prevent the program from stopping or failing to produce the correct result.

Errors occur for three principal reasons:
1) You write the program with an error in it.
2) The user does something wrong at the keyboard.
3) An event that is usually OK is interpreted by the computer as an error.

You should find most programming errors by running and testing the program. Usually, a few more will turn up later. When they do, you'll be very glad you took the time to put good remarks in your program.

You should anticipate every possible keyboard error and prevent the program from crashing. There are two common ways to do this.

One way is to ask the user to verify data as it is typed. But this does not always prevent errors! What if the user thinks his input is correct when it isn't? You can back him up by writing program lines that test the keyboard input before using it. For example, if the user is entering numbers, there may be an acceptable range of numbers. If a number is typed that is outside that range, ask for a new input.

The third class of errors includes events that are normally OK but look like errors to the computer in some situations. I'll show an example later.

There are standard error-trapping routines that prevent failure when you can anticipate the problem. Standard error traps use the following BASIC words:

ERR

This is the identification number of the error that occurred. If an error message is displayed, it is the number of the message.

ERL

This is the line number in the program where the error happened.

ON ERROR GOTO (line number)

This statement must be ahead of the line where an error is anticipated. It *turns on* an error trap. When the BASIC interpreter detects an error, it sends the program to the designated line number instead of stopping execution and going to the command or edit mode. At the designated line number, you do something about the error and then continue executing the program. *This statement remains in effect until canceled.*

ON ERROR GOTO 0

This statement turns off the error trap that's in effect. When an error trap is turned on by a statement such as

```
ON ERROR GOTO 3000
```

you will have a specific error in mind and a specific remedy at line 3000. But, ON ERROR GOTO 3000 is not selective. It will branch to line 3000 when *any* error of *any* type happens. Normally, the routine at line 3000 won't fix all possible errors.

As soon as your program passes the line where you anticipate a specific error, *turn the error trap off.* This is done by

```
ON ERROR GOTO 0
```

If you anticipate several errors at different locations in a program, you can set up an error trap for each of them and turn each one off after the risk of each specific error is passed.

RESUME

The ON ERROR GOTO (line number) routine is similar to a GOSUB statement. It branches to the designated line where you do something about the error. Then the statement RESUME *must be used* to return to the main program. There are several versions of a RESUME statement:

RESUME: Return to line number where error occurred.

RESUME NEXT: Return to the line following the line number where the error occurred.

RESUME (line number): Return to specified line number.

EXAMPLES OF ERROR TRAPPING

To see a simple error trap work, enter

```
NEW
10 CLS
20 ON ERROR GOTO 1000
30 GOTO 100
40 PRINT: PRINT "PROGRAM DIDN'T STOP"
50 LOCATE 20,1: END
1000 PRINT: PRINT "Error number is: " ERR
1010 PRINT: PRINT "Error line is: " ERL
1020 RESUME NEXT
```

Press F7 to enable TRON, then run the program. As you can see, it jumps from line 30 to line 1000. At line 1020, it returns to line 40 and completes execution of the program. Turn TRON off.

The error trap prevented the program from stopping and returning to the command mode. In the error trap, all it did was display the error code and the erroneous line number. This demonstrates how an error trap works, but it isn't a real-world example. What you should do is fix the program. Enter

```
30 PRINT X(50)
```

This simulates an error made by the user. It asks for item 50 in an array. That array has not been dimensioned, so item 50 is out of range. Run it. Look up Error 9.

A real-world error trap at line 1000 could tell the user the problem, ask for a new, valid number and return to the line where the incorrect number was input. Enter

```
30 OPEN "SOMETHIN" FOR INPUT AS #1
35 CLOSE #1
```

List and run it. Error 53, *File not found,* was discussed in Chapter 9 in the section entitled *THE NEW-PROGRAM DILEMMA.* Sequential files cannot be opened for input if they do not exist on disk. They can be opened for output, which will create the file on disk.

What this program "wants to do" is open the file for input, get some data from it and use the data. Lines to use the data would be between line 30 and 35 in this example. But, until the file exists, no data can be accessed. As written, it bombs each time you try to run it. Solve the problem in the error trap. Delete line 1020 and then enter

```
1000 OPEN "SOMETHIN" FOR OUTPUT AS #1: CLOSE #1
1010 RESUME
```

List it. When line 30 executes, it produces an error. The program jumps to line 1000, which opens the file for output and then closes it again. The file now exists on disk. Line 1010 jumps back to the line that *originally caused the error.* This time, the file exists and line 30 can execute without error. Run the program.

The advantage of doing it this way is that the error trap is used only once—the first time you run the program. After that, the file exists and line 30 can execute without any help from an error trap. List the files and you will see SOMETHIN. Kill it.

TRAPPING THE WRONG ERROR
You have an error trap that works fine for line 30. Enter

```
38 GOTO 500
```

List the program. Now there are two errors. Line 30 will produce an error because you killed SOMETHIN and it no longer exists on disk. The error trap should cope with that. Then line 38 produces an *Undefined line number* error. Run the program.

When you are reasonably sure something is wrong, press Ctrl-Break. List the program again. If you don't see the problem, turn on TRON and run it a while longer. Stop it with Ctrl-Break. Notice that the program is looping through line numbers 38, 1000 and 1010 repeatedly. List it again.

Line 38 causes an error. Line 1000 opens a file, which doesn't fix the problem at line 38. Line 1010 jumps back to line 38, causing the same error again. The program was in an endless loop that included the disk drive. The trap caught the wrong error and couldn't cope with it. To fix the program, you can either turn off the error trap or make it more specific.

TURNING OFF THE TRAP
The error contemplated at line 20 will happen or not happen at line 30. After that, *any detectable*

error will send the program to line 1000 and cause a problem—unless the error trap is turned off as soon as it is no longer needed. Enter

```
32 ON ERROR GOTO 0
```

That cancels the turn-on statement at line 20. Run it.

The program fails because of the programming error at line 38. That error is not trapped. However, it didn't get into an endless loop as it did before. Usually an error trap can't fix a programmer's mistakes. Line 38 should be fixed.

MAKING THE TRAP SPECIFIC

Instead of turning error traps on and off throughout a long program, you can merely let the first one remain valid. Then, at the error-trap location, you can have a series of fixes at different line numbers, one for each anticipated problem in the program. Each is specific to an error number and a line number and won't fix anything else.

For example, this line is a specific fix for a *File not found* problem at line 30. Don't enter it.

```
1000 IF ERR = 53 AND ERL = 30 THEN
OPEN "SOMETHIN" FOR OUTPUT AS #1: CLOSE #1: RESUME
```

You could then have a line 1010 that traps a specific error at line 170 in the program; a trap at line 1020 that is specifically for program line 230, and so forth. The last line in a series of specific fixes should apply when none of the others does. Use

```
1080 ON ERROR GOTO 0
```

That line will execute only on an error untrapped by an earlier line. It turns off the trap, stops the program and displays the error that you didn't trap.

Enter and run this example. How many errors are in it?

```
NEW
10 CLS:PRINT"Begin"
20 ON ERROR GOTO 1000
30 GOTO 77
40 OPEN "BADFILE" FOR INPUT AS #1
50 PRINT ARRAY$(1234)
60 PRINT "End at 60"
1000 IF ERL = 30 THEN PRINT "Error at 30": RESUME NEXT
1010 IF ERL = 40 THEN PRINT "Error at 40": RESUME NEXT
1020 ON ERROR GOTO 0
1030 PRINT "End at 1030"
```

The trap at line 1000 works for the error at line 30. It doesn't fix the error; it just resumes at the following line. The trap at line 1010 works for the error at line 40 and resumes at the following line.

The error at line 50 sends the program to line 1000 again because of the statement at line 20. This error has no home. It finds line 1000 unresponsive. Line 1010 ignores it. Line 1020 cold-heartedly turns off the error trap while the error at line 50 is still looking for help.

The only thing the computer can do is stop and announce the problem—which it does. Notice that neither line 60 nor line 1030 ever executes.

Lines 1000 and 1010 are specific to the error line, but not the error number. Rewrite them so they are specific to both error line and error number.

The problem at line 30 can't be fixed except by changing the program. The problem at line 40 can be fixed by an error trap. Rewrite line 1010 to solve the problem at line 40.

Add another specific error trap to continue running the program when the error at line 50 occurs. If it works, line 60 should execute.

In a real-world program, you would not simply skip a line and continue running the program when errors like this occur. If it's a programming error, fix it. If it's a program error, fix it. If it's a user error, fix it.

Don't Fall into Your Own Trap—Error traps can cause problems if not written correctly. Be sure to test each one carefully. They seem like housekeeping chores rather than programming action. After you've written a few programs that fail the first time somebody else tries to run them, you'll become a cheerful trapper.

DIVISION BY ZERO

Dividing by zero produces an error message but does not stop the program. The error can't be trapped by the method just shown. Enter

```
NEW
10 CLS
20 X = 11
30 LOCATE 5,30: INPUT "Enter Y: ", Y
40 Z = X/(Y-4)
50 LOCATE 8,31: PRINT "Z  = " Z
60 LOCATE 11,30: PRINT "Z/2 = " Z/2
```

Run it a few times, entering several values for Y. Then enter 4 and run again. In line 40, the denominator of the fraction is $Y-4$. When Y is 4, $Y-4$ becomes zero. The computer told you it divided by zero at line 40, but it continued to execute the program anyway. At line 50, it printed an enormous number called *machine infinity*. Then, at line 60, it used that number to perform another operation.

Some folks say that the result of dividing any number by zero is an infinitely large number called *infinity*. One definition of infinity is that it is larger than *any* number you can think of. Having just seen machine infinity, you can think of it. Therefore, machine infinity is not the real thing.

As programmer, you have three choices. You can adopt the standard mathematical view that division by zero is not allowed. Or, you can say that it is allowed, but machine infinity is not large enough. Or you can say that, in your program, machine infinity is large enough for practical purposes. That's why the computer doesn't stop running the program. You should write the program so it does what you want. If you don't want to divide by zero, test the value of the divisor and do whatever is appropriate.

DEBUGGING TECHNIQUES

Mistakes in writing a program cause problems. These problems are usually called *bugs*. Finding and fixing them is called *debugging*. There are several common debugging techniques. Sometimes you have to invent your own.

What You Need to Know—Usually, when a program doesn't work correctly, there are two kinds of information that will help find the problem: What path did the program take? What did the program do? If you can answer those questions, you can find the bug.

Where Did It Go?—In complicated programs, a bug may cause the program to take the wrong path. You can check the program and find nothing wrong—if you assume that program segments execute in the correct order. You can test each segment of the program and find nothing wrong because each works correctly when it gets the correct input. This can be puzzling.

When you can't find anything wrong with a program, run it and check program flow. One way is to use TRON. You can turn on TRON from the command mode, before running the program. This is usually OK if there are not a lot of loops and INKEY$ statements. If there are loops, the screen will quickly fill up with the line numbers in the loop and you will lose the line-number history of pre-loop execution.

If so, run it again and pause by pressing Ctrl-Num Lock as soon as line numbers in the loop start repeating. Then you have a screen full of line numbers leading up to the loop.

If you have a printout of the program, refer to the screen display to see the order of execution. Look at the printout to see if the program is executing in correct order.

If you don't have a printout, make a copy of the line numbers displayed by TRON. Then list the program on the screen to see what each line does. The best way to copy the screen is Shift-PrtSc, if you have a printer. If not, copy line numbers manually.

If you don't find the problem, run the program some more and then stop it again.

TRON and TROFF can also be used as statements on program lines. If you suspect that the program is branching incorrectly, enable TRON just before the branch point. You can put in temporary lines with STOP commands in each branch, or you can just pause or break out of the program after it has run past the branch point. Then check the program flow as displayed against the program itself to see if it branched correctly.

If the program isn't following the correct path, it is probably doing *exactly* what you told it to do. In this case, something is wrong with your instructions.

If a program branches by testing the value of a number, you may have used a "less-than" test when it should be a "greater-than" test. Or, you may be testing the wrong variable. Perhaps it should be X, but you made a mental error and told it to test Y.

If you are applying the correct test of the correct variable, and the program is not branching correctly, then the value of what is being tested is wrong. It may be calculated incorrectly somewhere else in the program.

String Testing—When a program branches by testing a string, an incorrect branch can be caused by the user using lower case when the program requires upper case. You know how to prevent that problem. Sometimes the problem is due to a space at the beginning or end of one of the strings being compared.

Here are two techniques that help when it seems that two strings should be the same but the computer says they aren't.

Stop the program and check the length of the strings being compared using LEN statements. "HELLO " is not the same as "HELLO". If that doesn't show the problem, test the string in the command mode with statements such as

```
IF B$ = "ABC" THEN PRINT "YES"
```

If the string is supposed to be "ABC" but the computer doesn't print "YES", then it isn't. Test the string again just after it is determined by the program. Find the reason and fix it.

What Did It Do?—The computer will print out the values of variables anytime you want to see them. A simple technique is to put in a temporary program line with a STOP statement. Run the program. When it stops, list that part of the program to refresh your memory. Then print the variables by typing PRINT statements from the command mode.

It may be necessary to calculate correct values manually or with a pocket calculator. If a value used by the program is not correct, you have a clue. Look at the segment that calculates the value. If it is a complicated calculation, put temporary stops in the program at several places and check each step of the calculation.

If you are displaying several values, it's easy to forget which is which unless you label them. Suppose you are checking both X and Y. A statement like this will avoid confusion:

```
100 STOP: LPRINT "X = "X, "Y = "Y
```

This stops the program and prints out both variables, each labeled so you know which is which.
Printing Variables as the Program Executes—It is not necessary to stop execution to see values of variables. You can see them on the fly. Put in temporary program lines such as:

```
100 LOCATE 23,40: PRINT "X = "X, "Y = "Y
```

As the program runs, you can see the values of these variables in the lower right corner of the screen.
Testing a Loop—Sometimes a loop doesn't work as you expected and the reason is not obvious. Put in a temporary program line to display the value of the counter and the values of variables affected by loop operation. Run the program and compare what is really happening in the loop to what you expected to happen.
Testing Data in Memory—When you are putting data into memory, and then using the data for something, there may be a bug in the way the data is read, or the way it was entered. Perhaps the order of the data as typed is not the order that the program expects when the data is used. Or, the program calls for data item 5, when it should be asking for item 4 or item 6.

It's easy to see what is in memory. You've done it several times in this book. You can see individual items by printing them from the command mode. Or, you can write a loop that will display them all.
The IF Barrier—Eventually, you will form the habit of putting multiple statements on one line. Eventually, you will make this mistake:

```
100 IF X = 20 THEN GOTO 400: X = X-1
110 PRINT Z
```

That line seems to say that the program should branch to line 400 when X is 20. Otherwise, it should subtract one from the value of X and then move to line 110, where it prints the value of Z.

The second statement on line 100 *will never execute.* If X is 20, it jumps to line 400. If X is not 20, the next *numbered* line executes, *not the next statement.*

When you write a program line like that, the mistake is difficult to see because you make the same mental error each time you look at it. You think that the second statement will execute because you wrote it that way.

Displaying the value of X by temporary lines both before and after line 100 will give you a clue. When this bug has bitten you a few times, you will decide never to put two statements on the same program line if the first one begins with IF.

Here is a different version of the same bug:

```
10 FOR I = 1 TO 25000: PRINT I: IF I = 20000 THEN GOTO 50: NEXT
50 PRINT "END"
```

How many times will the loop operate? What will it display on the screen? Enter and run it. Now, put each statement on a separate line like this:

```
10 FOR I = 1 TO 25000
20 PRINT I
30 IF I = 20000 THEN GOTO 50
```

(Program continued on next page.)

```
40 NEXT
50 PRINT "END"
```

Run this version until you are sure about what it will do.

With the loop on a single program line, it operates one time. The IF statement prevents it from reaching the NEXT statement. With one statement on each program line, it will execute 20,000 times—if you run it long enough.

String Too Long—Sometimes you end up with a string longer than 255 characters, which results in an error message. That can happen when you concatenate two or more strings, especially if one has variable length—such as something input from the keyboard.

A less obvious way to get into this kind of trouble is to concatenate fielded variables from a random file. A fielded variable is always as long as its field, even if some are blanks.

If you field a variable at 40 spaces, and then put in something that occupies only 10 spaces, it will have 40 spaces when you get it back from the disk. Thirty of them will be blank spaces, so you can't see them. Checking the length, using a LEN statement, will show you the problem.

Imponderables—Occasionally, you will do something that confuses or confounds the BASIC interpreter. Unless you are familiar with the interpreter program, you can't figure out exactly what happened inside the computer. But the mistake is not in the interpreter—it's in your program. You did something that didn't follow the rules of programming in BASIC. Here's a simple example. Enter and run

```
10 GOSUB 100
20 PRINT "Y"
30 GOTO 10
100 PRINT "X"
110 GOTO 20
120 RETURN
```

The computer says it is out of memory. What this program did is go to a subroutine repeatedly and then jump out of it without executing a RETURN statement. The computer isn't really out of memory. The BASIC interpreter could not cope with all of those GOSUB operations without any RETURNS.

Looking On the Disk—Sometimes you can diagnose a program mistake by looking at data records that it puts on the disk. If nothing is there, you are not opening the file correctly or you are not sending data to the file correctly.

You can see if the file was opened by using the FILES command in BASIC. If the filename is there, it was opened.

To see what is actually in the file on the disk, return to the operating system by entering SYSTEM. Then enter TYPE FILENAME, without quotation marks around the filename. If the filename has an extension, you must use it. What you see on the screen is what the program put on the disk.

When All Else Fails—As a last resort, retype the program lines that don't work right. Sometimes you will see something wrong that's obvious when you redo the line but invisible when you are just looking at it.

If that doesn't help, write that part of the program a different way. Use different variable names and a different program structure.

If that doesn't help either, you're on your own. Pluck and persistence will always win, but it may take a while. Sometimes it's best to stop fussing with the program. Return to it the next day, and you may find the bug immediately.

When to Suspect the Computer—If you keep track of mistakes, as though it were a game, the score will probably end up something like this: YOU:1,000,000   COMPUTER:1

When your brain is numb and you still can't find the bug in your program, you will suspect that something has gone wrong with your computer. Even though unlikely, it is possible.

Save the program. Load a different program that has run correctly before and try running it. If the program runs normally, the computer is probably OK. If the second program doesn't run correctly, that indicates a failure in the computer.

Turn the computer off and then on again. When turned on, it performs a self-check. If it reports an error, you found the problem. If not, follow the diagnostic procedures in the IBM book entitled *Guide To Operations,* in the sections entitled *Setup* and *PDP's.*

If you're still not sure, take the disk with your program on it to another IBM Personal Computer with at least as much memory installed. See if it will run. If it doesn't run on another computer, the problem is almost certain to be in your program. If it runs OK on the other computer, there is probably something wrong with your computer. Check with your dealer about repairing it.

HOW TO PLAN A PROGRAM

The first thing is to have something in mind that you want your computer to do. Spend time thinking about what information you will put into the program and what you want to get back. Think about how you would like to use the program. If it stores information, how will a keyboard operator ask for that information? How should the information be displayed? Make a sketch of screen organization.

Then make a plan. Divide the overall job into large pieces that establish a framework for the program. Here's an example:

Get file from disk
Input new data
Combine old data with new data
Display results
Optional hardcopy
Put revised data back on disk

Then break the program into tiny steps that you can do in a few lines. Make a list of these steps.

It's very important to decide on variable names when you make the plan. Make a note of what goes into each step of the program, what comes out and what the variable names will be.

THEN WRITE IT

Usually, the beginning is a good place to start. When you enter CLS, you've started. Sometimes it is better to attack a critical part of the program, such as a calculation or a subroutine. Then build both ways from there. Whatever seems logical is the way to proceed.

Renumber when necessary to make room for new lines. To write long programs, a printer is almost essential. Print out the program occasionally. Look it over and write on it. Use arrows beside the listing to show where jumps go and where subroutines return to. I use a yellow highlighting pen to mark the beginning and end of loops and other important lines.

Every time you complete a small segment of the program, save it on disk so you don't lose it due to a power failure. Writing a program takes concentration for a long time. When you get into it, you will have more of the program in your mind than in the computer. If you stop, you may forget the part in your mind. You'll find it tough to reconstruct. Don't try to program when you have less than an hour to spend on it. I recommend midnights.

Keep a list of variable names, arranged alphabetically, on a piece of paper. If you merely make up names as you need them, you will probably get some things mixed up and spend a lot of time retyping program lines to correct problems.

What Not to Expect—Don't expect everything to fall into place immediately. When you have a general plan that seems to make sense, start programming it. You will change and improve the plan as you go along. You will discover a lot of problems when writing and testing the program that you didn't anticipate when you were just thinking about it. That's normal.

Write the tiny steps of the program and test each one as you write it. Then test them in groups or program segments. Fix each problem as it occurs, even if it means starting over with a new plan.

About Flow Charts—Many programming books feature flow charts. These have specially shaped boxes and symbols to illustrate what a program does. The flow charts are always perfect. Practically no one can plan a program perfectly in advance. Perfect flow charts are made *after* a program has been written and all of the problems have been solved. If a book says you must use a flow chart to *plan* your programs, don't believe it.

Flow charts are optional. If another kind of plan is easier for you to make and follow, do it as you wish. Notes on a piece of paper work just fine. But *you must have a plan* of some kind!

When you write the program, put in a lot of remarks. Too many are much better than too few. If the program takes too much memory space with all of those remarks, make a second version of the program with the remarks left out. Run the second version. Keep the first version for reference.

Start with something simple because programming teaches programming.

SOME SIMPLE PROGRAMS YOU CAN WRITE

Address and phone-number lists are useful. An array is a good way to organize a list of names, addresses and phone numbers. Update it occasionally and print out a new list for reference.

Insurance people recommend keeping a household inventory: the item, serial number or other identification, when you bought it, from whom, how much it cost. If you do that, keep it up-to-date and keep the disk or a copy of the printout in a safe place.

If you want to know where your money went, write a program that adds up major categories such as Food, Frivolity and Fun. At the end of the month, enter your expenditures in each category. Total and print the results. Maybe computing will help you lead a better life.

It's handy to have a program that stores information about your credit cards, if you have some. You can put in the name of the issuer, the card number, the expiration date, the phone number to call if you lose it, and how many identical cards are in your family. Once you have such a program, keeping it up to date is easy. Then, if you lose one or more of your cards, you have the information needed to report the loss.

I've read magazine articles advising people not to program tasks that can be done with a notebook or a pocket calculator. In terms of efficiency, that's good advice. But it's bad advice if you want to learn how to program. The best programs to start with are simple enough to do with a notebook or pocket calculator. Programming teaches programming.

END OF LOOP

At the end of each chapter, I have asked you to review the stuff you just read. You may think that I am about to ask you to review the whole book. On the next page is a list of BASIC words. Please look them up in the IBM book *BASIC*.

If you haven't read the error messages in Appendix A, read them. You will get some insight into things that can happen. Look through Appendix J and the *Tips and Techniques* section of Appendix I.

You have a few programs on disk that you entered as examples. Please load them, starting with the simplest. List and run them. Then kill as many as you wish.

CONGRATULATIONS

I'm glad to see that you made it to this page—unless you're just peeking back here to see how the story ends.

I caught the programmer's disease by purchasing a computer, bringing it home and starting. When I got it to print HELLO, I was hooked. Then I spent a lot of frustrating late-night hours because I couldn't find a book that told me what I needed to know. Eventually, about 20 books didn't. They weren't written for ignorant louts such as I.

Learning to program from a book is very difficult. It takes a lot of motivation and a chair with a soft cushion. In this book, I intended to tell you what you need to know, when you need to know it. I left some things out that are not important to beginners. I'm confident that you'll discover them for yourself.

I had fun and hope you did, too. In my opinion, programming is about as much fun as a person can have while sitting down.

WHAT NOW?

You know enough BASIC to write useful and practical programs. To do that, all you need is diligence and ingenuity.

What you may not have is a feeling for program strategy and organization. Some of this is intuitive and some comes from the experience of writing programs. You will improve your strategic programming skill by programming.

There are lots of books on programming strategy that intend to give you the big picture without hanging up on details. They tend to be abstract and give the commanding general's view of the war, rather than that of the foot soldier. They have titles like *Program Structure* or *Program Organization*.

For a strategic programming experience, I'm happy to recommend another book in this series. It's called *Programming Techniques for Your IBM PERSONAL COMPUTER*. It uses segments of a large program as examples. After you have done the hard labor of typing in the examples, you get a reward: All examples fit together to make a program that you can use. The program is a versatile appointment and reminder calendar that displays a calendar page for any month and lists whatever you want to remember about each date.

The book focuses on programming strategy, but the examples are specific. You can see exactly how they work in a program. I am glad to recommend that book because it is from the same publisher as this book—and the same author.

BASIC WORDS TO LOOK UP

ERL	ON ERROR GOTO
ERR	RESUME
ERROR	SWAP
INKEY$	

Index

Cover Photo: Balfour Walker Photography

7.526330762479

Notes